D0206606

Conflict 101

A Manager's Guide to Resolving Problems
So Everyone Can Get Back to Work

Susan H. Shearouse

AMACOM

American Management Association

New York • Atlanta • Brussels • Chicago • Mexico City • San Francisco
Shanghai • Tokyo • Toronto • Washington, D.C.

Bulk discounts available. For details visit:
www.amacombooks.org/go/specialsales
Or contact special sales:
Phone: 800-250-5308
Email: specialsls@amanet.org
View all the AMACOM titles at: www.amacombooks.org

This publication is designed to provide accurate and authoritative information
in regard to the subject matter covered. It is sold with the understanding that
the publisher is not engaged in rendering legal, accounting, or other professional
service. If legal advice or other expert assistance is required, the services of a
competent professional person should be sought. .

Library of Congress Cataloging-in-Publication Data

Shearouse, Susan H.
    Conflict 101 : a manager's guide to resolving problems so everyone can
get back to work / Susan H. Shearouse.
        p. cm.
    Includes bibliographical references and index.
    ISBN-13: 978-0-8144-1711-9
    ISBN-10: 0-8144-1711-6
    1. Conflict management. 2. Interpersonal relations. I. Title. II. Title: Conflict
one hundred one. III. Title: Conflict one hundred and one.
    HD42.S54 2011
    658.3'145—dc22
                                                    2010043535

About AMA
American Management Association (www.amanet.org) is a world leader in talent
development, advancing the skills of individuals to drive business success. Our mission
is to support the goals of individuals and organizations through a complete range of products
and services, including classroom and virtual seminars, webcasts, webinars, podcasts,
conferences, corporate and government solutions, business books and research.
AMA's approach to improving performance combines experiential learning—learning through
doing—with opportunities for ongoing professional growth at every step of one's career journey.

Printing number

10 9 8 7 6 5 4 3 2 1

Contents

Acknowledgments

In writing this book, I have so many people to thank: all the clients over the years who have allowed me to assist them with their challenges, and my children, Jennifer, Eli and Jake, who taught me so much about myself and conflict resolution.

Thank you to good friends and colleagues who encouraged me along the way: Chuck Appleby, Jeffery Davis, Samantha Edwards, Jennifer Graves, Anne Loehr, Bob Mauer, and Pete Swanson. To the Sisters of the Bodhicitta Hula Hoop, who were unflagging in their encouragement: Robin Carnes, Sally Craig, Betty Deen, Laura Delaney, Laura DiCurcio, Antoinette Kranenburg, Allison Porter, Sandra VanFossen, and Lisa Zoppetti. I am grateful to Richard Alper, Ramona Buck, Will Edwards, Bob Mauer, Jim Meditz, Allison Porter, John Settle, Sue Warrick, Michael West, and Deborah Woodward, for their wise advice and editing. Chrystine Gaffney worked tirelessly tracking down permissions; Allison Shearouse translated my humble drawings to clear graphics; and Eli Stull provided technical skill so that the text finally emerged from my computer. Thanks to the patience and guidance of my agent, Grace Freedson, and the editors at Amacom, Christine Parisi, Michael Sivilli, and Carole Berglie.

For incredible support of all kinds, from believing in me all the way to spending endless hours listening to me and editing my words, I thank my husband, Tom Colosi.

The author gratefully acknowledges permission from these sources to reprint the following:

Reference to *The Thin Book of Trust, An Essential Primer for Building Trust at Work* by Charles C. Feldman. Copyright Feltman, 2009, Published by Thin Book Publishing.

Quote from radio program titled *Speaking of Faith, Getting Revenge and Forgiveness*, March 25, 2010, by M. McCullough. Reprinted with M. McCullough's permission.

Selection reprinted from *The Unlucky 13: Early Warning Signs of Potential Violence at Work,* W. B. Nixon, National Institute for the Prevention of Workplace Violence.

Quote from Larry Miller, comedian, reprinted by special permission from Mr. Miller.

Quote from Steven Gaffney reprinted by special permission from Mr. Gaffney.

Statement Based on Assumptions reprinted by special permission from Thomas R. Colosi.

Definitions of *conflict* and *culture* from *Merriam-Webster Online Dictionary*, reprinted from Web site with special permission from Merriam-Webster, Inc.

Excerpt from *Wherever You Go, There You Are: Mindfulness Meditations in Everyday Life*, reprinted by permission of Hyperion.

Quote from Daniel Dana, PhD, President, Mediation Training Institute International, *Managing Differences*, http://www.mediationworks.com/pubs/bookmd.htm. Copyright 1988. Reprinted with special permission from Dr. Daniel Dana.

PART I

Introduction

*As conflict—difference—is here in the world, as we cannot avoid it,
we should, I think, use it. Instead of condemning it,
we should set it to work for us. ...The transmission of power
by belts depends on friction between the belt and the pulley.
All polishing is done by friction. The music of the violin
we get by friction.... So in business, too, we have to know
when to try to eliminate friction and when to try to capitalize it,
when to see what work we can make it do.*[6]

—MARY PARKER FOLLETT

CHAPTER 1

The Joy of Conflict

Driving along a four-lane road several years ago, I came up over a small hill. I knew this road well, had passed this way many times. This time, I noticed a major construction project under way at the gas station on the right-hand side. Workers were digging a hole right next to the road. This hole was huge. I was amazed at how deep it was. I was fascinated.

Have I mentioned the traffic light that was some fifty feet over that rise in the road? Unfortunately, I was much more interested in the size of the hole than I was in the road. Several cars were stopped at the red light just ahead. Cruising over the hill, I smacked into a car waiting there. I rammed into that car hard enough to get the attention of the car in *front* of the car that I had rear-ended. Pretty soon we were all milling around the cars, inspecting the damage.

In that moment, everybody noticed me. The people in the car I hit certainly noticed me. Those in the car in front of the car I hit noticed me. The cops came very quickly—they had also noticed. Later that day, my insurance company noticed.

Since then, I have gotten my car repaired and am back on the road. What I realized then was how many cars I do *not* hit, and that nobody noticed. No one has ever gotten out of a car to come around and thank me for bringing my car to a complete stop before making contact with the rear bumper in front of me.

And so it is with us all. Throughout most of our days we successfully navigate differences, find solutions, and accommodate others' needs, building compromises and collaborations along the way. When it comes to resolving all of these conflicts, nobody notices. Our skills are taken for granted.

What everyone notices instead are the collisions—those times when our needs and expectations clash with others' needs and expectations. Someone says something, and we are sparked to anger. Suddenly we're standing in the middle of the room, yelling at someone else. Or slamming the door and stomping out of the room. The label "conflict" is slapped on the event, and we walk away embarrassed and ashamed. "How could I have said that to her?" "Why didn't I just let that go?" We turn these moments over and over in our heads, feeling lousy about who we are and what we have done and because of how we reacted.

Conflict Defined

Managers deal with conflict all the time. As leader of a group, the manager's job is to understand the mission of the workgroup—how it supports the mission of the organization—to articulate that mission to staff and to others inside and outside the organization, and to support staff in accomplishing that mission. Providing that support frequently involves resolving differences and disagreements with staff. Often we don't label this "conflict resolution" because we listen, respond, and resolve differences in the workplace before those differences kick up enough emotional dust to be visible. What, then, do we mean by the word *conflict*? Most dictionaries define *conflict* as the competitive or opposing action of incompatibles. In other words, conflict is when what you want, need, or expect interferes with what I want, need, or expect. It may be a disagreement over data or processes (how things get done); or it may be over resources (where the money and staff will come from to do the job); or it may be about relationships or our identities or values.

With this definition, we can consider the various levels of conflict,

from mild disagreements, to disputes that require much time and attention, to intractable conflicts where emotions run high and relationships
are broken. Resolving conflicts may be done so quietly and effectively
that the moment is not remembered as a conflict. You have probably
experienced this on a daily basis. Say, someone comes into your office
with a question, you talk it over, agree on an answer, and sketch out a
way to proceed. This is the job of management: conflict raised, conflict
solved. Other conflicts become much bigger, with tempers flaring and
any resolution seeming impossible. What I do in this book is help you
develop an understanding of the nature of conflict and its resolution so
that more of the conflicts you encounter can be resolved at the lowest
possible level—in essence, to manage better.

Most of us face challenges in dealing with conflicts in our professional and personal lives. As I often tell groups I work with, I earned a
life degree in conflict, as many of us do—at work, in my community, and
with my family. I knew there must be a better way. In 1985, I headed
back to school to get a master's degree in conflict resolution. I wanted to
work "between people." I wanted to help them develop skills to address
their differences, and use my own skills when they needed assistance
addressing those differences. My hope was that they could more frequently walk away from a disagreement feeling relieved—and maybe
surprised: "That went better than I thought it would."

Since then, most of my work has been inside organizations. A large
part of my time is employed mediating and facilitating within offices,
between bosses and direct reports—helping each to hear the other, so
that both can find a productive, mutually acceptable way to move forward. The rest of my time is spent teaching people the skills to manage
conflict more effectively themselves.

Learning to handle conflict is a lifelong journey. There will always be
differences between and among us. Much of the time, most of us work
our way through them effectively. We all also hit the wall on occasion.
Someone says something that triggers a response and we go off. Looking
back, we scratch our heads and wonder what happened. And we wonder
how we can keep that from happening again. What I love about my work
is that I see it as a key developmental task for all humans. There is always
more to learn, a new test waiting somewhere ahead on the journey.

Conflict in the Workplace

Many people I work with were hired for their technical expertise and promoted into management positions. Sometimes the change happens overnight. The job she left on Friday afternoon is not the job she starts on Monday morning. In that shift, the nature of the work changes dramatically, from dealing with "things"—data, spreadsheets, reports—to dealing with people. Instead of doing the work herself, now she must manage people so that they get the work done. More than once I have had a new manager, who is struggling with difficulties on her staff, look at me forlornly and say, "I'd like to have my old job back, where I knew what to do, where I didn't have to deal with getting people to do the work I used to do."

Managing people requires "people skills"—new levels of communication and conflict-resolution skills. Often these new managers or supervisors have new challenges that they had not imagined before. They find themselves in the middle of conflict with direct reports. Many times what the boss wants, needs, and expects from staff is counter to what the staff wants, needs, and expects. The boss also must stand up for the people within the organization, fighting on their behalf with other business units for scarce resources, managing expectations and workload, negotiating for positions, promotions, and opportunities. And the boss also stands between co-workers who are having their own share of conflicts, aiming to harmonize differences so that people can get back to work.

Understanding conflict—how it is created, how we respond to it, and how to manage it more effectively—is what this book is about. We all, at one point or another, find it challenging to handle the differences between us. We need to recognize what is happening and why, know when to walk away and when to stand our ground, and learn how to do all of that more effectively.

The cost of conflict in the workplace is high. Some of the ways that unresolved conflict affects productivity include:

- ► 42 percent of a manager's time is spent addressing conflict in the workplace[1]
- ► Lost revenue from staff time is spent unproductively

▶ Excessive employee turnover (replacement costs average 75–150 percent of annual salary)

▶ Over 65 percent of performance problems are caused by employee conflicts[2]

▶ High levels of absenteeism

▶ "Presenteeism," whereby employees are present but not productive, due to low morale

▶ High incidence of damage and theft of inventory and equipment as a result of employee conflict

▶ Covert sabotage of work processes and of management efforts because of employee anger[3]

The benefits to a manager, and to a workplace, of resolving conflict effectively, at the lowest possible level, result not surprisingly in minimized costs. While statistical studies are difficult to conduct directly on the relationship between effective conflict resolution and employee satisfaction, nevertheless by improving these skills a manager can expect increased productivity, improved employee morale, and reduced turnover and absenteeism. In a study linking employee fulfillment directly to business performance, "the single biggest contributor to these feelings of fulfillment, empowerment, and satisfaction lie in the day-to-day relationship between employees and their managers."[4]

Conflict is a broad subject; much has been written already and there is much to say. There are so many skills that managers must use throughout the day. This book is an introduction to these skills, providing tools and approaches that enable managers to deal more effectively with the conflicts they encounter.

One of the challenges for managers is *differentiating*: When is this question a disagreement that I need to engage others in resolving? When does this situation involve the supervisory responsibility to make decisions? There are times when making directive, unilateral decisions is appropriate for managers and supervisors. There are other times when communicating and collaborating (i.e., engaging conflict-resolution processes and skills) are essential in order to get the work done efficiently and effectively.

In this book, I talk about interpersonal conflict—when what you want, need, or expect gets in the way of what others want, need, or expect. Within an office, the wants, needs, and expectations of an individual may conflict with those of the group and its work. Often, interpersonal conflict in the workplace affects *more* than the two people involved. In an office I was working in recently, the supervisor and the team leader frequently had confrontations and loud disagreements. The tension between the two reverberated through the office. All of the employees became anxious about who was in charge, how decisions were being made, even what they might expect when they came to work the next day. This discomfort and distraction had a direct effect on morale and productivity.

In another office, the ongoing conflict between the manager and a staff member spilled over to the wider office as well, as the staff member spent much time badmouthing the boss. Not only was the employee's own work not getting done, but others picked up this virus of negativity and their work suffered, as well.

Understanding and managing conflict at this one-on-one level also gives the manager skills and insights to deal more effectively with larger conflicts—those involving more people. Each time you add another person to the equation, the web of interaction becomes more complex—just as individuals have their own wants, needs, and expectations within a group, so also groups become entities of their own, with their own wants, needs, and expectations that conflict with other groups. So, I start here, at this foundation, with an understanding of the dynamics between us as individuals, identifying some keys that help reduce antagonism and make it easier to resolve conflicts when they arise (and they *will* continue to arise, even after you have mastered all the skills in this book).

A word of encouragement: Small changes can yield big results down the road. As you read this book, identify small behavioral changes you want to make, and then make a commitment to practice them over a specific period of time, perhaps six weeks or six months. Step by step, you'll see incremental changes practiced patiently build upon each other. Later, look back at how well you have kept your commitment to change, and notice the shifts in behavior

> *True life is lived where tiny changes occur.*
> —Leo Tolstoy

and attitude that have occurred. As I watched the launch of the Mars *Exploration* Rover in 2003, I thought about the difference a small shift in the thrust of the rocket would make. A few degrees in one direction or another would send the Rover into totally different directions over time. Similarly, a slight modification in your attitude and approach may well bring you closer to resolving conflicts more easily.

Drawing from My Own Experience

Jon Kabat-Zinn, in his book *Wherever You Go, There You Are*, reminds us that we are all learners on life's path. As conflict has been the focus of my work for twenty-some years, I bring the lessons I have learned— and continue to learn—to you.

> In a wonderfully unfinished story called "Mount Analogue," René Daumal once mapped a piece of this inward adventure. The part I remember most vividly involves the rule on Mount Analogue that before you move up the mountain to your next encampment, you replenish the camp you are leaving for those who will come after you, and go down the mountain a ways to share with the other climbers your knowledge from farther up so that they may have some benefit from what you have learned so far on your own ascent. In a way, that's all any of us do when we teach. As best we can, we show others what we have seen up to now. It's at best a progress report, a map of our experiences, by no means the absolute truth. And so the adventure unfolds. We are all on Mount Analogue together. And we need each other's help.[5]

Here, I speak with my own voice. I use examples from others, but the perspective is from my own learning and observation. I learned a lot in completing the program for my master's degree. I learned even more in confronting my own "stuff" concerning the people closest to me, who challenged so much of what I thought I knew. The people I have worked with over the years continue to teach me even more.

All that said, even with twenty years' experience as a conflict-resolution professional, when it's about *my* stuff I still don't walk into a conflict saying, "Oh, boy, another growth opportunity!" In the pit of my stomach is a sinking feeling, a moment of dread. I must pull together inner resources because, in fact, on the other side of this moment is the possibility of reaching a better place, of finding some improvement in the relationship or in my own understanding of myself. As you consider the stories here and apply them to your own situation, you will see that the lessons come in small moments, in tiny packages, and from seemingly insignificant events.

The stories are true—that is, they are based on disagreements, disputes, and workplace challenges I have witnessed firsthand. The names and circumstances have been altered to protect the privacy of individuals. Also, as you will see in some situations I discuss, by the time someone has called me for assistance, the conflict is nearly impossible to resolve. My hope is that this book will provide you with tools and skills that you can use to address difficult moments before they reach this point.

How We Think About Conflict

When I teach, I often start discussions with a word-association game: "When you hear the word *conflict*, what do you think of?" As I write the responses of the group on a flip chart in front of the class, they continue to add words, quickly filling the page. Mostly, the words are negative.

stress	tension
war	disagreement
argument	miscommunication
avoidance	anger
hostility	win-lose
fight	battle

One of my personal favorites sometimes comes up: *dread*. Conflict? No, thanks. I have been there before and it was really ugly. People yelling. Doors slamming. Relationships broken. Destruction. A real mess.

Here are three more words to add to the list: *inevitable*, *growth*, and *progress*.

Conflict Is . . . *Inevitable*

Wherever we, as human beings, interact, it is *inevitable* that we will reach some point where what "you" want, need, and expect gets in the way of what "I" (or "we") want, need, and expect. It happens on the playground, in the neighborhood, at school, at work, at home, in the wider world of public policies and resources, and certainly between nations and nationalities. Pretending that it won't happen, or hoping that it won't, will not make it go away. Thinking that if you live long enough you get beyond it is another fantasy. We can, however, get better at responding to conflicts so that they are resolved with barely a ripple of discord.

I was raised on the standard fairy tales, each ending with that magical statement "And they lived happily ever after." Really? On the one hand, that sounds like bliss. On the other, it sounds incredibly boring. When I was a teenager, I remember thinking that as soon as I reached twenty-one, life would be a straight shot—I would have it all figured out, and everything would be easy after that. No more conflict, no more troubles. When I got to twenty-one, though, it was a big disappointment. So I raised the number to thirty—surely, by then. Well, thirty came, and I looked to thirty-five. Finally, at about thirty-seven, the light bulb went on: the learning keeps on going from here, until wherever the road ends.

In her mid-nineties, my grandmother told me, "Life is one adjustment after another." My first reaction to this was disappointment. Wasn't there some point we would reach when we could quit? When we would be done and could just sit on the porch and watch the seasons change? Then I saw the excitement and possibility of her wisdom. Life continues to unfold, giving us new challenges, new ways of thinking, and new means of relating to each other.

Conflict Is . . . *Growth*

Our personal realizations are steps to maturity. They come packaged as our needs and expectations, as well as our tools for getting those needs met, but they bump into the needs and expectations of others. Conflict brings me face to face with my own hostility and its effect on others. I resolve to change my ways—and I may resolve again and again to do it differently next time, as the growth that I seek slowly transforms my behavior.

I remember standing in the middle of the office when she accused me of not returning her phone calls. I felt my face flush, and I was about to set her straight, to tell her about all of the drama that had gone on in my life in the last two days, to justify my disrespect for her request. Instead, I stopped myself; I took a deep breath and asked her to tell me more. And then I listened to what she had to say.

This small act was a huge step for me—to move away from my usual pattern of reaction and try a new response. Learning to listen more and talk less is an ongoing effort. I can look back and see that I have grown over time by making that change. I am better able to hear others, to understand their concerns, to correct my assumptions, and to answer more calmly. And yes, as the people around me will attest, I am a work in progress.

I have learned something else about conflict—what happens when I go toe-to-toe with someone I care about and discover that he or she will stick with me through it. On the other side of the argument, we are still here together, closer than ever because we understand each other more and we know that the bonds that hold us are tighter than the demons that might tear us apart. We know that the relationship is stronger than all of this.

> *Fear of difference is dread of life itself. It is possible to conceive conflict as not necessarily a wasteful outbreak of incompatibilities, but a normal process by which socially valuable differences register themselves for the enrichment of all concerned.*
> —MARY PARKER FOLLETT

I learn from experience that avoidance or accommodation works against me sometimes, and so I look for ways to take on differences before they explode into bigger problems. With some amount of resistance and pain, I grow. For instance, arguments I was in before ended badly. The anger overwhelmed the room, until someone walked out—and often it was me. I was trapped by my fears, not daring to say what mattered to me, what I cared about. I lived much of the time behind a mask of politeness. I shrank further and further into myself, in some ways away from myself.

It is from learning this about myself that I began to understand forgiveness—that others are no more perfect than I am. We cannot function in life, as tied as we are to other humans, without forgiveness. And it is from this place of forgiveness that I learned the power of apology, along with the humility and vulnerability that such an admission takes. This, too, is growth.

When I say that conflict is inevitable, I do not mean that growth through conflict is also inevitable. Growth is optional—a matter of will and wanting. We all know people who don't seize the opportunities for growth that conflict can bring. It can be more comfortable to stay in denial, or to live in defensiveness and self-justification. The manager who is willing to step into the possibility of growth through addressing disagreements must have the courage to admit to him- or herself that maybe there is something the individual needs to acknowledge and change.

Recently I sat in on a meeting between an office director and his staff. Over the years that they had worked together, the staff had become more and more frustrated with this director's behavior. For instance, at a staff meeting, Sal, one of the staff, brought up a problem: "That new software has a serious glitch. A function we were counting on doesn't work." Sal had just begun to describe the problem when the boss cut him off. "Remove that program from everyone's computers. Let's go after the competitor's product, instead." Sal sat back in his chair and sighed. He had no chance to explore some possible fixes for the software. Rather than finding a simple solution, now the staff had a bigger project on their hands: negotiating a new contract, testing the new program, removing the old one, and installing the substitute across the company. Not only was this added work, it was a diversion from the other projects they were doing.

Sal had learned not to press the point. The director would sometimes start pounding on the table and raising his voice to make his position clear, and Sal didn't want to get that started again. Time after time, rather than listening to the staff's concerns and working through the problems with them, he would jump to conclusions and announce what would be done. He was quick to look for a person to blame for any difficulty, too. When a subordinate tried to talk with him about how his behavior was keeping the team from working together effectively, the boss became defensive. "It's my job. We don't have time to waste on those discussions. I'm just trying to keep this place going."

What Sal couldn't know was the extent of the pressure and stress that the boss was under to meet deadlines and quotas, and how that stress affected his response—why he often put a premium on hierarchic decision making. And what the boss didn't know was that often taking the time to listen, to find a solution with his staff members rather than imposing one, could make the work of the office easier. Treating team members and their ideas with respect, and building solutions together, could reap rewards through increased creativity and productivity.

Conflict Is . . . *Progress*

While "growth" is internal, progress is external—between people. Maybe new systems or agreements are developed. New answers are found to the problems that have become visible through the disagreement. There is little progress that is *not* preceded by some kind of conflict. Necessity is the mother of invention, and conflict is often the mother of necessity. And it is in the caldron of conflict that things get stirred up—and sorted out. We begin to look for solutions, for better ideas and possibilities, and we find them. Often we do not address a conflict until the status quo is so uncomfortable that the time and energy to resolve it seems bearable, though. Had we recognized the need earlier, the time and energy required would not have been so great.

In one office, the receptionist complained to whomever would listen. She never knew where this staff member or that staff member was, or when the individual would be back. After the phone rang repeatedly in the respective cubicles, the call would be automatically forwarded to the receptionist's desk. The tension mounted over months. The angrier she got, the harder it was for her to talk to the staff. When they finally came to a retreat, the group waded through a long discussion of various grievances and complaints. At last she had the opportunity to express her frustration. Eureka, a solution! Set up a sign-out board in the office so everyone would know who was available when. Could this solution have been found without the months of buildup? Maybe. Because the problem took so long to come to a head, and the group worked together to establish a new system, everyone recognized its importance and made a strong commitment to keeping that new system in place.

Here is another example of the progress that comes through conflict, this time on a slightly larger scale. Several years ago, a couple came to a large federal agency with a list of complaints. She was blind; he was her companion on life's road. The law says that all federal facilities must meet the needs of people regardless of their disabilities. Their complaints were that the parks they visited were quite restrictive for her. They met with the director, who said, "This is just not a priority for us. It's an unfunded mandate from Congress. We don't have the time or the money to do anything." The couple went away angry. After that meeting they visited 320 parks over a nine-year period, taking notes.

They sent a packet of their findings to the department. Their message was hostile and combative, threatening a lawsuit. The department answered in kind. E-mails flew back and forth, each one creating more animosity. Finally, a meeting was called. The new director said, "Let's sit down, listen to what they have to say, see how we might respond." What the staff heard from the couple was, "A blind person can't use the touch screen on the computer at the exhibit." "The person behind the counter doesn't know where the adaptive equipment is." "The little buttons of Braille that are cast in plastic break pretty quickly—and you can't read it after that." The staff leaned forward in their chairs, eagerly taking notes. Once they started listening, and walking in an unsighted world, their view changed. You could feel the shift in the room, from wary defensiveness and antagonism to receptive encouragement. The new mood was, "Here are two people with a huge commitment to the work we are doing. How can we help them help us do a better job?"

Finally, an example on a grand scale of progress through conflict. White Americans in the years after World War II viewed their world with contentment and optimism. For African Americans, though, the picture was disturbingly different. They were sent to the back of the bus; forced to use the rear entrances of public facilities and the "colored" water fountains; and barred from jobs and restaurants, hotels and stores. It took the courage of many people to challenge the status quo, to say loudly and clearly, over and over again, "This is not acceptable."

Recently I was in Atlanta. As I approached the building where I'd be working, I recognized its shape, even though it had been some fifty years since I last saw it. Everything else about the Atlanta I knew back then had changed. But there it stood, sturdy stucco with department store display windows facing the sidewalk, the decorative balustrades topping the nine-story structure. Rich's Department Store, it had been back then.

This particular morning, as I walked past those windows, long for-gotten memories were suddenly standing there with me. This was *the* place where my grandmother and my mother took me as a child for a grand outing—lunch and shopping for school clothes for the fourth grade. "Six, please." The smiling African-American elevator operator closed the door and up we went. Ordering a grilled cheese sandwich in the elegant dining room was an early lesson in how to be a "lady."

Today the store windows are filled with the history of Rich's: "The Store That Made a City." One of the displays stopped me in my tracks. There were pictures from 1960 of protestors outside of Rich's. I could almost hear the crowd in the old black-and-white photos. "Wear Old Clothes with New Dignity. Boycott Rich's," one sign read. As I stood looking in that window, I realized that when I was that little white girl sitting upstairs in the dining room, I had no idea that other children, lit-tle brown girls with their mothers and grandmothers, were not allowed into that room to eat. I was oblivious to the world of privilege in which I was growing up. It took some heroic, determined individuals who were willing to face conflict in order to achieve progress. Few of us are this far-sighted, courageous, or strategic.

Sometimes we need conflict—we need people who have the courage to stand up and say "This cannot stand." Those who are comfortable with the status quo can stay there a very long time. It took a strong dose of discomfort on the national news every night—conflict—to rock the dominant culture out of that comfort zone.

From the personal to the historic, progress has come out of the caldron of conflict. Conflict is inevitable. Progress and growth are possible. What moves the possibility into reality is our ability to work through conflict in a positive way, to use appropriate tools and skills. These skills enable us to have the courage to face the fears that often come with conflict.

Several years ago, I stood as facilitator in front of an angry church congregation. Churches are supposed to be places where people come together to share values, care about each other, and learn to love one another, aren't they? For three hours, members waited in lines at the microphones to register their complaints. The complaints they raised reached way back into the church's history. "Five years ago, she told me…" "I couldn't believe it when he showed up at the meeting with…" Clearly, these folks had been carrying around their resentments for a long, long time." Toward the end of the meeting, one participant stood at a microphone, looked around the room, and quoted Gloria Steinem to the crowd, "The Bible says, 'The truth shall set you free.' But first it is really going to piss you off." When I got back to my office, I hung that quote over my computer. It explained so much about conflict and growth.

Consider This

☑ Identify a conflict you have been a part of or witnessed that resulted in growth or progress.

Overview of the Book

Part I sets the stage for understanding conflict, beginning with this chapter. Chapter 2, "What Gets in Our Way?" explores what happens when a working relationship has gotten off track—how fear, assumptions, blame, and habits get in the way of resolving conflicts.

Part II, "Understanding the Dynamics of Conflict," provides an analysis of the dimensions of conflict, which points to the tools to understand differences and avoid needless contention. Chapter 3, "What We Need: The Satisfaction Triangle," describes three necessary components of satisfactory solutions. In Chapter 4, "Where We Are: Levels of Conflict," you will see how resolving conflict at the earliest opportunity is easiest—and strategies for dealing with conflicts that have escalated. Chapter 5, "How We Respond: Approaches to Conflict," enables you to gain a clearer understanding of your own approaches to conflict, and the approaches others around you use. From there, you learn strategies for beginning to change those approaches when they are not useful and to deal more effectively with other approaches you encounter at work. Chapter 6, "Who We Are: Cultural Considerations," explores cultural differences and the role these differences play in creating and resolving conflict. Chapter 7, "What We Are Arguing About Matters: Sources of Conflict," analyzes five sources of conflict in the workplace: information, interests, structural conflicts, values, and relationships—with a guide to using that understanding to resolve conflict more effectively.

Part III, "Keys to Resolving Conflict," introduces five concepts managers can use to create a more positive climate for workplace relationships. Chapter 8, "Building Trust," considers behaviors that build or wreck trust and how to rebuild trust that has been broken. Chapter 9, "Apology and Forgiveness," addresses the role that apologies and forgiveness play, and provides steps to take to apologize effectively and to move toward forgiveness. Chapter 10, "Rethinking Anger," explores the physiology of anger, as well as ways to manage your own anger or respond to others' anger. Chapter 11, "A Sense of Humor," focuses on the importance of keeping the ups and downs of working relationships in perspective; and Chapter 12, "Time," reflects on the importance of time in decision making and the resolution of conflict.

Part IV, "Putting It All Together," brings together concepts explored in earlier chapters, providing specific conflict-resolution tools and communication skills. Chapter 13, "Reaching Agreement: A Solution-Seeking Model," delineates a process for addressing differences, presents a solution-seeking model, and shows how to use it. Chapter 14, "Listening Is the Place to Start," focuses on listening skills and explores how managers can listen more effectively. Chapter 15, "Saying What Needs to Be Said," gives a guide and some tips for raising concerns and addressing issues so that others are more likely to hear your message. Chapter 16, "The Challenge of Electronic Communication," explores how to use electronic communication effectively in addressing workplace conflicts.

Each of the concepts and skills presented here will enable you to resolve conflicts more quickly and effectively, which will have an immediate impact on morale, productivity, and ultimately the bottom line.

Notes

1. C. Watson, and R. Hoffman, "Managers as Negotiators," *Leadership Quarterly* 7, no.1 (1996), http://www.conflictatwork.com/conflict/cost_e.cfm, last viewed August 25, 2010.

2. Daniel Dana, *Managing Differences: How to Build Better Relationships at Work and at Home* (Prairie Village, KS: MTI Publishing, 2006), p. 13.

3. Ibid., p. 18.

4. "Redefining Employee Satisfaction: Business Performance, Employee Fulfillment, and Leadership Practices" (Edina, MN: Wilson Learning Worldwide, 2006), http://wilsonlearning.com/images/uploads/pdf/employee_satisfaction_en.pdf, accessed September 4, 2010.

5. John Kabat-Zinn, *Wherever You Go, There You Are: Mindfulness Meditations in Everyday Life* (New York: Hyperion, 1995), p. 212.

6. Elliot M. Fox and L. Urwick, eds., *Dynamic Administration: The Collected Papers of Mary Parker Follett* (London: Pitman, 1973), pp. 1–20.

CHAPTER 2

What Gets in Our Way?

For many of us, *conflict* is a dirty word. Some of us try to escape conflict by burying our heads, turning away, not bringing it up. Others try to get out of the situation as quickly as possible by force of will—I'll just tell them what to do and be done with it. Why do we work so hard to get rid of conflict?

Again and again, business books and journals praise the advantages of engaging in constructive conflict resolution. Authors and researchers tell us how conflict can improve productivity and performance, strengthen teamwork, and become a catalyst for creative problem solving. We read and nod our

> *The easiest, the most tempting, and the least creative response to conflict within an organization is to pretend it does not exist.*
> —LYLE E. SCHALLER

heads in agreement. We attend seminars and workshops about it all the time. Yes, we believe all of this in theory. So why is it so hard to apply the theories in our own workplaces? This book is not about "Get over conflict so that you can get your team back to work." Rather, this book is about learning to see conflict as an inevitable, essential part of the work itself. But, first, a story.

. . . .

Outside the Deputy Commissioner's office—one of those large corner offices on the top floor of the government building, with huge windows looking out on the expanse of city below—dark clouds were rolling across the sky. A storm was coming. We could see it and feel it. The weather outside matched the mood of the room inside. I was sitting down to discuss the turmoil in the CFO's office with Debbie, the Deputy Commissioner, Jack, the head of Human Resources, and my partner, Pete. I had spent the day listening to the CFO's Senior Management Team (SMT)—three bright, strong, capable professionals. Pete had been having a serious conversation with Tre, the CFO.

What brought us to this meeting? Two weeks before, one of the SMT members had called HR with a long list of complaints about Tre. She ended the conversation with an ultimatum: "Either he goes or I go. And, by the way, the other SMTs feel the same way."

What??? Where had this come from? This team had been working together for over three years. Several months ago, in the annual employee satisfaction survey, Tre's office had received the highest rating of all the divisions. The organization could not afford to lose three of its top performers. And it couldn't simply fire the CFO out of the blue. Debbie and Jack were shocked. How had conflict been brewing so long without anyone's addressing it? What would we suggest now that they were at a point of crisis?

. . . .

I have said it before, and I'll say it again. Conflict is inevitable. When what you want, need, or expect gets in the way of what I want, need, or expect, we have a conflict. Why don't we resolve all of our conflicts when they first arise as mere disagreements, before they flare into bigger problems? Four stumbling blocks often get in our way: fear, blame, assumptions, and habits.

Fear as a Stumbling Block

We can easily address disagreements and misunderstandings. We listen, we find a way forward, we move on to the next item on the to-do list.

Unless that doesn't work. If we don't listen, or find a way forward, it can take time before we see the situation as a conflict. By that time, frustration has mounted, the problem looms larger, and fear sets in. That fear can spin us swiftly into panic or anger, driving us to take drastic action quickly.

> *There is nothing wrong with being afraid—but there is nothing more wrong than allowing that to be your master.*
> —BOBBY DARIN

Tre and his staff spent a couple of years reacting unconsciously to their fears. When confusion, contention, or indecision arose, Tre's immediate response was to kick into gear, yelling at someone on the team about what must be done immediately to fix the problem, to fix it his way and on his timetable. When the boss yelled at them, the staff's reaction was to get busy and to get quiet. What did Tre fear? What did staff members fear? In a conflict, what do we fear?

- ► We fear change and the loss that change might bring.
- ► We fear making a mistake and being seen as incompetent.
- ► We fear losing face—losing our reputation or our pride, honor, dignity.
- ► We fear being hurt. We fear being hurt physically. We fear the words that might hurt. The emotional memories of pain live in our hearts long after the physical pain has healed.
- ► We fear what the conflict might say about the other person, or about our relationship.
- ► We fear hurting someone else. We might fear our own physical strength and the damage we could do. We might fear saying something that can't be pulled back out of the air once it has been spoken.
- ► We fear how the conflict might affect the future, and our future relationships.
- ► We fear being disrespected or dismissed; we fear being embarrassed.
- ► We fear losing control; we fear feeling powerless.
- ► We fear being seen as weak, incompetent, or unworthy.
- ► We fear being abandoned. We fear being unlovable.

Consider this: Anger is a secondary emotion, often caused by the fears named here. In reaction to that anger, we have two automatic responses: fight or flight.

Some of us prefer the fight mode. Put your dukes up and start swinging. The best defense is a good offense. Win before they know what hit them. If a staff member disagrees with your idea, cut him off, let him know immediately that you are right, and the question is settled. To thwart the possibility of an argument, let him know, then and there, who is boss—in no uncertain terms. In the face of conflict with his staff, Tre came in swift and firm and demanding, leaving no room for further discussion.

Others of us take the flight option instead. It feels much more comfortable, much easier to avoid the difficult moments than to open up the possibility of differences that might explode into some unknown territory, where the monsters of unbridled emotion leap up to take over the discussion. Jack, the HR director, asked us how, if the SMT was so upset, could Tre have been given such positive ratings on the survey? The answer? Intimidated by his authority and the way he used it, they had chosen flight. Tre had warned them when the survey came out to give him a positive review. Fearing his wrath, they silenced their concerns and gave the "right" answers.

. . . .

In another office, I worked with a frustrated and fearful boss who preferred flight. After a couple of disastrous staff meetings, where there was a fair amount of dissension and disagreement, she decided that it was just not worth the risk having people in the same room who might argue about an idea. Her solution was to quit having staff meetings. "We've got too much work to do to waste time in meetings," she explained. Communication shut down. People within the office did not know what others were doing. They didn't know what new expectations were coming down from the higher-ups. They didn't know when new people were coming on board. By the time I arrived, they had not had a meeting in over a year. Rather than eliminate the dissension and conflict that made the boss anxious, the disagreements and conflicts had taken on a life of their own.

. . . .

In a heated dispute, if the fears are high enough, there is that moment in the middle of the fight where one person threatens the other. If we know each other well, if we've been working together long enough, or if one of us has a position of power or authority over the other, we've got lots of ammunition. Even the possibility of this kind of threat can create the fear of having any type of conflict.

Hanging over the employee's head is that nuclear threat, "You're fired!" The vagaries of the marketplace over the past few years have taught us that the security we count on from our jobs is not as secure as it once was. For Debbie, the Deputy Commissioner, the threat she heard from the SMTs was not "You're fired" but "I'm leaving." There are other catastrophic threats: "I'll kill you for that"; or "I'll take my friends with me when I go"; or "I'll steal the company clients or secrets, or destroy the computer database on my way out."

Fear can be a real showstopper when it comes to conflict. It stops even our willingness to entertain differences of opinion that may open up into a confrontation. The very thought of conflict is just too risky. The fight or flight options we turn to in response to that fear are often more likely to create increased conflict than to resolve it. We lose valuable opportunities to find creative solutions and build staff commitment.

Eleanor Roosevelt once gave this advice: "Do one thing every day that scares you." For those of us who are held captive by our fear of conflict, this wisdom can move us into taking positive action to address those situations that we are not handling well.

Consider This

- ☑ In your own work environment, what are the situations that you fear?
- ☑ In those situations, what do you fear?
- ☑ Identify one situation that's a little scary that you would like to address in a different way.

Blame as a Stumbling Block

Tuesday, May 11, 2010. Three executives in business suits filed into a U.S. Senate hearing room and took their places at a large table behind name tents and microphones. Each was committed to assigning blame to the other two. Meanwhile, 1,000 miles away and 1 mile below the surface of the water, oil continued to gush into the Gulf of Mexico at 60,000 barrels per day. BP Oil pointed to Transocean's blowout preventer, Transocean blamed the cement and casing that Halliburton supplied, Halliburton pointed back at BP and Transocean. Blame spewed in the hearing room almost as furiously as the oil from the broken pipe on the ocean floor. But blame did not fix the problem.

> *People spend too much time finding other people to blame,*
> *too much energy finding excuses for not being what they are capable*
> *of being, and not enough energy putting themselves on the line,*
> *growing out of the past, and getting on with their lives.*
>
> —J. MICHAEL STRACZYNSKI

When a conflict, a problem, or a disagreement arises, our first instinct is to figure out who is to blame. If we can pin the blame on someone or something else, then we don't have to deal with it any more—it's their fault, not ours. Let them figure it out. Watching the effects of this approach is enlightening—and disheartening. In an office where the boss hears any discussion of a difficulty, a mistake, or a problem and immediately

> *I praise loudly,*
> *I blame softly.*
> —CATHERINE II OF RUSSIA

begins to look for someone to blame, staff shut down. No one wants to raise an issue that needs to be addressed for fear of being blamed. Staff become demotivated as they grow anxious about who will be next.

In one office where I worked, the penalty for a mistake was banishment from the inner circle. Once blame was fixed, the project was assigned to someone else. That someone else would quickly become overloaded with work and then grow resentful, while others saw the boss's actions as favoritism. On the other hand, some of us are more inclined to take the blame. "It's my fault."

> *A good leader takes a little more than his share of the blame, a little less than his share of the credit.*
> —ARNOLD H. GLASGOW

"I don't have the skill." "I made the mistake." Here again, assigning the blame to one's self does nothing to address the conflict or the problem.

It is a fine line to walk between accepting responsibility, holding

> *Yet we act as if simple cause and effect is at work. We push to find*
> *the one simple reason things have gone wrong. We look for*
> *the one action, or the one person, that created this mess. As soon as*
> *we find someone to blame, we act as if we've solved the problem.*
> —Margaret J. Wheatley

people accountable for their actions, and shifting into blame solely for the sake of blame. In managing employees, holding them accountable for their actions and making clear their responsibilities in getting the work done is essential. However, many times, the "blame game" just keeps us from dealing with the real issues at hand.

Assigning blame to someone else is a delicious temptation. It looks like the conflict will be much easier to address or to resolve if we can first figure out whose fault it is. Then, if we can fix *the individual*, the problem is solved. When we look further into the conflict, however, nine times out of ten we have had some role in creating, contributing to, or exacerbating the situation.

In the opening story, the Senior Leadership Team came in with their lists of complaints about Tre, going back over the previous three years. Yes, there was a lot they could blame him for. But then the HR Director had a challenging question for each SMT member: "Why didn't you raise this sooner?" As frustrated as they were with their boss, they too had some responsibility to tackle the difficult issues before they became too big. Time spent assigning blame is only time *not* spent in finding a way forward.

. . . .

I sat in a small, windowless conference room interviewing all the staff of an office. The table took up almost all the floor space; several chairs were shoved into the room around the table. I had the schedule of interviews printed out, neatly placed on the table next to my legal pad, gel pen, and glasses. I worked my way down the list, with each staff member coming in right on time, taking a seat, and eagerly telling me all that was wrong with the office. These responses were about what the boss did or didn't do, or how co-workers weren't doing their jobs, who had offended whom, who you could count on and who you couldn't. The employees were quick to blame everyone else for all of the problems they had.

Number four on the interview list that day was Naomi. She sat down, carefully crossed her legs, and leaned forward, her elbows on the table. When she said, "You know, I think I might be part of the problem," I was stunned. She actually was willing to accept some of the responsibility rather than pointing a finger of blame at the rest of the team.

. . . .

Over the years, I have conducted hundreds of these interviews in all kinds of offices. My first task is usually to conduct an assessment, to understand what the issues and concerns are, so that I can put together a plan for helping everyone get back to work. Naomi was the first one, the only one, who did not start by blaming others for the challenges her office faced. It took courage for her to move out of the comfort zone of blame and begin to examine the situation to see what responsibility she might have.

Consider This
- ☑ How often do you find yourself assigning blame? When is it useful, when is it not?
- ☑ Instead of assigning blame, have you considered what part you play in this conflict?
- ☑ Given where you are now, how can you best address the situation?

Assumptions as Stumbling Blocks

Third on the list of stumbling blocks is our eagerness to make assumptions. We make assumptions unconsciously and take action without thinking. This creates conflict and makes working through differences more difficult. Consider this example.

. . . .

Winter, 1995. She had been to the Cosmos Club before. People in Washington, D.C., know what an exclusive society this is. The walls are covered with black- and-white photos of distinguished members, some living, some long since gone. Nobel and Pulitzer Prize winners, famous authors, political leaders, renowned businessmen (mostly men, really). Her dinner was delicious, the conversation bright and lively. When she was ready to leave, she went to retrieve her coat from the coat-check station. She saw an older man standing in the hall and as she asked for her coat, he pointed farther down the hall. "Ask someone over there."

She quickly snapped, "If you aren't getting my coat, you shouldn't be here." But she was speaking to Dr. John Hope Franklin. He was there attending a dinner honoring him for receiving the Presidential Medal of Honor for his life's work. This distinguished African American was a historian; his most celebrated book was *From Slavery to Freedom.*

• •

When I heard this story, I could only imagine how this woman's face flushed with embarrassment when she realized her mistake. We have all been there ourselves, making an assumption, stepping into our response, and quickly discovering how foolish we have been.

How quickly we move from seeing or hearing a piece of information and translating it into, *I know what that means*, then taking swift action—saying or doing something we may later regret. We each carry a host of built-in assumptions that inform our thinking and our actions. Many of these assumptions are useful in getting us through the day. We need to organize information into manageable categories and expectations. For example, we assume that equipment will work when we count on it, that others in the office will show up and complete the tasks assigned to them. Life would be too difficult to navigate if we didn't have sets of assumptions about how the world works and what behavior to expect from others.

We carry many assumptions—ideas that we take for granted—based on our experience or culture. Some of our assumptions are about conflict itself. For some of us, the thought of losing in a conflict is devastating. If we questioned that assumption, though, we might discover that often life goes on fairly comfortably even without winning every contest. We carry assumptions about how others see us and those assumptions often drive our behaviors. If we challenge those assumptions, we may discover that others do not even notice actions that loom large in our own minds. We may assume that if we stand up to someone who disagrees or if we say something the person doesn't like, that person will leave. But sometimes it takes courage to step out in the face of these assumptions, to change our behavior and see what the results might be.

Managers carry assumptions about information and communication. Sometimes managers assume that people in the office don't really need to know what is going on within the broader organization, that all they need to know is the task they have been given to do. Other times, managers assume that others know critical information, operating under some vague notion that "everybody knows that." These assumptions can be particularly appealing and dangerous for managers—appealing because communication takes time, and if people already know, or don't need to know, it can save a lot of time. It's also dangerous because, in the absence of accurate and timely information, employees will fill the void with rumors, gossip, and assumptions of their own making.

We have expectations or fixed ideas about people who talk differently or dress differently from how we do. Sometimes those assumptions morph into stereotypes, out of which we create prejudices. This often happens when we are dealing with people we don't trust or don't know very well. Our assumptions—the meaning that we unconsciously attach to our differences—lead us into saying or doing things that can be wrong, sometimes disastrously wrong, as in the story of the woman at the Cosmos Club.

"He's a narcissist." "She's just lazy." "He's rude." "She is a liar." "He's such a whiner, or a coward, or a bully, or…." Feel free to insert your own list here. It is perilously easy to slip into these fundamental attribution errors—deciding that the reason someone acts the way he does is because of a permanent character flaw, rather than for situational reasons. Before assuming and assigning some negative label, begin by considering that this person has good reasons for his behavior by asking your-

The least questioned assumptions are often the most questionable.

—PAUL BROCA

self: "Why might a sensible, reasonable person act this way?" Better yet, talk to the person to find out, in a nonconfrontational way, what's going

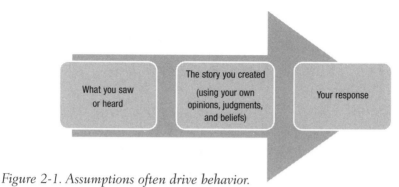

Figure 2-1. Assumptions often drive behavior.

on, or how he sees the situation. Don't assume you know why others are acting (or have acted) the way they do.

As managers, the lure of assumptions can carry more risk. In general, we assume that "we" are right and "they" are wrong. If you are a manager or a supervisor, it can seem even more important to *be* right, or to maintain the *appearance* of being right. Sometimes, managers feel that their authority will be questioned if they are not always right. The need to maintain this facade can undermine a person's credibility, rather than increase it. It takes more confidence and strength for someone to admit that she doesn't have all the answers than to try to look like she does. You might want to test this idea for yourself. Listen to the people whom you respect and admire. Are they willing to admit when they don't have an answer or when they make a mistake? At times it is assumptions that start a conflict in the first place. Someone hears or sees something, makes a snap judgment about it, and takes action. We may not find out for a long time that our interpretations of the event were dead wrong. Figure 2-1 illustrates this flow of action.

· ·

How easily we can create our own stories about what is happening, without clarifying our own assumptions. Some time ago I was talking to a group in a meeting. Out of the corner of my eye, I saw Cassandra write something on a piece of paper and hand it to the boss who was sitting next to her. (That's what I actually saw.) Almost below conscious thought, I thought, *That note must be about what I just said.* (I was beginning the story, based solely on my imagination—I had no way of knowing what she wrote.) *Cassandra doesn't like me much, and she thought she should have had this assignment instead of me,* I thought. (Again, my own judgments and beliefs.) *I must sound like I don't know what I am doing. The boss is thinking of shifting the assignment to Cassandra because I can't handle it.* (I create my own story.) Within seconds, I jumped from my observation of Cassandra's writing a note and sprang into action, becoming defensive about the job I was assigned to do. (My response.)

. . . .

Someone else sitting in that meeting could have seen the same incident and have created a totally different story about what was happening. Within a few minutes, the administrative assistant walked into the

> *The more we understand that we may be wrong the better our lives will be.*
> —STEVEN GAFFNEY

room with a birthday cake for another employee, and I realized what the note was about—and how foolish my own assumptions had been.

. . . .

Assumptions can stack up over time to create larger conflicts. Several years ago I was called in to a large corporation to address a workplace conflict. An African-American woman had filed a complaint of discrimination. Here is how the story unfolded.

Belinda was the wife of a pastor. Mary regularly walked down the hall, stopping to chat at each cubicle, until she approached Belinda's office. There, she stopped and went the other way. Belinda watched this happening day after day. She added her own meaning, her own opinions and judgments, and created her own story about what she saw happening. The story in her own mind was that Mary was avoiding her because of her race, and based on that belief, she took action, filing her complaint.

Then Mary told the story from her view. She knew she had an uncontrollable habit of using profanity, "a sailor's mouth," as she called it. She also knew that Belinda was a minister's wife. She felt uncomfortable talking to Belinda, fearing she might say something inappropriate and offensive to her. It was easier not to talk to her than to risk that embarrassment. When the subject finally came out in the open, Mary could see why Belinda felt singled out.

. . . .

These stories point out another dangerous set of assumptions: assuming that we know *why* someone is doing what he or she is doing. These assumptions sound like: "She's avoiding me because she doesn't like people like me." "He's trying to get me in trouble." "She wants my job." "He thinks I'm not very smart." "I know why she's doing that." As a mediator, I often have to remind people to speak for themselves, from their own experience, to describe what they saw or heard without taking the story into what they *thought* was happening or what they thought was intended.

> *Don't believe everything you think.*

Sometimes I help people imagine all of the possibilities about what else might be going on in a situation—to help them question the story they are telling *themselves* about what has occurred and how they have filled it with their own assumptions. In Chapter 13, "Reaching Agreement: A Solution-Seeking Model," and Chapter 15, "Saying What Needs to Be Said," I offer further guidance on examining your assumptions.

Consider This

Try this example: "She has the information I need. She didn't answer my e-mail because she wants me to fail. She's always wanted this project and resented me because the boss gave it to me. She is a snake. Don't trust her with anything."

- ☑ What assumptions is the speaker making about the information?
- ☑ What assumptions is the speaker making about the e-mail?
- ☑ What assumptions is the speaker making about the project?
- ☑ What assumptions is the speaker making about *her*?

In an argument, this swift conversion from observable facts to "story" to action can take over and fly far beyond any place for meaningful dialogue. As I discuss further in Chapter 10, "Rethinking Anger," when we are overwhelmed with our own emotions, we don't have access to rational thought. Our hearing is blocked. In those moments, someone says one thing and what we hear is something totally different. The difficulty, or the challenge, is that these assumptions can spring spontaneously to our minds, usually without our even being aware of what we have done.

How do you keep from being driven by your assumptions? You slow down. You start by getting curious. You ask lots of questions. And then you *listen* to the answers. Before you jump to conclusions, you think about what you are thinking and why—what opinions or judgments you are bringing to what you have seen or heard.

> *Begin challenging your own assumptions. Your assumptions are your windows on the world. Scrub them off every once in awhile, or the light won't come in.*
> —ALAN ALDA

Sometimes it's easier to start by looking back. You can think about a situation in which you had a difficult conversation. You can identify where it got out of control or started going in a direction you didn't want it to go. What happened there? What part did you play? What were you thinking? Reflecting on past experiences can help slow you down in future situations. Then you can more easily spot the assumptions you readily make before you act on them.

Consider This

- ☑ Think of a recent miscommunication you had. Briefly describe what happened. What did you see and hear? Identify just the observable facts, removing all of your opinions and judgments.
- ☑ What did you think and feel in that moment?
- ☑ What were your *assumptions*? What judgments or opinions did you have about the other person's intentions?
- ☑ What did you do?
- ☑ What else might have been going on? Identify several alternate possibilities or explanations.
- ☑ What could you do differently next time?

Habits as Stumbling Blocks

The fourth stumbling block to dealing with conflict effectively is habit. We have automatic responses and reactions when differences arise or conversations become tense. We are quick to spring into action and wonder later, "How did that happen?" My husband pointed out to me in the middle of an argument that I was physically backing out of the room. "Where are you going?" I realized it wasn't just with him that I left the scene whenever possible. I saw in this moment my sometimes unconscious tendency to avoid conflict. Once I could recognize this, I became more aware of my pattern in other situations as a habit and continue to work to change it.

From a very early age, we all learned how to deal with conflicts and disagreements. We watched parents and dealt with siblings. Through trial and error, and lots of practice, we found out how to get our needs met—what worked and what didn't. We discovered how to manage when what others (parents, siblings, teachers, aunts, uncles...) wanted got in the way of what we wanted. We were taught the unwritten rules of the house and the community. We also found out that what worked in our own home probably didn't work in someone else's home. We learned who we could turn to and how to get a response.

We learned what to value. Success? Winning? Harmony? Creativity? Hard work? Achievement? We also learned what was not important. We learned by noticing what got us attention or approval, and what didn't. We learned by watching our parents or others around us. Those who grew up with brothers and sisters learned a lot about how to get along— the oldest learned a different set of skills and strategies than the middle child or the youngest.

Often, when I coach people through conflicts in work situations, they begin to recognize the patterns from their past. Sammy will see that the difficulties he has dealing with his boss replicate the arguments and challenges he had with his father. Karen will realize that her problems with a co-worker are just like the ones she had with her sister.

By the time we were old enough to get jobs, those habits of thought and behavior had been deeply set. We had practiced the ones that worked, over and over again. We had abandoned the ones that didn't—in our home, in our position in the family, in our own culture. If it didn't work, if it wasn't rewarded, we pretty quickly stopped doing it.

All of us want attention; all of us want to be special. Some of us got praise and attention for performing well in school. Others of us were rewarded for being quiet, or friendly, or kind. There were others who got attention for being bad—for getting into trouble. Even if it was negative attention, at least somebody noticed. So that behavior, too, was reinforced. We bring those patterns and habits with us to the workplace, along with our briefcases and lunch bags.

Hence, someone who learned that avoiding conflict was the best way to get through the day will do the same at work. Another who got her needs met by being confrontational will use that same approach on the job when the chips are down. These patterns become well-worn behavioral grooves. In a moment of disagreement, we don't need to think; we just respond and move on to the next task. In Chapter 3, "What We Need: The Satisfaction Triangle," I explore further these patterns of response and give you some tips on how to manage them more effectively.

The challenge of these habits is made more difficult when the working relationship has not been working very well for a long time. When only one person in a relationship is aware of the problems faced in resolving differences productively, and tries to change that pattern by responding in a new way, using new skills and tools, the likely reaction will be resistance. The second person will often dig in, continuing to respond in a negative way because the dysfunctional dance of conflict has become comfortable, even if it is not productive. To change that dance, the first person will need to maintain a strong commitment to changing that behavior until the second may eventually shift as well.

I end this chapter almost where I began it. You can read and talk about better ways to respond to conflict, using books and journals and seminars, and with tools and processes and formulas for better managing conflict. Yet, do you still find yourself caught in dysfunctional conflicts? Until you understand the patterns and habits you have developed over a lifetime, and consider ways to put them aside, you are likely to continue repeating your mistakes. It's time to change.

Consider This

- ☑ Where are your most challenging conflicts at work?
- ☑ What triggers your automatic negative responses?
- ☑ What patterns and habits do you see reflected in these negative responses?

PART II

Understanding the Dynamics of Conflict

I believe in getting into hot water. I think it keeps you clean.

—G. K. CHESTERTON

CHAPTER 3

What We Need: The Satisfaction Triangle

H as this ever happened to you? You are embroiled in an argument about a matter that is important to you and also to an employee. After several back-and-forth exchanges, you finally say, "Okay, then, we'll do it your way." You do what you can to give that employee exactly what he is asking for, only to find out later that he is still ticked off. You are left wondering, "What is his problem? Isn't he ever satisfied?"

On the other hand, you may have had another experience as well. An employee storms into your office, upset about a policy that, as far as she is concerned, just isn't working. You listen. She continues talking; you continue to listen. In the back of your mind, though, you are thinking, "I don't know what we can do to fix that. It is what it is … nobody else has complained." She keeps talking and you keep listening. Finally she looks at you with relief and says, "Thanks for listening. I feel better. I'll talk to you later." You didn't *do* anything, and somehow the situation is now okay. You are left wondering what happened.

Usually in a conflict or disagreement, as we look for an acceptable solution, we focus on the *substance* of the outcome. Everyone wants something. The conventional wisdom tells us that getting that something means that the conflict is dissolved. Did you get what you asked for? If so, then you are happy. If you did not get what you wanted, then you are not happy. In the first scenario, your expectation is that, when you finally decide on a solution, the employee will be satisfied. In the second scenario, you do not expect the employee to leave your office satisfied unless you take some action that is acceptable to her. But the reality is often more complex than that. Just as important—sometimes more important—are the other two sides of the satisfaction triangle, shown in Figure 3-1: *process* satisfaction and *emotional* satisfaction. Understanding all three sides of the satisfaction triangle can provide managers with a more extensive set of tools for resolving conflicts.

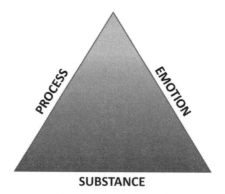

Figure 3-1. Satisfaction triangle.

The head of the Finance Office sent an urgent e-mail to the rest of the members of the executive leadership team. With only three months left in the fiscal year, the agency was facing a serious budget crisis, a $9 million shortfall. First, the team needed to understand where the money had gone; then, they would have to make hard decisions about how to reallocate funds to cover critical needs. For three weeks, they were in and out of meetings, gathering numbers, analyzing reports, looking for solutions. The meetings were long and the tensions ran high as each person protected his or her own department's priorities and looked for ways to cut back on expenditures. Keeping the goals of the agency paramount, and relying on the goodwill the team had developed, they were able to craft a new budget that satisfied the basic needs of each department.

. . . .

This example illustrates how all three sides of that triangle can contribute to satisfaction in a conflict. The final decisions that the group reached on budget allocations provided satisfaction on *substance*, though at the end of the process no one got all of what he or she wanted. Those long meetings they labored through, preparing charts and scrutinizing data, and sometimes arguing over specifics, answered their need for *process* satisfaction. Each person on the team understood how the decisions had been made, and where the final decisions came from. The respect for each other that they demonstrated in the midst of their disagreements and their willingness to listen to one another provided them with *emotional* satisfaction as well—each of them knew that he or she had been heard and had been treated with respect throughout the discussions, even as the meetings ground on and the outcome was elusive.

Substance Satisfaction

Satisfaction on *substance* is fairly easy to gauge. What are the answers? What are the solutions? What decisions are made? To adequately meet people's needs for substantive satisfaction, try the following:

➤ Move beyond initial demands and positions. Why does each of us take these positions? What are our interests, objectives, or concerns?

➤ Manage expectations. Identify what people expect, clarify realistic and unrealistic expectations, lower expectations that are unreasonable.

➤ Establish joint goals and common purpose. How does the question or disagreement relate to the work of the organization? Be clear that decisions ultimately are made to support the organization's work, not for any other agenda.

When a problem is solved, when a solution is found that meets the needs and interests of those involved, this is a satisfying moment, indeed. In the experience of the executive team responding to the budget crisis, each member reported that the solution developed by the team was satisfactory—that is, it met enough of their needs and interests to be acceptable to all.

Several years ago, a client showed me an article citing research conducted in the early nineties through the University of Minnesota, involving interviews of people who had appealed their court decisions. Of the people who go to court and lose, a relatively small number decide to appeal the decisions. The researchers asked randomly selected individuals why they decided to go through the appeals process. After all, appealing a court decision is costly, time-consuming, and emotionally draining.

The findings showed that, among the people the researchers interviewed, far more than half did not really expect a different decision at the next higher level. Puzzled, the researchers asked, "Why, then, did you choose to appeal?" Their responses were about *process* satisfaction and *emotional* satisfaction. Some felt that the process as originally described to them was not what actually happened in court. Others said that the appeal itself was part of their right to due process. For still others, emotional satisfaction was more important: They did not feel that they had been heard at the lower court level or else they felt that they had been treated disrespectfully during the trial.

Process Satisfaction

Process satisfaction involves clarity about how decisions are made, knowing where you can have input, believing that the decisions are fair and consistent, and accepting that the standards for decision making apply to others the same way as they apply to you.

Consider two employees from different organizations, each interested in a promotion. In Organization A, an opening is posted and several people apply; three are internal, four are external. The criteria for the position are clearly described, application procedures are carefully delineated, and notice is circulated about the position several weeks before the deadline. Candidates are interviewed. When Jim is not selected, he is sent a letter thanking him for his appli-

> *If you can't describe what you are doing as a process, you don't know what you're doing.*
> —W. EDWARDS DEMING

cation and providing some reasoning for the selection that was made. Jim is disappointed at not being selected, but satisfied that the *process* was fair and transparent. He recovers relatively quickly from the disappointment and refocuses on the job at hand.

In Organization B, no notice is given that there is a vacancy. The manager brings the new hire down the hall to introduce her to the rest of the staff. Jane is surprised: "How did she get that job? I have been working here for fifteen years. I know the computer system and our procedures, I know the history and all of the people we deal with. I will have to train her to do the job that I should have gotten. And I never knew about it!" Not only is Jane disappointed about not getting the promotion, but she is ticked off about the *process* itself. This employee expends considerable energy complaining to others about the new hire.

To provide process satisfaction, then:

► Be clear about how the decisions will be made, and who will make them.

► Have policies and procedures for decision making, and *follow* them. There are many organizations that have created volumes of policies and procedures that are not followed or, worse, that are only applied occasionally. This approach opens managers up to accusations of favoritism.

► Be consistent in decision making across departments and among employees. This can be challenging in a large organization. Employees talk to other employees working in other divisions. When one supervisor allows his or her employees to have flexible schedules or alternate work schedules, word passes throughout the building faster than the flu. Other employees want the same advantages and opportunities. They expect fairness and consistency when these policies are interpreted for them. Establishing clear criteria for these decisions provides a transparent policy.

► Provide opportunities for input into decisions, and let people know when and how that information will be used.

Further exploring the importance of process satisfaction in the workplace, Chan Kim and Renee Mauborgne identified three principles (the three Es) of fair process for employees:[1]

1. *Engagement.* When conflicts or problems arise, encourage input, allow others to question ideas, suggest their own remedies, or challenge proposals.

. . . .

One manager I worked with recently was notorious among her staff for making pronouncements of her decisions. When they approached her with suggestions from their own experience, her response was, "This is the way we will do it. I've already decided." They did not think that they had any opportunity for input into decisions that directly affected their work, and so their frustration was palpable and employee morale sank.

. . . .

2. *Explanation.* Yes, it is the manager's responsibility and authority to make decisions. When you have made a decision, close the loop. Clarify for employees the thought behind the decisions. Acknowledge their ability to understand by keeping them informed about your decisions. This acknowledgment demonstrates your respect for their efforts and expertise. It also allows them to let it go. Sometimes this is a step in process satisfaction that is too easy for a manager to overlook.

. . . .

When employees requested funding to attend a conference, the boss was unclear about how the training budget could be spent. He took the question to the human resources department. The answer was no—not for this particular conference. In his mind, everything was settled. The employees, though, were left wondering what the decision was, and how and where it was made. When they saw other employees' funding approved for a different conference, they were confused and indignant. Had the boss communicated with employees the answer to their question and how he arrived at it, they could have let go of the question as well.

. . . .

3. *Expectation clarity.* Be clear with employees about what is expected of them, what the "rules" are, what their areas of responsibility are, and the performance standards and penalties for failure. Giving

people notice and fair warning is essential to maintaining process satisfaction. With clearly identified job expectations, you can then hold employees accountable for their work. And that accountability is seen as fair. Additionally, the wise supervisor is clear with an employee in assigning a project: an unambiguous description of what is expected, a due date or deadline, (sometimes) designated milestones to be met along the way, and criteria for acceptable project completion. She then asks the employee to describe back to her what the assignment is so that she can ascertain that the assignment is understood and clarify any confusion that may have occurred in their communication.

When you become aware of the importance of process satisfaction to the resolution of disputes, you will see opportunities for process satisfaction in many situations. During the budget crisis described above (the $9 million shortfall), team members met for long hours poring over tables and data. At the end of each meeting, they identified data gaps and other areas for analysis. At the next meeting, they returned with more information. One reason they reached an acceptable solution was that each understood and participated in the decision-making process. In the end, each knew where the decisions came from because they had participated in creating them.

On the other hand, process dissatisfaction can take a toll on employee morale—and productivity. Recently an employee explained to me his frustration with his supervisor. He had put in extra hours while his boss was on leave. The supervisor's boss assured him, "Oh, yes, you can get overtime for this," which he did. When the supervisor returned and gave him a similar assignment, she said, "You will get comp time for this, not overtime." The employee's perception was that the decisions made by his boss were arbitrary and capricious, that he couldn't count on policies, or more importantly, on how the policies would be interpreted. When I met this employee, he was demoralized. "I'll work eight hours a day, but I am leaving at 5:00. I am tired of being jerked around."

Consider This

 Identify a conflict you have been a part of when a lack of clarity about the process contributed to the conflict.

 In this situation, what would have provided process clarity?

☑ Identify a policy or procedure within your organization that does provide process satisfaction when the outcome itself may not satisfy.

Emotional Satisfaction

Emotional satisfaction really comes down to, "Was I heard?" and "Was I treated with respect?" Everyone needs to feel listened to, respected, and safe. If, in the process of looking at a problem, people feel threatened or discounted, they are far less likely to accept any decisions that are made.

If we go back to the budget-crisis example, note that members of the executive team respected one another. When one spoke, others leaned forward and listened. They did not always agree. In fact, on some points there was strong disagreement. But they maintained their commitment to each other to respect their differences of opinion and to listen to one another. To put it another way, emotional satisfaction was an integral part of their problem-solving approach.

At the beginning of this chapter I cited the example of a woman who came into your office worked up about a policy issue. From your perspective, "All I did was listen." From her perspective, you respected her and her opinions enough to give her your time, to listen to her. That is just what she needed. To provide that emotional satisfaction, you need to:

▶ Create a safe place for difficult discussions. Some simple ground rules or guidelines can help: avoid personal attacks, keep an open mind, respect others' opinions, speak for yourself.

▶ Listen. Put aside your own thoughts and opinions. Turn away from the computer screen or the text message and give the person your undivided attention.

▶ Respect confidentiality. If you tell people that you will keep a conversation confidential, you must keep your word. If you determine that the information really must be shared with someone else, be clear at the outset that you cannot maintain that confidentiality—and talk about whom you will be speaking with, what information you will pass along.

▶ Of course, people have emotions, even at work. Provide safe ways for them to be expressed and heard.

Many times I have listened to a simple complaint that has taken on a life of its own within an office. "My supervisor doesn't even say hello to me. When we pass each other in the hall, she doesn't acknowledge that I exist." That manager may be caught up in her own thoughts. More often, the manager may not realize how important a nod, a smile, or hello can be to a subordinate. The employee carries those experiences of recognition and acknowledgment into times of conflict and disagreement.

Consider This

☑ Identify an experience you have had during which someone listened to you. What effect did that have on you? What effect did it have on the conflict?

☑ When someone disagrees with you, are you able to put aside your own thoughts and hear what the person is saying?

Understanding the satisfaction triangle can give you a powerful tool as a manager, especially when you cannot give your employees substance satisfaction. What they are asking for simply cannot be done. The resources are not available. A request may have to be denied because of policy. To maintain the supervisor's authority, the performance evaluation cannot be changed.

However, many times you *can* provide process satisfaction. You can develop clear processes and procedures for how decisions will be made, you can inform people of those processes, and then you can follow them. You can allow time for the employees to have input. When a decision is made, you must remember to close the loop: communicate what the decision is and explain what will be expected of them.

Virtually *all* the time, you can provide emotional satisfaction. The first step is to treat employees with respect—always. And when differences and disagreements arise, listen to what they have to say, and always treat them respectfully, even when you disagree.

Note

1. W. Chan Kim and Renee Mauborgne, "Fair Process: Managing in the Knowledge Economy," *HBR on Point* (Boston, Harvard Business School, 2003).

CHAPTER 4

Where We Are: Levels of Conflict

Big problems generally start off as small problems. In his *Poor Richard's Almanac*, Benjamin Franklin relates, "for want of a nail the shoe was lost;/for want of a shoe the horse was lost;/for want of a horse the rider was lost;/for want of a rider the battle was lost;/for want of a battle the kingdom was lost;/and all for the want of a horse-shoe nail." The rider could not foresee the price that would be paid for not fixing that horseshoe nail.

And not only do the small problems grow to become big problems, but the skills needed to solve them become more demanding as well. When you resolve problems early, you don't need additional tools to manage or resolve them. If you don't solve them early on, they fester. The challenge for the manager is to see the conflict early, and recognize that it needs to be addressed while it is still a minor disagreement.

In Chapter 2, I described the scene in a deputy director's office, after the senior management team had called human resources with a long list of complaints about the CFO, Tre. One of the seniors had ended the conversation with an ultimatum: "Either he goes or I go. And, by the way, the rest of the team members feel the same way." The response in the deputy director's office was stunned silence: "What??? Where had this come from?" This team had seemed to work well together for over three years. Clearly, small problems had become bigger problems over time, and the skills that could have addressed the smaller ones would not be adequate now.

In his work with conflict within churches, Speed Leas developed a model for understanding the development of conflict through a series of levels.[1] These levels of conflict are not confined to the church, however; they play out in all kinds of situations—in communities, in the workplace, in families, and in international relations.

Understanding these levels will help you identify appropriate skills to resolve differences. If a conflict has ripened to a fight, or is at the point of being intractable and dangerous, the communication tools that you use to resolve lower level conflicts will not be adequate or acceptable now. On the other hand, recognizing the potential for problems to escalate over time into intractable situations will encourage you to slow up, to take the time to resolve those differences while they are manageable.

The Five Levels of Conflict

LEVELS OF CONFLICT

1. Problems to solve
2. Disagreement
3. Contest
4. Fight
5. Intractable situation

The five levels of conflict identified by Leas are: problem to solve, disagreement, contest, fight, and intractable situation. But they are best understood through example. The following demonstrates the escalation of a conflict through these five levels and is based on a situation that played out recently between two of my neighbors.

1. *Problem to solve.* These seem easy—so easy that we probably don't consider them conflicts. We talk it over. We listen. We consider. We decide. We move on. Most, in fact, are resolved at this level.

. . . .

Mark and Miranda, and Rachel had together bought an older building, now a duplex. Mark and Miranda would live on one side of the duplex, Rachel on the other. Actually, the legal term for their purchase was "joint tenancy," which tied the neighbors together through a carefully crafted contract, except for one detail. Despite the consideration given to many shared matters, such as utilities and a common basement, the one thing the contract did not clarify was the exact property line between the two units.

Soon enough, they had a "problem to solve"—how to define the property fairly, either by hiring a surveyor or simply by walking around the property together with stakes and a measuring tape. As easy as this would have been to do early in their relationship, they just didn't get around to it. There were too many other pressing needs—hanging curtains, painting the kitchen, or planting the garden—that were easier and more fun to do than having this difficult conversation.

. . . .

2. *Disagreement.* This gets a bit more challenging. The parties begin to see that they have different views and each moves into the territory of declaring who is right, who is wrong. People take actions based on assumptions and perceptions.

. . . .

Rachel decided to build a patio, and she took down a trellis beside the existing patio when she did it. When Miranda looked out her kitchen window, she was surprised that the trellis was gone. This felt aggressive to Miranda: "But, Rachel, we never talked about this." To Miranda, the trellis and the area around it looked like a natural dividing point between the properties. Clearly, to her, that trellis was on her property. Meanwhile, on their side of the property line, Mark and Miranda did not want to get into an argument with Rachel, and they tried to take steps to avoid that. They did not have a further discussion with her about the trellis. What they didn't do was propose a sit-down conversation with Rachel so that each could hear the other's views and they could reach some mutually acceptable understanding.

. . . .

When we can solve problems and resolve disagreements at these lower levels, they dissolve easily. There is not that rear-end collision we described in the first

> *Honest disagreement is often a good sign of progress.*
> —Mohandas Gandhi

chapter—the quarrel that gets everyone's attention. But hindsight is 20/20. As we watch this dispute unfold, it is easy to see what the three of them *could* have done.

3. *Contest.* Ratchet it up a bit, and people swing into the next level of this model. Now it is about who is right, who is wrong, and the importance to each party of being *right*. Because—if we are wrong, then what? Are we less for it?

. . . .

After some time had passed, the question of the trellis and of Rachel's unilateral action gnawed at Miranda. These are her words describing the next step: "I drew plats, I made lots of drawings that offered what I thought were reasonable options to initiate discussion. I told her, 'Now that the trellis is removed, let's solve the rest of the property-line issue and compromise on the other divisions needed.' I'd drop these proposals off. Rachel intimidated the hell out of me. She shut me out of any conversation—she would get snippy and snotty."

. . . .

At this level, fear continues to rise, trust further erodes. Blame increases, along with negative assumptions and attributions. Because there is little communication, people create stories about what the other person is doing and why. The filters we use to make these interpretations are clouded by our own view

> *A long dispute means that both parties are wrong.*
> —Voltaire

of the situation—and about how right we are and how wrong "they" are. From this story we generate hostile attributions and characterizations.

4. *Fight*. The stakes are higher yet. A fight moves the parties to the possibility of pain. Someone will get hurt, maybe both parties—emotionally or physically. People move into defensive mode. How can they inflict pain on the other to the point that the other gives up? Fights are for winning. Fights are for *not* losing. (Sometime people define winning as losing less than the other guy.) In any event, compromise counts as a loss.

. . . .

By now the neighbors had stopped talking to each other—not for days or months, but for years. To avoid talking to each other, they would leave the utility bills in a common area, and write notes of complaint when a math error is caught. Rachel would watch Miranda water her garden, and seethe at the impact this would have on their joint water bill. Mark and Miranda left messages on Rachel's voice mail when they knew she wasn't home to answer the phone. They sent e-mails. E-mails were particularly satisfying because then they had *proof* of the message they had sent.

When Rachel came home with a German shepherd and when she put up shutters, Mark and Miranda took it personally: "Now, she even has a guard dog!" Then Rachel confronted Miranda: "Did you walk through my yard yesterday? You set off my dog." What Miranda heard was hostile and combative. Miranda's view was, "I felt like it was purposeful—she was putting together a plan to get me."

. . . .

At this point in a conflict there is no communication. Trust is nil. Blame and wild assumptions have taken over. Any action or statement made by one party is seen by the other as hostile.

5. *Intractable conflict.* This is the kind of conflict we all dread— conflict with a capital C. There is no going forward. Everyone is well beyond winning and losing. The parties are in a dangerous territory,

where the only answer anyone can see is annihilation, or at least complete separation.

. . . .

Rachel had had enough. She was selling her half of the house. She demanded that Miranda and Mark do the same, at the same time. As far as she was concerned, their joint tenancy contract required that solution. Selling their home was the furthest thing from Mark and Miranda's minds—they had a small child, they loved the neighborhood (except for their relationship with Rachel), and they wanted to stay put. Rachel finally said, "Sell your half when I do, or I'll take you to court."

The case ended up in front of a judge. Years after the event, the memory is still painful. Miranda continues to talk about the money that she and Mark lost and have yet to recover—in lawyers and court fees, in time away from work. Mark and Miranda cannot count the emotional toll all of this took on both of them, and the stress it created within their own relationship as well. Looking back, Miranda observed, "Avoiding conflict can cost more than just tackling it." They had gone from possibly uncomfortable conversations to the reality of the difficulties (time, money, emotional costs) of litigation.

. . . .

You can appreciate how this escalation may play out in a workplace situation. For example, the boss and the staff have had differences from the very beginning. The first week in her new position, Paula announced major changes in the work schedule. From her view, it was important to establish her authority early on. When a staff member questioned a decision, Paula was unable or unwilling to sit down and talk through the matter. Rather, when she heard the beginnings of a disagreement, Paula would make a declaration about what would happen, and then begin peppering the staff with e-mails to see if they were following through on her demands. The staff's efforts to talk to Paula about this ended in more directives. When three of her top performers gave notice, within days of each other, Paula was stunned. She couldn't understand what had happened or why they were leaving. The staff had reached level five—intractable conflict—and Paula had no idea how this had happened. Had she heard and responded to their concerns earlier, repairs might have been possible.

Whenever and wherever possible, find ways to resolve differences and disputes before conflicts get to level five. That will save you time, money, and an emotional cost that cannot be calculated. People often turn to the courts for the final settlement of their disputes, though courts often don't correct the problems that people have brought with them. The courts are littered with broken relationships—business as well as personal. I have mediated countless situations like these.

· ·

Two brothers opened a restaurant together. They had not clarified in the early days of startup who would be responsible for what. When the restaurant hit hard times, the two became entangled in a nasty legal battle that shattered their relationship, as well as destroying the business.

· ·

Five young men were eager to start a company together. They had been fraternity brothers; they stood in at each other's weddings. In those early days, when the problems were small and manageable, they were too busy to be concerned about minor disagreements. Over time, as their lives changed and the business and the disagreements grew, the conflicts became insurmountable, the distrust and fear became more than they could manage, and the business was destroyed as one filed lawsuits against another.

· ·

Yes, resolving differences earlier is better. Complete separation is often not that simple—and maybe not even possible. In the world of work, even after a termination, the boss and the employee can still find ways to inflict pain on one another, likely through lawsuits or assaults on one or another's reputation.

There are intractable conflicts, but still we press to find a way around and through them. At some point, the cost of keeping the conflict alive is no longer worthwhile. When each party realizes there is no winning, together they may begin looking for another way. Based on his experience in resolving the conflict in Northern Ireland, George Mitchell was sent as special envoy to the Middle East. As he took this assignment, he said, "There is no such thing as a conflict that can't be ended. Conflicts are created by human beings, and can be ended by human beings."

Strategies for Each Conflict Level

So, the earlier you resolve a conflict, the better. What can you do if the situation has moved up the scale? Is it hopeless? Not if you are willing to put considerable effort into repair. Depending on how far the conflict has gone, how long it has been deteriorating, and how important the relationship is to both parties, transforming a deep-seated conflict is possible, although it can take considerable effort over time. I often tell clients, "You didn't get into this quickly. You can't get out of it quickly, either."

When you are thinking about strategies for responding to problems at each of these levels, consider this: the level of conflict increases as the emotional involvement goes up and as the trust goes down. The following strategies are built on managing those changes.

> *If we are all in agreement on the decision, then I propose we postpone further discussion of this matter until our next meeting to give ourselves time to develop disagreement and perhaps gain some understanding of what the decision is all about.*
> —Alfred P. Sloan,
> as quoted by Peter Drucker in *The Effective Executive* (Oxford: Elsevier, 2007)

Resolving *Level 1*, "Problems to solve," calls for clear communication skills and a collaborative solution-seeking approach. I delve more into that approach and how to use it effectively in Chapter 13, "Reaching Agreement." However, at this point, know this approach begins with clearly stated issues or problems to solve, and it relies on good listening skills and the ability to identify interests. Agreeing on shared goals, even though individuals may have differing priorities, can help set a positive tone. Keeping conflict resolution at this level is possible when there is an atmosphere of trust within the office, there is a culture that views conflict and differences as healthy, and people are encouraged to raise questions and to disagree constructively, even in the face of difficulty.

At *Level 2*, "Disagreement," the tension and anxiety have begun to rise, and the fear of conflict is mounting. "What if the conflict becomes bigger?" "What if we can't settle it?" "What if I get upset, or she does?" What if? What if? What if? There is the potential for the difficult discussions to go badly—it is that potential that creates the fear. If you have had difficult, nonproductive conversations before, your fear of that happening again is even higher.

At this stage, you need more structure to create a safe place for dialogue. You need to specify some ground rules (guidelines, if you prefer) for how you are going to talk to each other. This can be as simple as, "Can we agree that one of us will talk at a time?" Or, "I'll listen to you, will you listen to me?" You will need to clarify a common goal or objective around which you are all looking for a solution. For instance, within the workplace, the productivity or the mission may be a common goal. Another may be maintaining an atmosphere where people can come to work looking forward to the day, rather than dreading possible interactions. These steps decrease the anxiety and difficulty of the conversation.

At *Level 3*, "Contest," the intensity and, hence, the fears are higher. Distrust is rising between the parties. As the drive to be right takes over, people in the workplace start reaching out for allies—people who support them in their position, who agree with how right they are, fanning the flames of conflict. A few people cluster at the coffee pot, or in one another's offices, talking about what has gone wrong: what he said, or what she did, or how badly "they" acted. As the distrust mounts, communication about the issue becomes more difficult, often disappearing completely.

At this level, you need a more structured process. To manage the distrust and anxiety, you need to ensure process clarity: what is going to be decided and how? What will the ground rules be? What data do we need and who will gather it? When will we meet and who will lead the meeting?

When you are at *Level 4*, "Fight," the fears are high and the emotions are running strong. Trust between the parties has reached such a low that neither party wants to participate in constructive discussion. Often the conflict at this point has grown larger and more diffuse. At an earlier stage, there may have been two or three issues to resolve; now even identifying specific issues becomes challenging, as fears and assumptions have been built on top of one another. The parties have gone beyond having a problem or issue to resolve. Distrust and suspicion have overwhelmed all aspects of the relationship.

At this point, you need external help. This help may be someone both of you trust within the organization, or someone hired from outside to serve as a mediator or facilitator. In addition to resolving the problems that were the origin of the conflict, the mediator may need agreement on new ground rules for how people will work together or interact within the workplace in the future. To be of any value, such commitments require a system for monitoring and accountability. These commitments may be written into performance plans or monitored through regularly scheduled follow-up meetings.

If the conflict reaches *Level 5*, "Intractable conflict," the people who are immediately involved are not able to make a joint decision. It is time to turn to an external authority to make that decision. At Levels 1–3, the conflict is at a level where the parties themselves can still negotiate with one another, if they have communication tools and skills to manage their differences. When conflict reaches Level 4, trust has deteriorated to a point that an external person whom both of the parties trust is necessary to provide a process for communication. Whereas at Level 4 an outside source can facilitate communication, Level 5 requires someone else to decide the outcome. The power difference between the parties may be too great, or there may be serious threats of harm to either or both.

Workplace bullying falls into this category and deserves special attention here. Over the past several years, my conversations with miserable employees have increasingly included claims of being bullied or subjected to hostile work environments. By workplace bullying, I mean behavior that is aggressive, unreasonable, and persistent. It can be verbal or nonverbal, and can be subtle and insidious. This behavior generally involves emotional or psychological abuse or humiliation. Bullying behavior occurs regularly over a long period of time, and includes verbal abuse, intimidation, regular threats of dismissal, character assassination, smear campaigns, and social ostracism. Most often, it's a boss who carries this out; occasionally a co-worker engages in this behavior.

In this or in other forms of Level 5 conflict, someone with clear authority needs to take appropriate action—as a decision maker and as a monitor to hold people accountable for their actions. This may be someone higher up within the organization, or it may be an external authority, such as a judge or an arbitrator.

Consider This

- ☑ How do you resolve problems when they arise?
- ☑ Do you promote an atmosphere where disagreements are encouraged?
- ☑ Consider the conflicts within your organization. At what level is each one? What can you do now to begin to resolve one of them?

Note

1. Speed Leas, *Moving Your Church through Conflict* (Herndon, VA : Alban Institute, 2002).

CHAPTER 5

How We Respond: Approaches to Conflict

W hen Sam gets an e-mail from his boss, giving him another assignment that is due this Friday, Sam reads the e-mail, shrugs to himself, and continues with the project he is working on.

When Tasha gets an e-mail from her boss, giving her another assignment that is due this Friday, she sighs, marks it down on her calendar, and scrambles to add it to her to-do list.

When Marvin gets an e-mail from his boss, giving him another assignment that is due this Friday, he picks up the phone and calls his boss to bargain. "I can't get that project done on Friday, but if you can finish that report I am working on, I'll get the new project mapped out so someone else can fill in the pieces."

When Louisa gets an e-mail from her boss, giving her another assignment that is due this Friday, she calls him on the phone and explains, firmly and clearly, "I can't possibly get that done by Friday. I already have a stack of work to do this week."

When Bernie gets an e-mail from his boss, giving him another assignment that is due this Friday, he puts aside the report he is working on and goes into the boss's office. "What do you need this project for? I need more information. And let me be clear with you about the projects I already have on my plate this week. Let's see if we can devise a solution that works for you and for me."

When we face differences and disagreements, we have choices about how we will respond to the situation. If you were to ask Sam, Tasha, Marvin, Louisa, or Bernie what their approach to that moment was, they may not be able to tell you. Each of them just responded in the way that made the most sense to them. We probably do not spend much time thinking about these choices; we may not even consider that we are making a choice. We respond in a way that we feel is comfortable and right for the situation. Most of us use only one or two approaches nearly all of the time.

Here is a short quiz that will help demonstrate the differences in these approaches. Picture yourself in the middle of a disagreement at work. Which of these statements sounds most like you?

1. I back off and let it go, even if it means that nothing is settled.
2. I prefer to do what others want for the good of the relationship.
3. I focus more on my goals and less on what others want.
4. Everyone should accept a little less than what he really wants so we can get on with the work.
5. I go to great lengths to understand what is important to others and to make sure they understand what is important to me.

Maybe the answer you give depends on whom you are having the disagreement with—your boss, your subordinates, or your peers or teammates. Maybe it depends on how important the disagreement is to you or to the office. Maybe it depends on other things going on in your life at the time, your mood, your health, the weather, the stock market, or what's happening at home. This list cites five such patterns: avoiding, accommodating, driving, compromising, and collaborating.

Most of us have preferences and patterns for the choices we make. Sometimes our approaches work well. At other times, these patterns may be limiting and self-defeating. The people we work with have their own patterns and preferences, as well. As a manager, understanding your own approaches to conflict can help you make better decisions in how to respond to conflicts you face. Further, understanding more about the approaches of the people you supervise gives you additional tools to manage conflicts effectively.

Over the past thirty years, various authors have written about these different approaches people take.[1] There are assessments available online that can help you identify your own preferences. One of the most accessible of these guides is *Style Matters: The Kraybill Conflict Style Inventory* at http://www.riverhouseepress.com.[2]

In this chapter I present in depth each of these five approaches to conflict listed above. Figure 5-1 is a visual way to understand these different approaches and their relationships to one another. The vertical axis represents concern or energy for one's own goals (wants, needs, expectations), or the goals of the group one belongs to. The horizontal axis represents concern for the relationship or for the other person (or people), his or her wants, needs, and expectations. While the figure helps to explain and understand these differences, bear in mind that there are no distinct boundaries between these approaches.

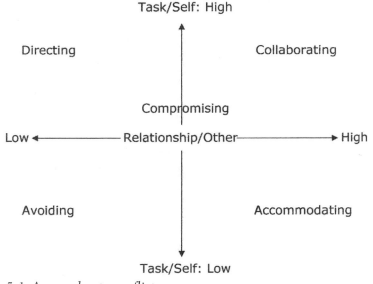

Figure 5-1. Approaches to conflict.

Consider This

☑️ As you read the descriptions below, think about your own choices. When things are going smoothly, how are you inclined to respond?

☑️ How do you respond when tension rises in a disagreement? Does your reaction pattern shift?

There is no one *right* way to approach conflict. Each of these styles is appropriate in some circumstances, inappropriate in others. One challenge is to learn to use different approaches depending on different circumstances. As behavior specialist Abraham Maslow said, "When the only tool you have is a hammer, every problem looks like a nail."

Another dynamic to recognize is how your preferred style might shift when you are in a stressful situation.[3] If your approach shifts dramatically when the tensions rise, you are likely to create confusion and distrust in those you work with. For instance, if your preferred style is accommodating under normal conditions, and your behavior shifts to directing when your anxiety rises, others are likely to be wary, finding your reactions unpredictable.

For each of the five approaches mentioned earlier, consider how that style can be an appropriate response to conflict. Then look at the downsides of overusing that style. Finally, for each approach, there are tips for working more effectively with another person who uses that approach.

Avoiding

The first example in the quiz, "I back off and let it go, even if it means that nothing is settled" is a statement of *avoiding*. It sits in the lower left-hand side of Figure 5-1: low energy for or attention to either the relationship or the task, as well as your own concerns. At times, there are good reasons to choose avoidance:

▶ Don't sweat the small stuff. Let go of problems that, in the grand scheme of things, are just not that big a deal. Sometimes you have so many bigger problems to deal with that it's better to let this one go. Suppose someone leaves a coffee cup in the office sink; it is easier to wash it out than to either chase down the culprit or create signage to hang over the sink.

▶   It's just not worth it. You can spend a lot of energy banging your head against a brick wall, to no good end. Let it go—avoid the conflict. Suppose, for example, that when a new policy on comp (compensatory) time comes out, you as manager read it and groan. Now, you will have to explain to staff that the extra time they are putting in during this crunch won't be compensated the way it was last year. People are not going to like it. They will complain, but there is nothing you can do about it. You don't waste energy and effort trying to get the policy changed. You know from past experience that once something like that has been decided, the decision is final.

▶   Sometimes people need time to cool off. Or you need to cool off—or to get more information, or to consider what is going on, or to better understand what the problem might be. This is tactical avoidance; it is a short-term response, a postponement. You will revisit the conflict when you are better prepared.

On the other hand, some of us avoid problems, differences, and disagreements when the situation really needs to be addressed. A manager who always avoids conflict creates a very difficult workplace for everyone. For example:

▶   Small problems get bigger. Problems that start small or are manageable can grow into situations that are much harder to deal with—or even become insurmountable barriers. Avoidance seems like the best route to take—until a negative behavior becomes a pattern. For example, one coffee cup in the sink is a small thing; however, when staff consistently leave their dirty dishes stacked in the sink, expecting someone else to clean up their mess, the problem needs to be addressed.

▶   The appearance of unfairness. Overuse of avoidance in the workplace can create significant difficulties. On survey after survey, the biggest complaint workers have is the perceived unwillingness of managers to take action against poor performers. Those who do pull their weight in the office, who are dependable and productive, watch another who is not held accountable. Their motivation and morale drop as they begin to wonder, "What is the point? Why am I expected to be responsible when others are not?"

▶   No paper trail. A manager who avoids confronting a poor performer often creates a difficult scenario. After weeks, or months, or even years, of not holding the employee accountable for the quality of his work or her tardiness, of avoiding the confrontation, and perhaps even of giving this person, year after year, positive performance reviews, the manager reaches a tipping point of exasperation, and calls the human resources office, wanting to terminate the employee. HR's response? "You can't fire this person. You have no justification in his personnel file."

▶   No visible presence. I have worked with a few managers who seem to have perfected the ability to get from their own offices to the elevator without making contact with anyone else in the office—so, they never have any problems. At least, none that they can see. Others who work with them, however, are increasingly frustrated. Problems that could be resolved can't even be raised.

Simone and Luis were really ticked off with their boss, Mike. Over the past year, they had met with him several times, presenting a carefully written, long list of their frustrations—support that the office needed, projects that were not getting done, and the like. Each time Mike listened to them, and then explained, "Right now I am really busy; I'll get to that in a couple of months." Months came and went, and he never addressed any of their concerns. One Monday morning, Mike came in to work only to hear the news that both Simone and Luis had found other jobs. Mike avoided, again and again, issues that could have been resolved. Now he faced a crisis in the office that he could not avoid.

Why do people avoid conflict even when avoiding as a technique is really not working for them? Often, it is fear: fear that their emotions will get out of control, or fear that they will hurt someone's feelings, or someone will hurt theirs, or fear that they will do the wrong thing, or make a mistake. To move away from avoiding when you recognize a situation that you need to address, find ways to create a safe place for people to talk (see Chapter 13 for more detail):

- ► Set up a time to talk that allows both parties to express their ideas and concerns.

- ► Find a neutral place. If you are having a difficult discussion with an employee, come out from behind your desk. Talk over a conference table, or consider a more informal setting.

- ► Allow people (yourself included) time to think through their responses or decisions.

- ► Develop guidelines for the discussion so everyone knows what behavior is expected from one another. Simple statements like, "One person talk at a time" or agreeing to listen to one another can set a tone for productive discussion.

- ► Establish a common goal or purpose. Clearly state the problem to be solved, or question to be answered, rather than state the answer you want someone to agree to.

- ► Stay focused on issues, not on personalities or on assigning blame.

If you are working with an avoider, alert the individual early on to potential problems or issues that may need to be addressed. Also, give the person time to think and consider, rather than demanding an answer in the moment.

Consider This

☑ Do you find yourself avoiding conflict more often than you'd like? Are there problems you can't talk about? People you avoid?

☑ Are there conversations you are not having?

If so, identify the steps you will take to address one issue that needs attention.

Accommodating

In the short quiz at the beginning of the chapter, the second response "I prefer to do what others want for the good of the relationship," is about *accommodating*. In the lower right-hand corner of the chart (Figure 5-1), accommodating places higher importance on "the other" or "for the group" than for what may be "important to me."

There is a lot that is positive about accommodation as a strategy:

▶   Accommodating behavior often springs from feelings of compassion and empathy: "Their needs are great, my needs are small. What can I do to help?" For example, when Tom's young daughter was diagnosed with leukemia, others in the office stepped in to cover his workload, no questions asked. The needs, expectations, or goals of the group are more important than those of the individual. Being a team player often means putting aside your own desires for the greater good of the whole group.

▶   Sometimes accommodating can be like money put in the bank. "What you are asking for here is important to you, less important to me." There is a spirit of cooperation within the office. When one employee has a daunting deadline looming, another person will offer to help out. So accommodating others sometimes gives you the leeway to ask for favors in the future. With team spirit, there is an unspoken expectation that favors will be reciprocated down the road.

▶   Customer service is all about accommodating the customer. "What can we do to help?" "Certainly, we'll take care of that right away." My boss, other departments, and different offices in the organization have needs and requests, as do external customers. It is your job to respond, to deliver, to give them what they need when they need it.

There are limits to accommodating, however:

▶   Unlimited accommodating can't be sustained over time. You run out of resources or energy to take on every task that is requested or expected of you.

. . . .

The boss put a report on Carole's desk, saying, "I need this completed by Friday afternoon, close of business." Carole, ever accommodating, did not tell him that she was already swamped with tasks, all of them urgent. Rather than disappoint him, Carole said okay. As the paper sat on Carole's desk, she considered her choices: (a) I can run myself ragged, rearrange child care so that I can be at the office until 11:00 on Thursday night; (b) I can deliver an insufficient report; (c) I can call in sick; or (d) all of the above. What she couldn't do was tell her boss that she could not get all of the projects on her list completed on time. Something would have to move from top priority status. Not only was she paying the price for her over-accommodating, but as a burned-out employee she was also not much use to the boss. Better that he should know what she was struggling with and find another way to get the work done than for him to lose a good employee to overload.

· ·

▶   Sometimes, accommodating just encourages others to take advantage. Then, they don't take responsibility for their own work.

· ·

Mara in operations needed an emergency order filled. She called procurement. Fair enough; everyone has emergencies sometimes. Joe, the head of the procurement office, frequently advocated for customer service, and Mara was, after all, the customer here. So, Joe jumped through a few hoops, circumventing the usual process to get the order delivered. On the operations side, the message Mara learned from this experience was that she didn't really have to go through the standard procedures and fill out all that paperwork. She discovered that if she simply called procurement and declared, "It's an emergency," Joe could make it happen. It took a little time for Joe to realize that he was now always acting in crisis mode and he began to wonder how he got to this point.

· ·

Why do people overuse accommodation as a response to conflict? Why do they allow their high concern for the relationship to override their own interests? The manager or supervisor who is desperate to be liked by her subordinates can slip into accommodation mode more often than is healthy for the organization, failing to hold staff accountable for their time or work products. "I want you to like me" "I want you to see me as a good person ... a good worker ... a good boss ... a good guy." Likewise, the subordinate who is too accommodating to the boss risks burnout and resentment as the assignments keep piling up.

A manager can also overuse accommodation when dealing with his or her own superiors or the external customers, committing the staff to more tasks than they can handle, and thereby losing sight of the priorities he or she has already established for the team. The result may be promises that cannot be kept, staff burnout, and important priorities not receiving adequate attention.

Consider This

☑ Do you find yourself saying, "Yes, I can do that" when in your heart you are saying "No, I can't possibly take on one more thing"?

☑ Do you hear someone's request with some agitation: How could they be asking me to do that *again*? And still find yourself agreeing to the task?

☑ If your answer is yes to these questions, identify one issue that is important to you. What strategy can you use to raise this issue without concern for damaging the relationship?

If you find you are over-accommodating, try the following:

➤ Acknowledge the importance of the relationship.

➤ Identify the issue at hand that needs to be addressed.

➤ Build the relationship so that, as future problems arise, you can work through them without fear of rejection.

➤ Learn to say no to a request, perhaps by giving the other person alternative solutions.

If you are working with a person who is a strong accommodator, try the following:

➤ Pay attention to the relationship, as well as to the issue at hand.

➤ Ask nonconfrontational questions about the person's concerns, preferences, and opinions.

Living on the Bottom Half of the Chart

Working with an avoider or an accommodator can seem like a pretty good place to be—or at least it can feel comfortable for a while. With avoiders, you don't have to talk about difficult issues because they never come up. As long as no one voices a complaint, there is no problem to solve. And with accommodators, you can get what you need. As long as you make it clearly known, the accommodator is ready and willing to comply. What is not seen, under the surface, is the simmering resentment that can come back to bite you in uncomfortable places. That resentment can lead to passive-aggressive behavior, or what we call "the grits factor."

Sometimes people who overuse avoidance and accommodation resort to passive-aggressive behavior. What do we mean by *passive-aggressive behavior*? On the receiving end, you may know that something is not right, is not working, but you can't quite put a finger on it. The passive-aggressive person may go to great lengths to avoid or to accommodate—or to appear to avoid or accommodate, while undermining your efforts or policies, hoping that you get the message or feel the pain. Since the issues that need to be addressed are not on the table, you can't work together to find solutions, or even any way to move forward toward finding those solutions. The person's anger and resentment grow—and are often fed by—his or her reluctance or inability to address difficult issues.

. . . .

When Sarah, her old boss, left, Mary was really disappointed. Mary and Sarah got along so well. Sarah really understood people, was organized and responsive, and was lots of fun to work with. When Sid came in to replace Sarah, he just was not the same. He didn't talk much with Mary. He kept irregular hours. He didn't tell her when he was coming or going, or what was going on. He didn't ask about her job or concerns or life.

Unaddressed, Mary's list of complaints grew. She didn't discuss them with Sid. Instead, she spent lunch hours with other members of the staff, telling them in the smallest detail every misstep she saw Sid make, criticizing every decision he made or initiative he began. It wasn't long before she had quite a followng in the lunch room. They could all complain about the boss, and nobody had to take any responsibility for the situation. Others didn't know where all of the animosity came from. And Sid? He had no idea what was going on or how to change the situation. He only knew that he walked into a mounting wall of hostility every morning.

- -

Passive-aggressive behavior can be pretty costly. On the factory floor, there is an expression, "malicious compliance." Workers who are ticked off at management have the last word, "Yes, you can tell me to do this, and I will do it—and when it fails miserably, you won't know who to blame." Passive-aggressive behavior: you can't get a firm grip on what is going on but you know that something is wrong.

On the other hand, it's a lot like cooking grits. Some of us have cooked grits the old-fashioned way—not microwave grits, but the real kind, simmered on the stove in a pot. The process goes something like this: Bring the water to a boil. Slowly pour in the grits, stirring constantly to keep them from lumping. Turn down the heat, and continue to stir so the grits don't stick to the bottom of the pot. Experienced grits cooks all know that, at this point, you must stand back from the pot. While the grits are simmering, they have an uncanny way of popping up in the most unexpected places, spitting bits up into the air. If you are not careful you will have boiling hot grits on your face.

Sometimes people who live in the world of avoidance and accommodation are like those grits in the pot. Suddenly they erupt in the most unlikely places. Wow! Where did that come from? He was always such a quiet guy. Well, "that" came from gobs of resentment that have been simmering over time, maybe years, until they pop up in your face. If you are working with someone who has these tendencies, it is in your best interest as a manager over the long haul to give the individual ways to be more open, honest, and forthcoming about voicing his or her concerns. There is more on this in Chapter 14, on listening.

Similarly, as a manager you may be guilty of passive-aggressive behavior. If you recognize your own tendency to hold onto resentments and engage in passive-aggressive behaviors or have blow-ups (like those grits), you can develop the necessary skills to become more direct with your employees, raising issues and addressing differences and needs as they arise. That kind of behavior change takes time and a lot of courage and commitment, but it can be done.

Consider This
- ☑ Do you see yourself sometimes engaging in passive-aggressive behavior?
- ☑ Do you find yourself in the middle of a grits explosion, wondering yourself why you blew up so quickly?

Directing

In the short quiz at the beginning of the chapter, the third statement is about *directing*: "I focus more on my goals, and less on what others want." Looking again at the Figure 5-1 chart, you'll see that the vertical axis represents concern for oneself or for getting the task done. Directing is in the upper left-hand corner and represents high concern for what you want, need, or care about, or high concern for "getting it done," and less concern for what others want, need, or care about. Directing is an appropriate approach sometimes, and it is inappropriate at other times. First, let's see the many ways that directing is an appropriate response to disagreements and disputes:

► If you can state in clear terms what you want, need, or expect, you greatly enhance the possibility of getting what you need. A good manager will say, "Here are my priorities, here is why, thought through and listed." When the manager clearly states the vision, the mission, the work to be done, the team appreciates the clarity and the direction they are being given.

► Healthy directing brings out the best in each of us. When the office puts together a proposal for a project, many people expend a lot of effort. What does this project need? What do we bring to it? How can we deliver in a way that stands out against the others? The energy and the thought processes that go into this direction raise the standard for everyone.

▶ Solid direction—even a good argument—can bring everyone closer together. This has been a huge lesson for me about conflict. That is, going toe-to-toe with someone who matters to you (boss, subordinates, or coworkers), and working through a difficult issue shows you that the other person will stick with you through it. You demonstrate your commitment to the work and to each other by engaging one another fairly. Likewise, you are still working together, often better than ever before, because you understand each other and you are assured of mutual loyalty to the mission and goals.

On the other hand, there is danger in *always* being in directing mode. A person who is always directing, who lives by the axiom "My way or the highway," creates unnecessary challenges for him- or herself and for everyone else as well. Here are some of the downsides of always being in competitive mode:

▶ People who are *always* in competitive mode are often fixated on being right. Other people's ideas are not solicited or considered. When others raise concerns or questions, they can be shut down immediately.

▶ Or one person (sometimes the boss) takes credit for the work of the entire team. As he or she briefs higher-ups at the conclusion of the project, the report sounds as if that person completed the project single-handedly. All the work that the team has done is disregarded.

▶ Every disagreement can become a win-lose contest, with the competitive person committed to winning no matter what the cost. Sometimes this strong commitment to winning at the other's expense degenerates even further to lose-lose: "Maybe I'll feel some pain, but if I can make you lose more than me, it will be worth it." As Coach Vince Lombardi famously said, "Winning isn't everything. It's the *only* thing." This works really well for a football team, but in working relationships the "losers" do not simply walk away from the game. In disagreements or conflicts, over time the others who are not being heard or acknowledged for their contributions, or who are made to feel inept or unvalued, start looking for ways to even the score.

▶ The manager needs the support of others to implement ideas. If you are *always* in competitive mode, you will find pretty quickly that you are hanging out there by yourself. Others may become hostile and combative, or give up and withdraw. Or, as one of my favorite baseball caps says, "I'm their leader; which way did they go?"

Consider This

    ☑   Are you eager to confront—so eager that others may back away from working with you, or avoid discussions with you?

    ☑   Do you insist on having the last word?

    ☑   How important is *winning* to you?

If you see yourself using this style too often, identify one disagreement and commit to using the solution-seeking model in Chapter 13, "Reaching Agreement."

If you see yourself being overly competitive, try the following:

▶ Slow down.

▶ Rather than rush to give the answer, or give directives, practice listening; become curious about others' ideas and views. You will find less resistance to your own ideas when you can take others' views into account.

People who are *always* in directing mode want to be seen as competent, smart, and, above all, *right*. They want to be respected for who they are and what they know. How do you respond to someone who seems to be stuck in directing mode? Give them respect, and talk in terms of *their* interests. Both can go a long way toward opening up the competitor's ears to what you have to say.

Similarly, demonstrate respect for who they are, what they know, and where they have been. You will read more on this topic in Chapter 15. Suffice it to say here that a person who is always in competitive mode wants to be seen as valued and worthy. Make certain that your tone of voice, your nonverbal communication, and your words convey that. At the same time, talk in terms of *the other person's* interests. Talk about why what you have to say may be important. Think WIIFM— "What's In It For Me"—from *the other person's* perspective. Before you raise an issue, ask, "Why might he want to hear about what I have to say?" "What does she need from me?" This is the difference between "I need a raise" or "I deserve a raise," and "Here is my value to *you*," or "to the organization."

Compromising

At the beginning of the chapter, the fourth statement was "Everyone should accept a little less than what they really want so we can get on with the work," and this represents the *compromising* approach. On the Figure 5-1 chart, compromising is right in the middle. Yes, there is concern for what is important to you, as well as what is important to others, but in the interests of getting things done, everyone gives a little. I don't get all of what I want. You don't get all of what you want. We split the difference, meet somewhere in the middle. Traditional bargaining is one example of compromising, and it has several strengths to handling conflict:

▶   Compromise is useful when there are built-in limits to the resources available. The phrase that is often used in negotiation is "fixed pie." If you are dealing with a fixed pie, a limited resource, compromise has the potential to give each party an acceptable partial resolution. For example, the management team working with the $9 million shortfall found themselves with limited resources—even more limited than they had imagined at the beginning of the year. Compromising was the approach they used to find a solution. After gathering as much information as they could, ultimately the group decided that each department could manage with something less than they had expected in order to come up with a viable answer to the budget problem.

▶   Compromising can yield a fairly quick, "good enough" answer. Suppose the front counter schedule was challenging for an auto service facility. With a limited staff and the need to offer coverage in the evening hours, the manager set a schedule that seemed to fairly distribute the workload, including the 6:00 to 9:00 P.M. time slot. Everyone worked one evening a week, a compromise that provided no one person would be responsible for handling this less desirable period.

But, sometimes compromising doesn't yield the best decisions. For example:

▶   People can be too quick to jump to an intermediate solution and get a less than satisfactory result. In the standard budgeting process, a small amount of money may not be adequate to accomplish anything meaningful. Rather than pursue decision making through compromise, whereby each component receives a small allocation, setting priorities and assigning the limited resources to a single project may achieve better results.

▶   Compromising can become more of a game than a good decision-making tool. When we know that decisions will be made through compromise, we tend to raise our goals at the outset, anticipating the compromise and perhaps thwarting the process.

. . . .

The budget process for the Jones agency started in January. Each office submitted its request for funds for the next fiscal year. After everyone finished the arduous process of justifying staffing needs and new initiatives, budget analysts sat around the conference table cutting those requests, considering other possibilities, and adding a little here or there if they could until they met the target number. Each office knew, as everybody at the conference table knew, that the requests submitted had to be higher than the actual dollars needed; it was how the budgeting game worked. Sam, the naive director who submitted a budget that was too finely tuned to the actual needs of his office, was disappointed when the final budget was delivered; there would not be enough money left to do what needed to be done.

. . . .

Consider This
    Are you sometimes in too much of a hurry to get an answer and move on?
    Might you be missing important information that could help everyone get to a better solution?

To move away from too much dependence on compromising, to keep from smacking your forehead later for missing a more comprehensive, less obvious solution, slow down. Get more information before thinking about an answer. Explore the possibilities. Find out what is important to the parties involved. Discover what is important to you—what this decision is really about—before making the decisions.

Collaborating

In the beginning of this chapter, the fifth statement was "I go to great lengths to understand what is important to others, and to make sure they understand what is important to me"; this statement describes the approach of *collaborating*. On the Figure 5-1 chart, collaborating is placed in the upper right-hand corner. It translates to high concern for what you and the relationship, as well as high concern for what is important to others. Breaking the word *collaboration* down to its parts, it is easy to see the "co-labor" in it— or, working together. In collaborating mode, both parties first spend time understanding the situation from both perspectives, then together they build a solution that works for both. When both the relationship and the decision are of high importance, taking the time that collaborating requires is well worth the effort.

The positive side of collaborating behavior is obvious:

▶ Everyone has his or her needs and expectations met. For instance, in the earlier example of the auto service front-counter schedule problem, the manager consulted each member of the staff about his or her preferences and personal situations. One member was taking classes at the local college, giving him a split shift through the week around his classes, and the evening hours every day really would work well for him. Another employee was juggling child care and her husband's work schedule, and coming in later and working later each evening would work well with her. The solution was achieved through collaboration.

▶ Collaborating on a solution builds support for the decision. By working together to find a solution, both your needs and the others involved are appropriately met. When everyone leaves the room, people have a stronger commitment to implementing your decision. Each has ownership for problem solving when anyone hits a stumbling block.

➤ Collaborating builds the relationship. Building a mutually beneficial solution through collaboration requires listening to one another and respecting each other's views and opinions. When you engage in this approach, the trust bond among manager and staff is strengthened. When there is another disagreement, you all engage one another in finding a solution because finding the last solution went so well.

When I first saw the Figure 5-1 chart, I naively thought that collaboration was the answer to all of the world's problems. We talk until we find a solution that meets your interests, needs, and expectations as well as mine. But when I applied my newfound enthusiasm to practical, real-life situations, I found that there were downsides to always collaborating all the time.

➤ Sometimes collaborating takes more time than the decision justifies. Perhaps you have attended those seemingly endless meetings, as I have, where everyone's opinion is sought ad infinitum on a relatively trivial question, as everyone looks for a solution that will make everyone "happy." What would make me happy at that point is for someone to make a decision so that we can get on to more important things.

. . . .

Kelly was responsible for purchasing a new printer for the office. Should it be wireless? Was inkjet sufficient or did they need LaserJet quality? Should they combine the fax function with the printer and eliminate the office fax machine? Kelly spent valuable staff meeting time soliciting others' ideas and input, presenting various cost proposals and options to the group. Members of the group were impatient. "Kelly, we trust you to make a good decision. Can we move on?"

. . . .

➤ Sometimes collaborating may take more time than anyone has. In an emergency or a crisis, the leader needs to give directions so that staff can take action.

► Sometimes the manager is reluctant to step in and make a tough decision, preferring to rely on a collaborative approach for fear of making a mistake. But making a decision too slowly in the search for consensus can be a bigger mistake.

► Collaborating can be used to avoid making any decision at all. "We'll wait until everyone agrees," becomes another way of saying, "We're not going to make any decision."

► Collaborating simply may not be possible. Where the disagreement or conflict is over limited resources, there may be no way to "expand the pie," to build a solution that answers everyone's needs.

By the way, I don't use the term *win-win* when discussing collaboration. It is a popular phrase, but it can mislead people into expecting to win—getting back into that mode of "winning" at all costs. Decision making is often more complicated than win-win.

Consider This

☑ Do you sometimes agonize over getting to a decision — looking for everyone's agreement before moving forward?

If you tend to overuse collaborating, the best solution is to create realistic deadlines for decision making. Solicit input from others, with the understanding that, if you can't reach a solution together within this time frame, then you will make the decision. If you are working with someone who overuses collaboration, encourage the person to make decisions and provide deadlines.

Understanding these style differences in approaching conflict can help us to hear each other and respond to our differences more effectively. Remember, each person brings strengths as well as weaknesses to any decision-making process. In complex conflicts or disputes, resolution requires using each of these approaches appropriately along the way. As a manager, there will be times to clearly state and hold to your own needs and priorities, times to accommodate the needs of others, times when the only solution to a problem is to compromise, and times when you can work with others to achieve a collaborative answer.

STYLES OF CONFLICT RESOLUTION

AVOIDING—"Conflict? What Conflict?"

▶ Often *appropriate* when the issue is relatively unimportant, the risks of harm are too high, time is short, or a decision is not necessary.

▶ Often *inappropriate* when negative feelings may linger, resentment may build, or problems that need to be addressed are not resolved.

▶ Often the choice when people fear the consequences of raising issues.

To respond to avoidance, create a safe environment for solving problems.

ACCOMMODATING—"Whatever you want is okay with me."

▶ Often *appropriate* when issue is more important to the other person, tasks involved are part of your work responsibility, favors and requests are traded over time.

▶ Often *inappropriate* when others could benefit from your wisdom and experience, or habitual use builds resentment.

▶ Often the choice when people are concerned about the relationship.

To respond to accommodation, raise issues without confrontation, assure others that the relationship is not the issue.

DIRECTING—"My way or the highway."

▶ Often *appropriate* when differing ideas and opinions need to be expressed, when an immediate decision is needed, or when energy is generated for accomplishing tasks.

▶ Often *inappropriate* when cooperation from others is important to implementation and buy-in, win-lose dynamics are created, or others are treated with disrespect.

▶ Often the choice when a person wants respect or control of the situation.

To respond to directing, respect the person's knowledge and experience, help the person identify how it is in his best interests to cooperate or collaborate.

COMPROMISING—"Let's split the difference."

▶ Often *appropriate* when finding some solution is better than a stalemate, cooperation is important but time and resources are limited.

▶ Often *inappropriate* when you can't live with the consequences, finding solutions that better meet the needs of those involved may be possible.

To respond to compromisers, slow down. Make sure you understand what the issue is, and identify the interests before jumping to a solution.

COLLABORATING—"How can we solve this problem together?"

▶ Often *appropriate* when the issues and relationship are both significant to those involved, cooperation and buy-in are essential to implementation, there is reasonable expectation of addressing the concerns of everyone.

▶ Often *inappropriate* when time is short, the issues are unimportant, finite resources make it impossible to create a solution that meets everyone's needs.

▶ Often the choice when a person or group wants joint ownership of decisions.

To respond, set realistic, definite deadlines for decision making. Encourage individuals to take responsibility for decisions without unreasonable fear.

Notes

1. Various authors have created similar charts for understanding these different approaches along a continuum of assertiveness and relationship, including Kenneth W. Thomas and Ralph H. Kilmann, *Thomas Kilmann Conflict Mode Instrument* (Tuxedo, NY: Xicom, 1974); and Robert Blake and Jane Mouton, *The Managerial Grid* (Houston: Gulf Publishing, 1964).

2. Ron Kraybill, *Style Matters: The Kraybill Conflict Style Inventory* (Harrisonburg, VA: Riverhouse Press, 2005).

3. Ibid, p. 12.

CHAPTER 6

Who We Are: Cultural Considerations

M rs. Bingen taught us a lot in the fourth grade that was beyond reading, writing, and arithmetic, such as how to answer the telephone, how to introduce ourselves to someone new, how to introduce a friend to another friend, and so on. The lesson on how to shake hands stuck with me: "When you hold out your right hand, squeeze the other person's hand firmly. That shows that you are strong and confident." All my life I have practiced this lesson. And when I have shaken hands with someone who did not respond with a firm grip, I secretly wanted to teach that person the right way to do it.

> *Strangers in a new culture see only what they know.*
> —ANONYMOUS

A different lesson waited for me on the Pine Ridge Indian Reservation in South Dakota, where I was volunteering during the summer several years ago. Larry Peterson, a Presbyterian minister, had lived on the reservation with the Lakota Sioux for twenty some years and he had become the cultural interpreter for our group.

One night Larry told us about a time when he took several young Native Americans to a church function in a neighboring town. On their way home, the children complained about their aching hands. They explained to Larry that they dreaded shaking hands with "those church people" because of their "hard handshakes." The children viewed these handshakes as aggressive. As they explained to him, "You should offer your hand with no resistance, so that others will know that you come in peace." Here was a surprising lesson for me on the differences among cultures. For many years, I had assumed there was but one way to shake hands—the *right* way—which just happened to be my way. I was startled to realize that others who had a different approach were equally logical in their own reasoning.

My summer visit to the reservation gave me a taste of how our cultural differences shape our worldviews, and how those views direct our behaviors. Larry had moved to the reservation with his own European-American upbringing and its set of cultural norms. But he was unaware of many of these norms and beliefs until he lived among people who did not think the way that he did. When he arrived, an elder of the tribe said to him, "If you are not going to be here at least twenty years, it's just not worth it." Not enough time, in other words, to get to know him and for him to get to know them. Clearly, this was a different sense of time than Larry held.

Another story from Larry concerns a young member of the Lakota, who was away at college in California. He received a phone call; his grandfather was seriously ill. Without question, the young man left school to attend to his dying grandfather. Family was the most important thing in his life, and there would be no missing this last chance to be with someone so important to him. Larry reflected on his experience as a young man, away at college many years earlier. His mother called; his grandfather was facing death. But his mother reassured Larry, "Your grandfather knows how much you love him, and knows how important your studies are to your future. Stay at school and finish your exams. You can come home to mourn with us later, even if you miss the funeral." Those cultural differences in values can play out in the workplace as well, in the ways a manager and his staff face difficult decisions.

Culture Defined

Culture is generally thought of as an integrated pattern of human knowledge, beliefs, and behaviors that characterize a group of people—the customary beliefs, social forms, and material traits of a racial, religious, or social group. The continuance of a group's culture depends on the group's capacity for learning and transmitting its knowledge to succeeding generations. Generally, a group's culture consists of unwritten rules about how its members (however they identify themselves) do things.

These rules vary from group to group. How a family expresses affection—or doesn't; how children address adults; how people in the neighborhood drive their cars or view law enforcement—these are just a few of the subtle, day-to-day interactions that teach us what is important in life and how people should treat one another. These rules and values are not formally taught. We acquire them as we grow up, as we learn and practice interactions within the group. The values we embrace may be defined by where we were born, where we live now, our educational background, our religion, and our gender, race, or ethnic group, to name a few factors.

Consider This

☑   List as many cultural groups as you can that form your identity. (Consider where you were born, where you were raised, your family's heritage, your sex, your sexual orientation, your religious beliefs, your level of education and where you went to school, your ethnicity.)

We Are Products of Our Groups

Each of us belongs to several groups that help to define the rules of life we understand and live by. This makes it difficult to make broad general statements about how this person or that person will behave in a given situation. For example, I was born in the American (U.S.) South and I have a Southern accent. But my father was in the army and we moved around quite a bit, so the assumptions of my cousins, who grew up in the South, are not the same as mine, though we may sound alike. An Asian woman who was raised in San Francisco may look very much like someone raised in Taiwan, but her cultural experiences, and hence her attitudes and beliefs, will be quite different. That said, there are tendencies and preferences that can help us understand some of the differences between us.

Inevitably, in the workplace these cultural differences meet one another and sometimes clash. These differences can unconsciously shape the preconceptions we have of each other, and may create conflicts. They also may inform opposing ideas about how to approach addressing those conflicts. Similarly, our cultural differences can create distrust. What you have done or said may make perfect sense in your worldview, in your understanding of what is important and your perception of how people should behave toward one another. In a workplace exchange, my reaction to what you have done—because I don't see the world exactly the way you do—may be confusion or bewilderment, or even anger. In my view, you have not met an expectation, or have broken a commitment—even an assumed expectation or commitment. We have never talked about our cultural expectations and differences, often because we didn't even know what they were.

. . . .

When Cynthia was growing up, the house was very quiet in the mornings. Family members got up, got ready for the day, and went on their way, being careful not to disturb their father, whom they all knew as someone to be avoided until at least noon. Angelo's house growing up was a bright, noisy place from morning until night. When he came down to breakfast, everyone said good morning. It was the accepted way to start the day.

Cynthia became Angelo's boss. When she came to work, she walked past Angelo's desk, straight to her own office every day. It never occurred to her to interrupt her own thinking to say "Good morning." Over the months that they worked together, Angelo watched Cynthia walk by his desk each morning and continued to wait for, to expect, Cynthia to greet him like, in his mind, "any civilized person would." Angelo put many interpretations on Cynthia's behavior: that she didn't like him, that he was not doing a good job, that she was cold and unfriendly. When Angelo finally told Cynthia how her behavior affected him, she was taken aback. It never occurred to her that he would react negatively to what seemed to her to be normal behavior.

. . . .

A Caution

Be careful: The temptation to generalize is strong. If we can fit people into neat models and boxes, they can seem much easier to manage: "You know how those Italians are," or "Of course, she's a woman. You know how they overreact"; or "[insert group] always does [insert stereotype]." Remember, culture does not account for all of the differences among people in the workplace. Sometimes the differences between people within a given culture may be greater than the differences between groups! With that caveat in mind, the next time you find yourself in a confusing situation, ask yourself how your own cultural assumptions may be shaping your reactions, and try to see the world from the other's point of view.

. . . .

When I walked into the meeting room, I could feel the tension among this team of managers. The conflicts between them had been brewing for some time. In this first meeting, I could see and hear the cultural differences: the manager was from India, one team member was African American, two appeared to be European American, and one described himself as "born in Iran, lived in India as a child." What impact did their cultural differences have on the conflicts before them? I was never exactly certain how this belief or that worldview created the situation in which they now found themselves, though I knew that they were dealing with differences that were probably deep and wide. My work, as I saw it, was to understand and respect their differences rather than label their attitudes.

. . . .

While volumes have been written on culture and cultural differences, our intention here is to highlight a few of the ways that cultural differences impact disagreement and resolution in the workplace. With this information, you can begin to develop an understanding of the impact of these differences.

Culture Examined

Many authors have created models for understanding the dimensions of culture as a way of better understanding the differences among us. In the 1970s, Geert Hofstede, a sociologist from Belgium, worked with IBM at its facilities around the world. Though the corporate culture of the company is the same wherever its offices are, he saw that the workers in different locations held different attitudes about how they worked together. From his extensive research, he developed country-by-country assessments of beliefs and values that shape workplace behavior.[1]

Based on his experience with the Hopi and the Navajo, and then his travels in Europe and Asia, Edward T. Hall popularized the concepts of "high-context" and "low-context" cultures in his book *Beyond Culture*.[2] High-context cultures are more collectivist—that is, people view their relationship to the group as very important; reliance on nonverbal communication is high. In general, cultures in Latin America, Africa, the Middle East, Asia, or indigenous groups in the United States are in this high-context category. Those in low-context cultures are more individualist—that is, individuals make choices and decisions with little concern for what is important to the group. Generally, in the United States and Western Europe, the individual is seen as the most important component of society. Though most people in modern society have some experience with both of these modes, these different worldviews play out in myriad ways in our approaches to conflict and in our communication styles.

In yet another model, Craig Storti, in his lively workshops on "Communicating Across Cultures" for the U.S. Department of State, uses several dimensions of cultural difference to help people identify the various preferences that they have as individuals and as members of particular cultures.[3] He calls these the locus of control, concepts of rightness and fairness, management style, attitude toward uncertainty, and communication styles.

As we explore the ways that culture shapes our belief systems and our behaviors, bear in mind that there are many ways to look at, listen for, and understand these differences. In an argument or debate, some groups often refer to authorities or experts to legitimize points; for others, their own experience is more persuasive and convincing. In short, it is a cultural thing, learned within the group one was raised. So, we arrive at our truths from different directions, each convinced that *our* way of understanding is the *correct* way.

My own European-American view of time is linear. This is so deeply ingrained in me that when I read of other groups, for whom the construct of "past, present, and future" has no meaning, I cannot wrap my brain around their perspective, no matter how much I try. In another example, for some cultural groups time is of the essence. Punctuality is important. To be late for a meeting is an insult to others. But for other cultural groups, time is a much more fluid concept. The intention to meet is what is important, the designated time is approximate. "Let's meet at 10:00" has two very different interpretations, though each assumes that the communication is clearly understood by the other.

A missionary working in Germany once told me of her experience of Germans and Ghanaians meeting together at a local church. In the Ghanaians' view, church started as you were preparing to go to the service, stopping at neighbors' homes to gather them up and bring them with you. For the Germans, church started at 11 A.M., whether you were in the building or not. As she related this story to me, by the time the Ghanaians arrived, the German service was almost over.

Another worldview difference that has a dramatic impact on our life choices and expectations in the workplace is the view of destiny. In some groups, there is a strong belief that one controls one's own destiny. Yet other groups hold the view that fate and external forces control where people are and what they can expect. We see this in disagreements ranging from the workplace to the community to the political arena. "Pick yourself up by your own bootstraps" runs smack into "It is my lot in life."

Five Dimensions of Cultural Difference

To give us more of an understanding of the nature of culture, let us examine five common dimensions of cultural difference: communication, tolerance for uncertainty, power, identity, and time.

Communication: Direct or Indirect

How do we talk to one another? This ranges from direct to indirect. Those on the direct end of the spectrum speak what is on their minds. Their preference is to tell the truth (as they see it) rather than spare another's feelings. Communication is strictly about the transfer of information. Yes means yes. No means no. Those on the indirect side prefer to show more deference to the group or other individual, likely to spare feelings or to preserve harmony. Their speech may be hesitant, slow, or quiet. "I was thinking maybe if you had time for lunch, we could...." "I don't know about this, but I think...." In this indirect pattern of speaking, there is a rising intonation at the end of every statement, making each sentence sound like a question. The emphasis is on building relationships.

In cultures where indirect communication is the norm, people have many ways to say no without ever saying no. They use phrases like "I think so," "Probably," "We'll look into it," "We'll see," "Maybe." All these can mean no without using the word *no*. Harmony is preserved by avoiding being definitive or using what may sound like a harsh negative. In individualistic or low-context cultures, however, people tend to be verbally direct. They value communication openness, are willing or eager to self-disclose, and prefer clear, straightforward communication. In low-context cultures, direct approaches are seen to contribute to a positive management climate. In collectivist or high-context cultures, indirect communication is preferred because the image of group harmony is essential.[4]

In the United States, directness is often seen as the dominant or preferred style in the workplace. In her book *Talking from 9 to 5*, Deborah Tannen, who once said, "communication between genders is cross cultural," explores the differences between the direct style and the indirect style as it is experienced between men and women, as well as between national cultures.[5] In Tannen's book, as well as in Malcolm Gladwell's *Outliers*,[6] the problems that sometimes result from indirect communication styles can be life-threatening. Both authors cite airplane-cockpit dialog that led to airplane crashes.

Gladwell, for example, describes a disastrous interaction involving a Columbian co-pilot, the airplane pilot (also Columbian), and the air traffic controller in New York. Gladwell describes the incident:

> "Imagine the scene in the cockpit. The plane is dangerously low on fuel. They have just blown their first shot at a landing. They have no idea how much longer the plane is capable of flying. The Columbian co-pilot tells air traffic control 'That's right to one-eight-zero on the heading and, ah, we'll try once again. We're running out of fuel.'" Gladwell refers to this as "mitigated speech": "when we're being polite ... or when we're being deferential to authority."

> The thing you have to understand about that crash is that New York air traffic controllers are famous for being rude, aggressive, bullying. . . . They handle a phenomenal amount of traffic in a very constrained environment. . . . The way they look at it, it's "I am in control. Shut up and do what I say." They will snap at you. And if you don't like what they tell you to do, you have to snap back. And then they'll say, "all right, then." But if you don't, they'll railroad you. (pp. 194–195)

It can be seductive to put our own interpretations on these style differences—to make assumptions such as, "Direct communication is more powerful," or "A person who uses indirect communication is insecure." These assumptions are not always true. The manager may give a direct and clear (not necessarily harsh) message: "Have that report on my desk by 5:00." Bosses may also communicate effectively with subordinates indirectly to accomplish tasks. "I would like to see that report before you leave today"; from the boss, this may be indirect, but the employee can still receive the intended message. On the other hand, the manager who uses indirect and unclear messages is not likely to get the needed results— for example, "How is that report going?"

Power differences especially affect direct and indirect communication, how it is given as well as how it is received. The direct may be, "I'm going to lunch. Cover my calls." The indirect would be, "I'm going to lunch. Would you mind covering my calls?" A boss can comfortably use either the direct or the indirect style to communicate with an employee. But that same direct tone from a subordinate may not be received by the manager as acceptable because it implies an incorrect power relationship between the two. Within your own organizational structure, you may talk to employees with a more direct style, and yet with your boss you will use a more indirect style. A subordinate's saying, "Get that report to me by 5:00 today" to his boss would be heard quite differently from a boss making that same statement to her employee.

Understanding how these cultural and power differences impact communication includes responding to them appropriately:

- ▶ Avoid assuming that a person who uses an indirect style is weak, or that a person who uses a direct style is domineering or arrogant.
- ▶ Manage your own style preference and modify it when appropriate.

Tolerance for Uncertainty: High or Low

How comfortable are you with taking risks—and with the possibility of failure? On the high end of the scale, some people are willing to take risks. They set up new businesses, move to a new places, question the existing rules. These people are often the early adopters of new technology, eager to take on the newest smart phones or digital equipment. Their preference is for fewer rules, and they are generally more tolerant of differences in values, opinions, and beliefs. On the low end of this scale are people who value tradition, for whom new is not necessarily better, and who feel taking a risk can be dangerous. For these people, beliefs and values are firmly held. There is *one* right answer. Rules and structures are tight.

Embracing a new career or developing a new business line or product, investing in a new venture or moving to a new town where the job market is better—these are more comfortable options for those at the high end. At the low end, maintaining traditions and respecting the rules are stronger inclinations. In the workplace, there are those who are eager to jump into new assignments, and they do so with the attitude, "I don't know how to do it, but I am eager to figure it out." Others are more cautious, with the hesitation, "I don't want to commit to doing something unless I am certain I can succeed."

Alfie (at the high end) was willing to step up and challenge the boss's ideas, even though he knew it could be risky. The boss might get upset and respond negatively. But Alfie would take the risk. "What is the worst thing the boss can say? He's not going to fire me." Some of Alfie's peers were really glad to have Alfie around. They had the same questions, but it was a lot safer to sit back and watch what happened to Alfie, then decide whether to join him or not. Alfie complained to me, "When the boss isn't around, they are all agreeing with me. Then when I say something, nobody in the meeting backs me up."

Hannah (at the low end) knew the rules. Whenever her boss proposed a new approach or procedure, she was quick to quote the manual. She knew the SOP upside down and backwards. She resisted change, and preferred to keep things as they were. When the boss announced that she would need to move her workspace, Hannah was full of questions. "Why do I have to move? Here is just fine." When I asked her what she liked about her job, she answered, "The security of it."

As a manager, you need to understand employees' differences in dealing with uncertainty, risk, and change. Try to do the following:

➤ Be responsive to their needs either for stability or for risk taking.

➤ With those on the low end of this dimension, avoid too much change when possible, provide explanation when necessary, and give advance notice.

➤ For those on the high end, provide stimulating opportunities to take on new projects.

Power: Egalitarian or Hierarchical

Who has the power or authority to make decisions, and how does that individual use that power? Of those on the egalitarian side of this scale, people expect to have some control or influence over the decisions that affect them. There is a spirit of inclusion: we are all in this together, and everyone's voice is valued. On the hierarchical side, people expect that those with power or authority will make the decisions. The lower ranking people give deference willingly to those above them. So, this is a dimension of culture that particularly impacts management.

The egalitarian boss will engage the staff in decision making on significant policy decisions, usually through staff meetings or one-on-one conversations. For subordinates who also hold the egalitarian view, this is as it should be: "We should be consulted on these issues." For those on the hierarchical side, however, this egalitarian approach can be frustrating. These employees are often more comfortable saying, "You are the boss. Tell me what to do and I will do it." The egalitarians among us may find themselves making the same statement, but that is because they believe it is what is expected of them, though they will not be happy about it. They really want and expect to have input.

Cultures develop within organizations. I think back to my graduate program in conflict resolution; it was notorious for our vocal participation in all the decisions that the faculty made—or tried to make. But that was the culture of the program—the worldview of the students: we should have some way to participate in the decision-making process. Across campus, in other graduate programs, there was much less activism. The culture of the math and science programs or the nursing programs was more hierarchical—students read the catalog and the syllabus, and then followed the course of study as it was laid out.

Organizations have different cultures, different operating systems. A person functioning effectively within the military for twenty years has a clear understanding of the importance of hierarchy, as do all of the people she works with. When she retires and takes a job in a civilian workforce, though, she discovers that the unwritten rules are different in an egalitarian system. If she is the boss, she may have difficulty adjusting to employees who expect to negotiate assignments. Indeed, she may be frustrated by the (in her view) inefficiency of the more egalitarian approach.

As a manager, you need to understand the nature of egalitarian versus hierarchical perspectives. Consider doing the following:

▶   Allow opportunities for those who value egalitarian principles to provide input into decisions that may impact their workplace or responsibilities.

► Practice providing clear guidance and organizational structure for those who are more comfortable with a hierarchical approach.

Identity: Individualist or Collectivist

Is your identity defined more by your own accomplishments or by your membership in a group? Those of us on the individualist end of this spectrum make choices and decisions based on questions we ask ourselves, such as "What do I want? What do I need? What do I care about?" Those of us on the collectivist side are concerned with the good of the group, asking questions like, "What is best for the group? What does the group need or want or care about?"

> *We all know we are unique individuals, but we tend to see others as representatives of groups.*
> —DEBORAH TANNEN

This topic relates to a discussion earlier in this chapter, in regard to the concept of high- and low-context cultures. In general, we can pair the attributes of the individualist with the low-context culture, while the collectivist view is aligned with the high-context culture.

In the previous chapter, I introduced a model for considering the typical approaches to conflict resolution (Figure 5-1). Using this model, we see that those on the collectivist side often show a preference for avoidance and accommodation. They approach disagreement with high concern for the group or the other person. As reported by Stella Ting-Twomey, it is rare in Asian cultures to have open conflict because conflict appears to disrupt group harmony.[7] In contrast, in American culture, the individual is often considered the most important component of society: there is a high concern for individual rights and freedoms. Those on the individualist side are more likely to respond according to the vertical axis (high concern for self or the task at hand), in directing mode.

Looking at the diagram in this light, you can see the stereotypes that pair up with these behaviors. Individualist people on the vertical axis are often considered arrogant and egotistical; collectivists on the horizontal axis are likely be seen as weak, as pushovers. But these are stereotypes, not prescriptions; they can limit our ability to understand one another and to appreciate the contribution that each type of person makes to a healthy workplace.

Privacy, personal space, and individual accountability are emphasized at the individualist end of the scale. In collectivist cultures, group accountability dominates. Several years ago, in responding to lessons learned from Japanese industry successes, U.S. businesses showed a strong movement to apply these collectivist lessons to teamwork in various industries. It didn't always work—the cultural change required was too great.

For example, the Library of Congress reorganized its organizational structure into teams. Previously the work had been assigned to individuals, and their performance was evaluated as individuals, based on the number of titles cataloged and quality of the work. Shifting to a team structure was a huge cultural shift for these employees; they would now be evaluated based on the productivity of the team. This created more conflict than predicted. At the implementation level, team members argued over who was carrying their weight and who wasn't, who was doing their fair share and who wasn't. Management eventually abandoned the approach, in part because of the contentions and conflicts that were created.

This dimension of individualist versus collectivist identity also helps us understand different attitudes about saving face. "Face saving" refers to the importance of maintaining a good image and the strategies we use to save face in conflicts. Those on the individualist side are most concerned with reputation, credibility, and self-respect—all related to the ego. Ting-Twomey explains that American subjects, for example, tend to adopt self-face preservation and maintenance, focus on self-face issues, use control-focused conflict strategies and confrontational strategies, and display stronger win-lose orientations. For Americans, loss of face means personal failure, loss of self-esteem, or loss of self-pride on an individual attribution basis. On the collectivist end, however, saving face is related to honor, on how the incident reflects on the family, the group, or the organization. Asian subjects tend to use face-smoothing strategies, mutual-face preservation strategies, and conflict-avoidance strategies. For Japanese and Korean subjects, loss of face means disrupting the group harmony, bringing shame to their family, classmates, or company.[8]

How might this dimension of culture play out in the workplace? As one example, consider the individualist boss who may want to recognize individual effort in order to demonstrate appreciation for a job well done. The collectivist employee may find being singled out in this way embarrassing, rather than as a moment of pride.

In understanding the individualist and collectivist preferences, the manager needs to:

➤ Be aware of the needs and expectations of employees.

➤ Appreciate the contribution to group cohesion that the collectivist makes.

➤ Allow opportunities for those on the collectivist end to express concerns, assured that they will not hinder the harmony of the group.

➤ Provide rewards and appreciation appropriate to the preferences of the people you manage.

➤ Recognize the individualist's desire for acknowledgment.

Time Orientation: Short Term or Long Term

The dimension of time, as described by Geert Hofstede, refers to the adherence to, or pursuit of, "traditional values."[9] At the short-term end of this spectrum, a person's view of life and decision making takes place within a short time frame. For example, the short-term thinker will view shareholder interests in terms of the next quarterly report. He might propose laying off 2,000 employees because this will make the financial statement look strong. But it may have negative consequences for the long term, as it could leave the company short-staffed, unable at the end of a downturn to respond quickly to a growing market. Getting things done fast is important, but the focus is on short-term rewards. There is little concern for how a decision fits into the longer view of history. The short-term thinker says, "Time is money, you know."

On the other hand, the person with a long-term orientation views decision making in a broader context. There is no hurry to make a decision; more consideration is given to history and long-range future implications. Rather than rush into a decision, the long-term thinker slows down her decision making. Decisions will have far-reaching implications; let's not be in too much of a hurry to make a change that could have long-term consequences. "Slow and steady wins the race." In Japan, people take out hundred-year mortgages for their homes. It is hard to imagine that kind of long-term thinking in the United States.

. . . .

Several wine makers from California visited Bulgaria to advise the Bulgarians on how to produce more and better quality wine. As they began to share their wisdom, one Bulgarian looked at them in amazement at their audacity, "Gentlemen, my wine cellar is older than your *country*!"

. . . .

As a manager dealing with people's differing concepts of time, you need to:

➤   Recognize the perspectives others may bring to the decision-making process.

➤   Be responsive to those differences: the urgency of the short term, and the patience of the long-term.

Consider This

☑   On this spectrum of cultural differences, what are your preferences?

Communication

Direct   Indirect
_____

Tolerance for Uncertainty

High   Low
_____

Power

Egalitarian   Hierarchy
_____

Identity

Individual   Collective
_____

Time

Short-term orientation   Long-term orientation
_____

Power and Culture

In the United States, the management level of corporate America is heavily populated with Americans of European cultural origin.[10] Among this group are people with a strong tendency toward the left-hand column of this cultural scale. Working with, managing, and supervising people who bring a different worldview to the workplace can challenge their beliefs. We often want to work with people who act like ourselves, who do things the *right way*—which means doing things "like we do." Those in power often subconsciously reward and recognize those who reflect the dominant culture's view.

As a European American myself, it is often difficult for me to see the world from others' points of view. I carry my own biases from my own belief system, whether I am aware of those biases or not. Within the dominant culture, there is often an unconscious expectation that "they should all be like us." Somehow, our thinking goes, we can put up with their little quirks and quaint customs (i.e., their cultural views) and maybe one day they will become enlightened and see the world as we do.

The diversity of today's workforce (race, gender, ethnicity, religion, and so on), which reflects the changing demographics of the U.S. population, creates disputes and conflicts that are often driven by cultural views. The behavioral differences between the dominant group and minority groups can result in an "us versus them" mentality, whereby we see ourselves—whoever we are—as doing things the *right* way and others as doing things the *wrong* way. As demographics shift further, the dominant group can feel threatened, and the opportunities for conflict and distrust will increase. In addition, this growing diversity forces change, sometimes slowly, sometimes dramatically, and change inside an organization is always hard. Frequently, it is change itself that creates conflict. The effective manager of the 21st century has the ability to see that diversity can bring strengths as well as challenges to the workplace, and has the skills necessary to manage the inherent differences.

Notes

1. Geert Hofstede, *Culture's Consequences: Comparing Values, Behaviors, Institutions and Organizations Across Nations* (Thousand Oaks, Calif.: Sage 2001).

2. Edward T. Hall, *Beyond Culture* (New York: Anchor Books, 1976).

3. Craig Storti, *Figuring Foreigners Out* (Yarmouth, Me.: Intercultural Press, 1998).

4. Stella Ting-Twomey, "Cross-Cultural Face-Negotiation: An Analytical Overview." Paper presented at Simon Fraser University, Harbour Centre, Vancouver, BC, Canada. April 15, 1992.

5. Deborah Tannen, *Talking from 9 to 5: How Women's and Men's Conversational Styles Affect Who Gets Heard, Who Gets Credit and What Gets Done at Work* (New York: William Morrow, 1994).

6. Malcolm Gladwell, *Outliers: The Story of Success* (Boston: Little, Brown, 2008).

7. Ting-Twomey, "Cross-Cultural Face-Negotiation."

8. Ibid.

9. Hofstede, *Culture's Consequences*.

10. Thomas Kochman and Jean Mavrelis, *Corporate Tribalism: White Men/White Women and Cultural Diversity at Work* (Chicago: University of Chicago Press, 2009).

CHAPTER 7

What We Are Arguing About Matters: Sources of Conflict

Y es, what we are arguing about does make a difference. What do we disagree about? Is it the terms of the contract? Are we struggling with how we can get the task done? Or who does what and when? Or does the argument touch on our very core values and principles? Standing back and thinking about a disagreement before you begin to discuss the matter with someone else can help you find your way through the conflict to reach a resolution.

Figure 7-1 shows most sources of conflict on the left-hand side, arranged from those that are easiest to resolve to those that are hardest to handle.

Information conflicts can be relatively simple to resolve, once you recognize them as such. Conflicts of interests and expectations take a little more time to understand. Once you do, however, you often can open up options that will meet the needs of each person involved. Structural conflicts are often out of the control of the parties involved, so resolving them requires new strategies. Conflicts in values are by and large not

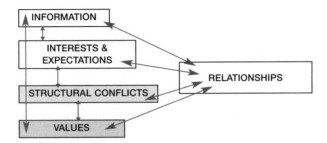

Figure 7-1. Sources of conflict.

negotiable. You must first identify that the differences are about core values themselves, then you can begin to find a way to the other side of the conflict. As you see later in this chapter, however, conflicts may not fall simply into one category or another, and often have effects on each other.

Now, take a look at the right-hand side of Figure 7-1: "relationships." Arrows point back and forth between relationship conflicts and all of the other types of conflict because relationship conflicts make all of the others more difficult to resolve, and because other conflicts can complicate relationship conflicts. In this chapter, I first describe all of the conflict sources in the left-hand column, then I tackle the challenges of relationship conflicts.

Information

Information conflicts are disagreements about facts or data: the numbers written in the report, what the policy or the contract says. These can be the easiest conflicts to address. If the disagreement is about information—I have one set of facts and you have another—once you identify that as the problem, you and the other party can agree on where to get information that you both will accept.

. . . .

"Request denied." Karyn read the message on her screen, too stunned to think. She was beyond exhaustion; her mother was still at home, sick and frail. Karyn had submitted a request for advanced leave to deal with this most recent round of trouble.

Just a few minutes before, Richard was in his office, scrolling through the day's endless list of e-mail requests and directives. Projects were piling up, staff were calling in sick. How was he supposed to get the work done with the round of flu that was sweeping through the office? And here was Karyn's appeal, one more in a nagging stack of requests. Couldn't she see that they were already shorthanded? She'd already used up all the leave she had, how could she be asking for more?

Karyn was convinced that there was some way to get advanced leave. She had seen others do it. She would pay it back. She just needed help this one time. She was desperate for time off to get her mother settled into a nursing home. Meanwhile, Richard knew he was right. It was the supervisor's prerogative to allow leave or not, especially advanced leave.

When Karyn finally walked into Richard's office, they both reached for the dog-eared manual on his desk. They could read the policy from Human Resources. If the answer wasn't clear there, they would call to get clarification. A common understanding of the information was all that it took to find a way through their disagreement.

. . . .

Often, the key to resolving information disputes is to agree on which authorities or sources of data to use, or on the methods used for gathering the data.

> ### HOW TO ADDRESS INFORMATION CONFLICTS
> ► Agree on a common source of information.
> ► Agree on a process for gathering data or facts.

Interests

Conflicts over interests and expectations generally take more effort to understand and resolve. To begin, what do I mean here by *interests*?[1]

Most of the time, when people discover themselves in disagreement, they declare their positions—they make demands or stake claims. Each of us presents our own answer to the conflict. You can begin by arguing who is right and who is wrong. And then you can move into how *right* you are and how *wrong* the other person is. You present your justifications for the demands you are making. Often those justifications are based on principles: "Because I am the boss." "I deserve it." "I need it more than you do." "We did it your way last time." "Mom always liked you best." "Possession is nine-tenths of the law."

Interests are your underlying concerns, desires, and needs in a disagreement. Generally, interests are less apparent in a conflict than demands or proposed solutions. Therefore, in a contentious moment, first identify your own interests: What is important to you? What it is you are trying to accomplish? Why does this matter? And then try to understand the interests of the other person: What is important to him? Why? What is he trying to accomplish? What is he concerned about? When you can shift your discussion from arguing over positions—who is right and why—to each other's interests, you can often discover solutions that are satisfactory to both.

HOW TO ADDRESS INTEREST CONFLICTS

➤ Focus on interests, not positions.

➤ Identify the underlying concerns and the needs of each person.

➤ Build solutions that meet the needs of everyone.

For example, within a company, presumably everyone across all departments is working for the same goal. One and all are there to make and sell as many cardboard boxes as they can. Their goal is the same, but they have different interests in meeting that goal. The sales manager gets a commission based on the number of orders placed each quarter; so, her interest is in maximizing the number of boxes she sells. She may be frustrated by calls from customers waiting for delivery on promised orders.

The manager of operations is responsible for making the boxes to meet the orders coming in. He has to see that the machines are maintained and adequately staffed. He makes certain that someone at the end of the line checks the boxes for quality before they are shipped out. His bonus comes from keeping production costs (including overtime) low. His interests are in maintaining steady production, keeping the machinery running at an optimal rate, and promoting high staff morale and therefore high productivity. He is tired of being constantly nagged by Sales for greater production when Sales has sold beyond the capacity of the equipment.

. . . .

Yes, they both are in the business of making and selling boxes. They have mutual interests. For instance, they have a common interest in keeping the customers happy. But their separate interests sometimes collide. To resolve their differences, they need to recognize their mutual as well as their competing interests, rather than arguing over who is right or wrong. Ultimately, each of them is right. Selling more boxes is of primary importance to the company; and maintaining equipment and staff to ensure a quality product is also of primary importance to the company. They resolve their differences by creating an improved communication system between the two departments, so that operations is informed in a more timely way as customer orders are placed, and the sales manager can track production, including breakdowns, backups, and shipping dates.

Structural Conflicts

Structural conflicts generally involve limited resources, or structures that are beyond the control of the people in the conflict. In interest-based conflicts, solutions can be found through "expanding the pie"—finding solutions that meet the interests of both at the same time. In structural conflicts, however, the pie is fixed—the answers must be found within built-in limitations.

Here are some examples of structural conflicts:

► Three offices with windows, four staff members with the same level of responsibility. Who won't get a window office?

- ➤ Five people applied for the promotion, and there is only one opening.

- ➤ An administrative assistant reports to two bosses.

- ➤ Two positions have overlapping roles and responsibilities.

- ➤ Does the water in that river belong to the people at the headwaters, or to those whose land borders the river—on which side of the river?

To resolve structural conflicts, we must look to the ways that decisions are made. There are several ways to do this. For example, you can raise the matter to a more appropriate level of authority.

HOW TO ADDRESS STRUCTURAL CONFLICTS

- ➤ Raise the issue to an appropriate decision-making level.
- ➤ Establish fair and transparent decision-making processes.
- ➤ Reallocate ownership and control of decision making.

· ·

As the group gathered for the meeting, the tension mounted. Those who arrived early for donuts and coffee wondered aloud if Carla would come. Ted was particularly anxious. Over the past several months, he and Carla had had a few bitter phone conversations and numerous hostile e-mail exchanges. In fact, everyone knew that these two division directors had frequent arguments with one another over policies and priorities.

Before the meeting, their boss explained to me that theirs was a personality conflict. Once they started talking about their differences in the meeting, the true conflict emerged: One division of the organization was assigned by region, the other was assigned by functional focus. When a food crisis erupted in Haiti, Ted, the regional director for the Caribbean, was clear that the decisions were his to make. After all, he knew the region and the resources available there. Carla, the director for food relief, was equally clear that, since she had the technical expertise, she would be making the decisions.

In the meeting their boss finally heard the dispute (rather than relying on secondhand reports about each of them) and acknowledged, "When the Executive Committee created the reorganization, we didn't take time to clarify who was in charge of what; we figured somebody could work that out later." The solution for this structural conflict then was readily apparent. The boss, working with the rest of the Executive Committee, created a clear definition of the roles and responsibilities for these two positions.

. . . .

Another strategy is to establish fair and transparent decision-making processes. Define the criteria for decision making and inform the people involved as to how those criteria will be applied. When the available solutions are limited and the rewards—whether financial or other recognition—are significant, people become competitive, contentious, and suspicious of the decisions that are made. In particular, promotions can result in structural conflicts, as can performance awards or contract decisions. But fairness and transparency can be powerful forces in resolving structural conflicts.

. . . .

Dean filed an Equal Employment Opportunity (EEO) complaint against the agency. Four times over the last five years he had applied for promotions and had been denied. Surely, he reasoned, he had been denied because he was deaf. In a mediation, the human resources specialist carefully described step by step the agency's decision-making process for promotions. (This was a written policy within the agency. However, because he was deaf, he was not aware of much of the informal communication within the office.) First, the hiring manager would create the job description. Then, someone with experience, but outside of the component, created from the job description a list of specific criteria for meeting the job requirements. Next, another person from outside the agency reviewed each application, giving a numerical score according to each of the criteria. Based on the total scores, a hiring panel interviewed those most qualified and the selection was made.

As Dean processed all this information, his questions changed from "Why wasn't I selected?" to "What can I do to improve my qualifications?" Once he understood the decision-making process, he dropped the EEO complaint.

. . . .

Additionally, you can reallocate ownership and control of decision making. Look for ways to turn decision making over to those who will be directly affected by the decision.

. . . .

The awards process within a local government office had employees buzzing like hornets. Those who didn't receive awards were incensed. "Clearly," they thought, "we have worked as hard as others, so why haven't *we* been recognized?" Those who had received awards were embarrassed and defensive. At the awards ceremony designed to acknowledge effort and boost productivity, they did not know how to react. "Don't call out *my* name!"

A committee was formed that included both those who had gotten awards and those who hadn't; they would decide what to do with the program. After several meetings, the committee unanimously agreed to terminate the awards program. As they searched for a policy that would be perceived by all of the employees as fair and transparent, they could not find one. Because this decision was made by the employees themselves, others acknowledged that the decision was appropriate.

. . . .

Values

When we talk about values, we refer to the principles or qualities that we hold dear. As discussed in the previous chapter, values are shaped by the identity groups that we belong to, whether ethnic, religious, regional, class, race, gender, or other. A few values might be considered universal, however the way they are interpreted, recognized, or demonstrated might be quite different across cultures.

Everyone you work with or know requires that certain basic human needs be met.[2] How these needs are satisfied varies widely around the globe, however. Whenever a conflict or disagreement puts these values at risk, the first task is to address the needs.

- ➤ Respect—a sense of worth, to be acknowledged as a valued human being
- ➤ Identity—a sense of self in relation to the outside world
- ➤ Security—safety, freedom from harm and the fear of harm, freedom from danger
- ➤ Belonging—the need to be accepted by others and to have strong personal ties with one's family, friends, or identity group

Other values vary from individual to individual, or from community to community. These principles and qualities—what we believe in and what we care about—define who we are. Our values are not negotiable. If you are arguing about value differences, you will not change my mind and I will not change yours.

Consider This

☑ Consider the list of words below, and mark the five values that are most important to you.

Achievement	Creativity	Honesty
Advancement	Curiosity	Humor
Adventure	Effectiveness	Independence
Autonomy	Equality	Innovation
Balance	Excitement	Integrity
Beauty	Family	Knowledge
Belonging	Freedom	Learning
Challenge	Fun	Leisure
Competition	Growth	Loyalty
Cooperation	Health	Power

Prestige	Serenity	Teamwork
Productivity	Service	Variety
Quality	Social responsibility	Wealth
Relationships	Spirituality	Wisdom
Self-actualization	Strength	
Self-reliance	Structure	

Now, give the list to others you work with, and ask them to do the same. What values do you share? Which are different? This can be an eye-opening exercise with people whom you think you know very well.

Because our values are so closely tied to our identities, it is hard to imagine that others would not hold the same values that you do. This makes the territory of values conflicts particularly rough terrain. Perhaps you have been caught in endless arguments about politics or religion with co-workers or friends, or even within your own family. It is better to find a way around those differences rather than continuing to try convincing others of how right you are and how wrong they are.

HOW TO ADDRESS VALUES CONFLICTS

► Search for super-ordinate goals: the mission of the office or organization, the value of diversity in the workforce, etc.

► Allow parties to agree and to disagree.

► Build common loyalty.

Often in a values-based conflict, you can shift the focus to higher ground, where you both can agree on a bigger goal. The manager who can clearly state the mission of the organization, and within that mission, how the work of the office or department or team is key to meeting that mission, gives employees a clear sense of purpose around which to focus their own efforts. This is what it means to focus on super-ordinate goals—goals that are beyond the needs or interests of the individual.

How do value differences affect the workplace? Here are two examples that illustrate the challenges.

Several years ago, I was cruising down an interstate behind a cute little red Jeep. Its license plate read "LV2PRT." I was behind this vehicle for quite a while, so I had plenty of time to consider it. Did the plate say "Love to Party"? Maybe it said, "Live to Party"? In either case, obviously partying was really important to the driver of this car; he really valued having fun. And then I thought, *I have worked with someone a lot like him. He's the one who comes into the office bleary-eyed on Monday morning, regaling everyone with wild tales of the Saturday night bash that rolled into Sunday morning.* After I heard his stories, I was sometimes tempted to step into lecture mode. "You are ruining your life. Can't you see that this is no way to succeed?" Any time I was tempted to do this, though, I also remembered how others had tuned me out when they heard me launch into another sermon.

I concluded that there was nothing that I could say that would change his mind about the fun he was having and how important it was to him. What I could do was turn my own thinking around. Rather than trying to change his mind about his values, I could meet him on his own ground. Instead of trying to change his values, I could focus my efforts on the goals of the office and how his work supported that mission. I thought, *He needs to keep his job to be able to support his partying ways; that may be a way to motivate him to get the work done.* I also thought that we might also be able to tap into his energy to bring some fun to our own office. In short, it was better to put my efforts there than to try to change his mind about his values.

The boss presented a big project to an employee: "We've got a new mandate coming down from headquarters. A whole new system to get up and running. It's going to take a lot of extra work to get this done. Nights. Weekends. But if you do a good job, there is a real opportunity for you here. Maybe a promotion. And it'll look great on your resume." The employee reacted, "I don't care about a promotion or building a resume. I am willing to give you a solid forty hours a week, but that is all I committed to. At the end of the day, I am going home to my family. It's why I have this job."

For the boss, his value was that "career achievement is really important. I have spent my life working for it." For the employee, though, his value was, "I have this job so that I can take care of my family." Neither would convince the other about which value was the "correct" one. To find resolution, they first had to quit arguing over their differing values and consider how best to achieve the greater good.

. . . .

Relationships

On the right-hand side of the Figure 7-1 chart is the category "Relationships." These types of conflicts are about the history we have had together, how we communicate, the stereotypes we hold, and most important, the level of trust between us. All of those arrows point from relationships to the other sources of conflict because relationships affect everything else. If you and someone else have a positive relationship, the two of you can work through just about anything, from disagreements about information to different values. Often, because you have a positive working relationship, you want to preserve it. Working through the conflict is worth the energy and effort it may take.

The arrows in the figure point in both directions. That is, other types of conflicts also have an impact on relationship conflicts. This is particularly true of structural conflicts and values conflicts. In the story earlier in this chapter, of the boss with the regional directors, Ted and Carla, who barely spoke to one another anymore, the boss's explanation to me was quick and definitive: "They have a personality conflict." We dug further down to the roots of that conflict, and we discovered that there was a legitimate structural conflict underlying many of the arguments they had. Certainly the structural conflict created by overlapping responsibilities contributed to the relationship conflict.

Whenever someone tells me that they have a personality conflict, I begin sniffing around to see what else might be going on. The neat and tidy explanation, "they have a personality conflict," is often masking another source of conflict. It's easy to declare the situation hopeless once the "personality conflict" diagnosis is made, but that diagnosis leaves little hope for improvement. People shrug their shoulders, "There is nothing you can do about it."

Never underestimate the power of trust in a relationship. Trust is essential. If I am asking something of you—or you of me—we each need some assurance that the other will fulfill the commitment. Sometimes the level of trust needed is small. For instance, in the exchange of money for goods at the grocery store, you give your credit card to the cashier, trusting that the package of meat will be fresh when you get home. Driving down the highway, you count on the other car not to change lanes without signaling. With more important investments—our hearts, our livelihoods, our lives—the level of trust we need increases. In the workplace, we depend on others to perform consistently, to deliver on promises and commitments, in small ways and in significant ways, every day.

There is good news and bad news here. The good news is that, when people trust one another, they can work through virtually any conflict or difficulty. When mistakes are made, they give each other the benefit of the doubt. If I trust you, I will generally accept what you tell me—your excuses or explanations. I will give you information that you need in a timely way. Communication is fairly trouble-free. Information flows between people in an easy exchange.

The bad news is that, when there is no trust, communication becomes much more difficult. The simplest disagreements can become unsolvable. If I don't trust you, I will doubt your motives and intentions. I will dismiss what you have to say, and I will withhold important information for fear of what you may do with it. When trust is gone, we cannot resolve the simplest issue. In a simple information dispute, I will not believe your data. I will be suspicious of what you have to say and why you are saying it. You will have the same reaction to statements. Figure 7-2 shows the interlocking relationships involved in conflict resolution.

The Effects of Distrust in the Workplace

You can see the lack of trust in many business and government offices. This lack of trust can paralyze business operations.

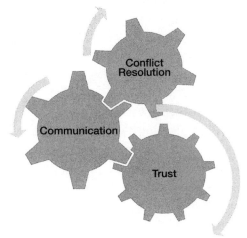

Figure 7-2. Trust, communication, and conflict resolution.

Recently I returned to an office to mediate a disagreement between a supervisor and an employee. In July, the two had worked together easily, talking with and about one another in positive and productive ways. Each was clear about his responsibilities. Each counted on the other for support, information, and decisions. Then their relationship hit a wall. At the mediation in February, it was clear that things between them had soured. The employee had filed a grievance against the boss; his list of complaints was long. As I sat between them, I listened for clues as to what had changed.

In the employee's explanation, he told me, "My boss doesn't respect my decisions. He doesn't listen to me." I replied, "Tell me more about that."

"It really started two months ago. The boss overheard my conversation on the telephone with a board member. He didn't ask what was going on so I didn't have a chance to explain. He just announced loudly, 'I can't trust you,' and walked away. Since that moment, nothing I have done has been good enough for him." For a few minutes, the room was silent. Then they began to talk. The two of them could now confront the real challenge that they had: to work toward rebuilding the trust between them.

Another employee described the challenge of the distrust that he experienced. When the boss went into a meeting with someone else, the employee's imagination would fill with the worst possible scenarios of the conversations going on inside the room. But when trust was reestablished, he let go of that anxiety, confident that whatever the discussion was, his own relationship with the boss was secure.

> *The chief lesson I have learned in a long life is that the only way to make a man trustworthy is to trust him; and the surest way to make him untrustworthy is to distrust him and show your distrust.*
> —HENRY L. STIMSON

Time after time, when I am called in to assess an office dispute I find that distrust is at the heart of the problem. My job then becomes that of helping staff and management find ways to rebuild some rudimentary levels of trust so that the other issues can be addressed. On the other hand, sometimes I find terrific relationships of trust.

Every morning Paula drives an extra thirty minutes to her job. Every afternoon she retraces that same drive, adding an extra hour to her work day. Every day! She has passed up equivalent jobs that are twenty miles closer to home. Why does she do this? Because, to hear her tell it, she has such a good boss, someone she can really trust.

When she talks about Tameka, she talks about trust—that each trusts the other. Paula trusts Tameka in no small part because Tameka trusts her. And that trust is so valuable to Paula that she will go to great lengths to maintain it. Here are some of the things Paula says about her boss:

"I don't want to lose her trust in me. Tameka gives me assignments and trusts me to get them done."

"If I tell her something in confidence, she keeps it confidential."

"When we disagree, she listens. She may not agree with me in the end, but she listens. After she has made the decision, she gets back to me to tell me what she agrees with and what she doesn't."

"She looks out for everybody here. When someone needs help, Tameka looks for ways to provide it."

When I hear Paula talk, I think of so many other bosses I know who dream of having the loyalty and commitment that Tameka gets from Paula. The foundation of that loyalty and commitment is trust.

• •

Consider This

☑ Use a survey like the one below to determine the level of trust within your own office.

1. My boss keeps promises and commitments.

Strongly agree				Strongly disagree
5	4	3	2	1

2. Co-workers keep their promises and commitments.

Strongly agree				Strongly disagree
5	4	3	2	1

3. My boss listens to me, even when he/she disagrees.

Strongly agree				Strongly disagree
5	4	3	2	1

4. Co-workers listen to me, even when they disagree.

Strongly agree				Strongly disagree
5	4	3	2	1

5. My boss communicates with me openly and honestly about significant information.

Strongly agree				Strongly disagree
5	4	3	2	1

6. My co-workers communicate with me openly and honestly about significant information.

Strongly agree				Strongly disagree
5	4	3	2	1

7. My boss demonstrates confidence in my skills and abilities.

Strongly agree				Strongly disagree
5	4	3	2	1

8. My co-workers demonstrate confidence in my skills and abilities.

Strongly agree				Strongly disagree
5	4	3	2	1

9. In our office, we look for ways to work together cooperatively.

Strongly agree				Strongly disagree
5	4	3	2	1

The Dynamics of Trust

In the beginning of a working relationship, most of us give others the benefit of the doubt. From there, trust builds slowly over time. For some of us, trust is easily given. Others take much longer before they will trust another.

We often think of trust as a savings account. Each time a commitment is made and kept, each time a promise or a confidence is maintained, or each time information is passed on in a timely way, managers are making deposits into the trust account. Each time a manager tips off an employee about a change that is coming, or gives staff credit for the work that's been done, or trusts someone to accomplish a task, the manager adds to that account. The manager's actions tell employees that the boss is looking out for them, and that the boss values the work they do. The manager confirms that this relationship and the staff's contributions to it matter.

Every manager will need to draw upon that savings account, at one time or another. Inevitably, there are times when the manager will make a mistake. If the account is strong, when there are fumbles there is that buildup of trust to draw upon. Employees will forgive you and the relationship and the work will stay on track. They will continue to believe in your intent and your ability. Communication will flow as before. Staff can talk about those things over which you disagree. When they are concerned about some new direction, or have a difference of opinion, they feel it is safe to come to you to talk it over. Figure 7-3 portrays the trust-building mechanism and a subsequent loss of trust.

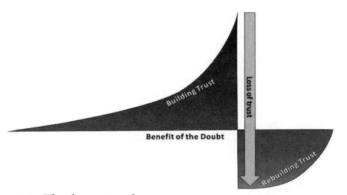

Figure 7-3. The dynamics of trust.

Trust is built up slowly, over time. It can be broken quickly, however. If an employee believes that you have been deliberately misleading or have withheld critical information, or have broken a confidence, the trust between you and that employee, or perhaps the whole staff, can plummet. But, as Figure 7-3 shows, it does not simply return to the level at which the relationship began; it slips below that line where one extended the benefit of the doubt to the boss. To return trust to that level requires energy, effort, and attention.

Trust can also be chipped away over time, not in one event, or one day or one month, but through a steady piling on of disappointments and broken commitments. When trust has been broken, communication is damaged and may shut down completely. As noted earlier, when communication tanks, trust sinks even lower. This downward spiral takes the working relationship with it down into the vortex. Productivity suffers. Informal communication doesn't happen—there's no more of the casual conversation as people pass one another in the hall or in the cafeteria. It's easier and more comfortable to just walk on by. People sit in meetings, withholding significant information. Phone calls are not returned. Messages are ignored. When trust is low, people hide behind e-mails. *Rather than talking to that person*, the thinking goes, *I'll just send her an e-mail*, even if her cubicle is ten feet away. (Chapter 16 has more on electronic communication.)

. . . .

The years I spent working with Jack and Howard were difficult ones for all of us. They had had a falling-out that they didn't repair. When Jack saw Howard coming down the hall, he would duck into my office to avoid any possibility of having to talk to Howard. Here, the simplest communication was lost and even basic information was not exchanged. In one instance, because they were not speaking, Jack didn't know that Howard would be out of the office for two weeks on vacation. It turned out that this information was critical. Jack was preparing a presentation, and Howard had vital information that Jack needed but could not include. They both looked worse for the omission.

. . . .

Trust is particularly challenging when a staff member is promoted from within the office to a supervisory or management position. Others can hold grudges about the decision. Additionally, sometimes there is uncertainty about previous relationships—or lack thereof—that creates distrust with the person who was promoted.

. . . .

Wanda was one of several staff members in a small office. Two other women in the office were her good friends. They did everything together: they ate lunch together, took breaks together; they talked about their weekends, laughing and joking at each others' desks. Others may have felt left out, but then again they had their own circles of office friends.

Then Wanda was promoted to supervisor. She left the office on Thursday afternoon as one of the team. When she came to work on Friday she was the boss. Her circle of friends was unchanged, but suddenly the distrust among the rest of the group exploded. Others felt excluded. They watched for any sign of special treatment for Wanda's friends, keeping score and growing more and more resentful.

• •

In this situation, Wanda did not start off with the benefit of the doubt. Trust was way below that line, from the beginning of her job as supervisor. As a new supervisor, she didn't recognize how important rebuilding that trust would be to her ability to be successful in her new position. We can't blame her for that. Nobody ever taught her about that part of her job. She knew what the office was expected to do—the tasks to be completed, delivery deadlines, backlogs, and benchmarks. But she'd never been given the skills for the much more difficult job: managing the people she supervised. By the time her boss called for help, little work was getting done, and the distrust had become a significant barrier to any collaboration or cooperation.

The Manager's Challenge

For staff members with no supervisory responsibility, trust is important. With a healthy trust between co-workers, the inevitable conflicts that arise may be resolved before anyone describes the situation as a conflict. Disagreements are discussed and resolved without anyone ever thinking there was a "conflict" at all.

For managers juggling relationships in all directions, trust is even more important in resolving conflict. Sometimes I think of managers as "the knees" of the organization. The older I get, the more I realize the stress my knees take from the bottom up, as well as from the top down. The manager has relationships to maintain with direct reports, between staff, with bosses, and across departments. That manager is then balancing his or her own needs with the needs and demands of staff and with the expectations and requirements of higher-ups. Maintaining trust in all directions at the same time can sometimes feel impossible.

. . . .

Sasha was caught in that squeeze with her subordinate, Harold. She promised Harold that he would be getting a bigger space when the new office opened. At least, that is what Harold heard: "She *said* I'd get a bigger space when the build-out was finished!"

From Sasha's point of view, she promised to *try* to get him bigger space. When Sasha took the request to her own boss, she felt she did everything possible to secure the space for Harold. The answer came back, "No. He'll have to stay where he is now."

Sasha was stuck. To Harold, it looked like she had broken a promise. But she needed to protect her boss, his authority, and her relationship there. As far as her boss was concerned, Sasha would have to take responsibility for this decision herself so that he could maintain a positive image with the department. So, what could Sasha do? At this point, she was caught between that proverbial rock and a hard place. What might she do differently next time?

To protect the trust between them, she could be very clear to her employee, Harold, that she would *recommend* a change. This often requires a clear inquiry: "Just to be sure we're on the same page, tell me what you are expecting from me." Then, Sasha could restate her intention to *advocate* for a change, and to clarify what she could not promise at that point. That is a promise she could keep while still protecting herself and her boss.

. . . .

Fixing relationship conflicts requires energy and attention over time: repairing and rebuilding trust, giving apologies and seeking forgiveness, managing anger, and maintaining a sense of humor. The next four chapters provide some tools that you can apply to these relationship conflicts.

Consider This

☑ Think of various disagreements or conflicts you have faced recently. Analyze them to determine their sources: Information? Interests? Structural? Values? Relationships?

☑ With that understanding, what tools can you use to address similar situations in the future?

Notes

1. Roger Fisher, William Ury, and Bruce Patton, *Getting to Yes: Negotiating Agreement Without Giving In* (Boston: Houghton Mifflin Harcourt, 1992).

2. John Burton, *Conflict Resolution and Prevention* (New York: St. Martin's, 1990).

PART III

Keys to Resolving Conflict

Between stimulus and response, there is a space.
In that space lies our freedom and power
to choose our response. In our response
lies our growth and freedom.

—VICTOR FRANKL,
MAN'S SEARCH FOR MEANING

CHAPTER 8

Building Trust

The evening news shows footage of the most recent earthquake. Stunned crowds are wandering through the streets. The security and safety they had once depended on is gone. The house that protected them is not trustworthy. They are sleeping in the streets, fearful that another tremor will bring the house down.

Maybe you have known that feeling of freefall when you discover that someone you counted on has broken your trust. The earth has shifted under your feet. You may have spent months or years developing a solid relationship, and suddenly the things you counted on before you can't count on anymore. You are left wondering, *Where do we go from here? This changes everything.* You become protective, and put up a wall to keep from being hurt again. You become more cautious and circumspect. You find yourself looking over your shoulder, checking with others to make sense of what has happened, and anxiously wondering what might happen in the next day or week or month or year.

The Components of Trust

Many authors have created models for understanding the dimensions of trust as they exist in the workplace. Dennis S. Reina and Michelle L. Reina, in their book *Trust and Betrayal in the Workplace,* describe three components of transactional trust: contractual trust, communication trust, and competence trust.[1] In *The Thin Book of Trust,* Charles Feltman divides trust into four components: sincerity, reliability, competence, and caring.[2] Whatever system we use, thinking about trust in terms of its various categories can help us understand better what builds trust and what wrecks trust. And when we commit to rebuilding trust, the discussion is more productive when we can describe the past destructive behavior by putting it into a category, rather than making a flat statement like, "I don't trust you." In this chapter, I discuss three categories of trust—reliability, competence, and caring—first showing how they relate to trust, then considering how to wreck trust and how to build trust.

Reliability

Reliability as a trust component is about keeping commitments. Building reliability begins with clarity: being clear about the commitments you are making, and being clear about what you expect of others. The circle of reliability is completed by following through—by keeping those commitments you make.

> **Warning! Dates on the calendar are closer than they appear.**

Reliability also includes *not* making commitments you can't keep. Saying, "I'll have that report to you by Friday" assumes that you can get the information you need from another department by Thursday. Sometimes it is easy to make one commitment on top of another, without realizing there is simply not enough time in the day, the week, or the month to keep all of them. Before making a commitment, check the practical realities of fulfilling your commitment.

I speak here about the commitments *you* make. In building trust within the team, however, you also need to be clear about the commitments that staff makes to you. Those questions that are the journalist's friend are also useful for managers and employees.

- ▶ *Who?* Who needs the requested item? Who is responsible for getting it done?

- ▶ *What?* As specifically as possible, what is expected? What is requested?

- ▶ *When?* Every request, every project, every assignment needs a due date. Let people know when you expect an answer or a deliverable.

- ▶ *How?* Do people have the resources to complete the assignment? Are there special concerns and requests that need to be met?

- ▶ *Why?* Having an explanation of why the task needs to be done can motivate a person to get the job done. It also demonstrates respect for another's competence to provide information about how his or her contribution fits into the wider effort.

Reliability also refers to consistency in general mood and demeanor. Employees look to the boss to provide stability. Being able to count on that person being on an even keel increases their level of trust. In truth, managers sometimes do not realize the effect their outbursts of anger have on people's sense of trust. She screams. He picks up a paperweight and throws it against the wall. She bangs her fist on the table and storms out. He slams the door to his office. Afterwards, their reactions are: "Get over it; it's just the way I am." What they don't realize is the long-term effect this behavior can have on others. The flare-ups can be for dramatic effect but they also can create a climate in which others become wary, uneasy, and anxious about when they may happen again. Trust erodes.

How do you deal with differences and disagreements among people? How do you handle yourself under stress? As was stated in Chapter 5, when your responses shift dramatically between calm and stormy, the people around you are confused, surprised, shocked, or hurt.[3] And then they become distrustful. The behavior leaves others wondering when it will happen again, and where and how.

Competence

Competence with regard to trust refers to the ability to do the task at hand. Generally in the workplace, we assume that people can meet the established standards of performance. A person is hired based on her knowledge, skills, and ability to take on a set of job responsibilities.

Sometimes a person is hired for one set of responsibilities and has the requisite technical expertise to do that job well. He does the job so well, in fact, that he is then promoted to a supervisor's position. The technical skills that served so well at the staff level are not nearly so important in the supervisor role. Rather, what is needed at this level of responsibility is people skills: the ability to provide leadership to motivate effort, the ability to work with people to keep them productive, and the ability to provide guidance and feedback when people need direction. For a new manager or supervisor, this is a completely new skill set. The wise new supervisor or manager recognizes the differences in position, and acknowledges the need to develop new abilities. Then he finds within the organization or outside the organization the tools and education necessary to be effective in this new role. Demonstrating competence in this new role builds trust among staff that the manager has the needed leadership skills to handle the task.

Caring

As a component of trust, care refers to having concern for the needs and interests of others. Caring may be the most important component of trust. If employees know that their needs and interests are important to the manager, they will trust that manager to take action, to do what needs to be done. In this way, managers need to demonstrate interest in the work the staff is doing, their career development beyond their immediate jobs, and to some extent their personal lives. Even when the manager has to make hard decisions that may directly affect the staff's work or schedule or personal life, if employees trust that the manager cares, they are much more willing and able to go along with those decisions.

Care in this trust context applies to the team and its work, as well as to individuals. The manager who builds trust in this dimension is aware of the priorities of the team and protects those priorities from the barrage of requests that may come from other departments or from external customers. Having their backs in the face of conflicting demands is a powerful trust builder.

Consider This

  Observe others you work with. Whom do you trust?

  Why do you trust them? What actions do they take, what do they say, and what do they do that makes them trustworthy?

How to Wreck Trust

Let's see how you can wreck trust, turning those three components of trust upside down. In terms of *reliability*, you can lie. You can withhold the truth. You can break your word. So what if you are late for the meeting? They'll wait for you. Don't bother making certain that you can get something done before you promise to do it. Nobody's perfect, right?

You can surprise them. It always pays to keeps them guessing—they'll never know what to expect or when. You can make vague commitments. Then, when you fail to keep them, you can claim they just didn't understand you. And, you don't have to follow through. Maybe they'll forget—after all, you know how easy forgetting is, you do it all the time. And you can lose your temper. You can blow up when things get tough—they'll get over it. You are who you are. That's not *your* problem, right?

As for *competence*, you can wreck trust by accepting assignments that you don't know how to do—but don't tell anybody you need help. Fake it until you make it, right?

And as for *caring*, remember to gossip. Information is power, after all. Having the scoop, the latest skinny on someone else, being in the know, gives you power. And you can look better by making others look worse. Talk behind people's backs. Spend your lunch hour talking about other people in the office. What do they know? You'll be a lot more popular when they see how much you can dish.

Then there are some other ways to wreck trust. For example, you can use other people's work to get ahead. No need to give them credit for what they have done—you take the credit, take *all* the credit. Sure, it was a team effort. Everyone on the staff pulled together to get the job done. But you are the boss, so, ultimately, you are responsible. If it went well, it's because you did such a good job of keeping them all on task. And don't ever listen to your staff. Don't spend the time getting to know them. All they need is their next assignment. Give it to them as quickly as possible and move on to the next task.

. . . .

I learned a lesson in high school. There were three girls standing in the hall, arms loaded with books, waiting for the next class. Vicki told Paula, "That is a pretty dress you're wearing." When Paula walked off, Vicki turned to me and said, "That dress was really tacky. I just wanted to see what she would say." As I turned to walk on to my class, I wondered what Vicki would be saying about me once my back was turned. In the workplace, this scenario plays out again and again.

. . . .

How to Build Trust

On the other hand, maybe you'd like to try using those same three categories to build greater trust. Building trust takes energy, effort, and attention, but the effort you put into building trust will be repaid many times over when conflicts arise—which they will. With trust established, it will be much easier to communicate honestly, to seek solutions, and to know that you can count on others to keep their commitments.

Reliability

By demonstrating your reliability, you, as a manager, can establish and build a trusting relationship with your staff.

▶ *Be honest.* Even in the best of times, as a manager you may need to change course based on changing circumstances. If you have demonstrated over time that you are as honest as you can be, when these changes happen, people are much more likely to believe you and accept your best intentions.

▶ *Keep commitments.* Do what you say you are going to do when you say you are going to do it. Even in the small things. If you will be late for the meeting, let someone know. If you are bringing someone else with you, let them know that, too.

Commitments can be tricky things. When you, as supervisor, say, "Sure, I think we can do that," others are likely to hear, "Yes. You've got my word on that. I'll make it happen." Don't give your word if you cannot *keep* it. To protect others' trust in you, promise to recommend, then check with your own boss before making any final commitments.

▶ *Avoid surprises.* For every move you make—even surprises you think will be pleasant for your staff—tip them off first, particularly when trust is low. When they are not sure they can trust you, your every move and motive can be suspect. "What does she mean I can have the afternoon off? What is she going to do while I am gone?"

▶ *Be consistent also with your mood.* Not many people are bright and chipper all the time every day. But if your mood swings wildly from day to day, others will be tiptoeing into the office, wondering what kind of mood the boss might be in today.

HOW TO BUILD TRUST

- ▶ Be honest.
- ▶ Keep your word.
- ▶ Avoid surprises.
- ▶ Be consistent.
- ▶ Do your best.
- ▶ Demonstrate respect.
- ▶ Listen, listen, listen.
- ▶ Communicate.
- ▶ Speak with positive intent.
- ▶ Admit mistakes.
- ▶ Be willing to hear feedback.

> ➤   Maintain confidences.
> ➤   Get to know others.
> ➤   Practice empathy.
> ➤   Seek their input.
> ➤   Say "thank you."

Competence

Trust in others is built on recognition of their competence to do the job at hand. Your employees will trust you to do your job competently if you remember the following:

➤   *Do your best.* If you have been given an assignment that is beyond your ability, admit it. Talk it over with the person who gave you the assignment. Then *get help.* Look around for the resources that surround you. Find others you respect for their knowledge and expertise. Ask for their advice.

It often takes courage to admit that you don't know everything there is to know. Hold on to the confidence of knowing that you do have valuable skills and abilities. You were assigned this project because they believed you were able to do it. To build your competence, look for other resources as well: books, classes, online information.

➤   *Learn new leadership skills.* Building trust as a manager with your staff depends as much on your ability to motivate and support employees as it does on your technical skills.

Caring

Expressions of caring about others are critical to all relationships, but as a manager there are particular things you can do to show you care for the staff, thereby building trust:

➤   *Respect the other person even when your views differ.* Consider that others think their views are well grounded, they want to do the "right thing," they can see things that you miss and miss things you can see, and they recognize that you may have different information than they do.

Demonstrate respect for who they are, what they know, and where they have been. Respect comes through the words you use and your tone of voice, as well as your body language as you talk and as you listen.

▶ **Listen, listen, listen.** One of the most powerful skills you can cultivate is the ability to listen well. (There is more information on how to listen in Chapter 14.) Put aside your own thinking in order to hear what is going on with someone else—whether it's your own higher-ups, or a peer, or someone you supervise. Take the time, expend the energy, focus your attention on what they are saying, and that will speak volumes to them about the value you put on your relationship.

▶ *Communicate, communicate, communicate.* As a manager or supervisor, there are times when you have information that you cannot share. That is a given, and one of the challenges of being a manager. When you hear something from above of a sensitive nature that will have a direct effect on your employees, talk to your higher-ups about what you can discuss and what needs to be held closely. That said, there is a lot of information you *can* give to people. In the busyness of your day, stop to consider how people are kept informed, who is getting what information and how they are getting it. Is everyone on the staff receiving the same information? The more you can communicate in a timely way, the more each of them will feel that they can trust you.

As Dale Carnegie famously said years ago, first you tell them what you are going to tell them, then you tell them, then you tell them what you told them. Find as many ways as possible to keep the information flowing: e-mails, staff meetings, and one-on-one conversations. I can hear the groans when I suggest another meeting, but telling people face to face and to as many as possible at the same time give people a sense that they know what is going on, of feeling included, and that they are important enough to know what is afoot. Use the variety of electronic tools at your fingertips: e-mails, voicemail, Facebook, and Twitter. (In Chapter 16, I discuss some dos and don'ts of effective electronic communication.)

▶ *Speak with positive intent.* This is the opposite of talking behind people's backs. When you talk about others in the office, present or not, find ways to acknowledge their contributions and skills.

▶   *Admit mistakes. Nobody is perfect.* You get credit for trying. And being able to admit your mistakes goes a long way to being trust-worthy.

· ·

The conference program had gone to print. Finally, we were ready to drop it in the mail to our mailing list of 5,000. I opened my copy one more time and realized to my horror that the conference fees were wrong. This financial section may have been the most important piece of the printed program. My heart sank. I called my boss. The last thing I wanted to do was to admit that I had not caught this huge misprint earlier. The first thing that I needed to do was to tell him about it so we could strategize some solution. I felt embarrassed and foolish. Months later he told me, "One thing I really like about you, Susan, is that I can count on you to tell me when things are going wrong." It's a good thing he valued that, because I was in a new position with lots of responsibility but little experience, and I made more mistakes than I want to remember.

· ·

▶   *Be willing to hear feedback.* Listen to others without inter-rupting, without launching a counterattack, without becoming defen-sive. Talk about a hard criticism—this one is a real challenge! (I'll talk about it more in Chapter 14.)

▶   *Maintain confidentiality.* As a supervisor, you have additional responsibilities regarding confidentiality. Sometimes someone may say "keep this confidential" and when they start talking, you realize you can't keep *that* confidential. It is better to avoid promising confidentiality until you know more about the content. You might list general topics about which you cannot promise confidentiality. If you realize the information you have heard is something you must tell someone else, explain your decision and your concern—and strategize with the person about how you will share that information and with whom you will share it.

▶   *Get to know others as people.* Let them get to know you, as well. Maybe nothing demonstrates that you care as much as taking the time to express a personal interest in employees and co-workers. Managers and supervisors are generally strapped for time, so when you read this, you may protest. I am not suggesting that you have lengthy conversations with staff about the ins and outs of their lives. But if you spend time finding out what their hopes and dreams and aspirations are, as well as what they may be struggling to juggle inside and outside of work, you can instill loyalty in them that will be well worth your investment of time.

▶ *Be consistent.* Treat all the people you supervise with equanimity and fairness. It is inevitable that there are some people you will get along with better than others. They speak your language. You feel comfortable around them. You like their style, maybe because of the skills they bring to the job, maybe for other intangible qualities. Know that other employees are keenly, maybe jealously, watching the time you spend with each of them. You don't have to be perfectly balanced in some mechanical clockwork fashion. You do, however, need to be conscious of creating some balance of your attention among those with whom you work. You can be friendly without being friends.

▶ *Practice empathy.* Try to understand the situation from their point of view.

▶ *Seek their input.* Provide ways for them to develop and learn new skills.

▶ *Say thank you.* Thank people privately and publicly for a job well done, an effort made even if it wasn't successful. Sincerity is important here—they must believe that you really mean it. And be specific with your thanks: "Thanks for the extra hours you put into the Houston project." "I appreciate your response to that difficult caller yesterday." "We really needed the research you provided for that proposal. Thanks." A vague "Great job, Harry" leaves Harry wondering what you are talking about or why you are saying it. And work hard to be inclusive—to acknowledge positive contributions from each employee.

Here are a few extra ways to say thanks:

1. Acknowledge hard work during staff meetings.

2. Catch people doing good. Sometimes we put more energy into finding the mistakes and correcting them. Look for opportunities to appreciate their efforts.

3. Keep a stack of note cards in your desk and make a habit of writing thank-you notes each week to deserving staff members.

4. Leave a sticky note on someone's desk saying thank you—be specific.

5. Send thank-you e-mails—be specific. Consider copying your boss on the message.

6. Create a "wall of thanks" in the office where you can post notes for jobs well done.

How to Rebuild Trust

Rebuilding trust is a challenging task, but it is not impossible. Remember that rebuilding trust will take demonstrated commitment over time. Here are some steps to take if someone else has broken your trust:

1. Before approaching the other person, ask yourself a few critical questions: Am I willing to have a conversation about what has happened? What might I lose if I don't? What might I gain if I do? What might I lose if I do?

2. Identify the specifics of what happened. Did the person miss an important deadline? Does he or she miss deadlines frequently? Did the individual make a commitment and not keep it? Did you expect the person to have the skill to complete the project and yet that person didn't meet the standards you expected? Did he or she talk to you disrespectfully in a meeting? Is this a matter of reliability, or competence, or caring?

3. Set up a time to talk about it. Make sure that both of you have adequate time to give the conversation your full attention.

4. Be clear before you get into a discussion about the nuts and bolts of your concern and why being able to trust the other person is important to you.

5. Talk about the incident or incidents that concern you. Be specific.

Identify one or more of the components of trust—reliability, competence, or caring—that has become a problem. It is much more productive to talk about one of these components: "I didn't get your last three reports until I called and reminded you to get them in each time. I am concerned about your reliability," than it is to say: "I don't trust you." Maintain a calm, businesslike, factual approach with the focus on behaviors, not characterizations.

6. Listen. Ask, "What happened?" Give the person time to think about what you have said and to respond. He or she may have an explanation that clarifies what has happened. The person may apologize.

7. Describe specifically what the person can do to improve the situation.

If you have broken another's trust and want to rebuild it:

1. As soon as possible, set up a time to talk about this particular issue. Again, make sure that both of you have adequate time to give this conversation your full attention.

2. Express your concern for the importance of the relationship and your positive intention for the conversation.

3. Ask if the person has concerns and then listen. Give the person time and space to think and to talk. Avoid becoming defensive. If the person is able to express concerns, all you need to do is say, "Thank you for telling me."

4. Apologize. Take responsibility for your part in the situation. You may want to take some time to think about what you have heard before you respond. (The next chapter, "Apology and Forgiveness," discusses this further.)

5. Explain what steps you plan to follow so that what has happened won't be repeated.

Consider This

☑ How trustworthy are you?

1. *Sincerity*: Do you explain to people what values and principles are important to you? Do you demonstrate your commitment to those values and principles in your actions?

    2. *Reliability*: Do you keep the commitments that you make? What do you do when you realize you have made a commitment you can't keep? Do you clarify commitments and promises so that others know what you expect of them? How? Do you clarify commitments and promises so that you know what others expect from you? How?

    3. *Competence*: Make a list of the areas where you feel you are competent. How do you demonstrate to those you work with, manage, or report to that you have the competence to handle job requirements? How do you ask for help or training when you are given a job that exceeds your experience or competence?

    4. *Caring*: How would the people you manage finish this statement: "I know my boss really cares about the team because …"? Do team members know that you support their efforts and are working for the good of the team? How? If there is a problem in the workplace, are people willing to raise the issue? If not, why not? If so, how do you know? Are you comfortable receiving help from others?

Review your responses to these questions. What steps will you take to improve your trustworthiness among your subordinates?

Notes

1. Dennis S. Reina and Michelle L. Reina, *Trust and Betrayal in the Workplace: Building Effective Relationships in Your Organization* (San Francisco: Berrett-Koehler, 1999).

2. Charles Feltman, *The Thin Book of Trust: An Essential Primer for Building Trust at Work* (Bend, Ore.: Thin Book Publishing, 2009).

3. Ron Kraybill, *Style Matters: The Kraybill Conflict Style Inventory* (Harrisonburg, Va.: Riverhouse, 2005), p. 12.

CHAPTER 9

Apology and Forgiveness

"Apologize? We don't need to apologize! They are the ones who made the mistakes." This was what I heard from a group of managers at a large corporation. I stood in front of the room in amazement. I knew the company had high standards for employment and promotion. I didn't know that being perfect was one of the necessary qualifications. I assumed that because they were human, they also would sometimes make an error.

Wherever people are interacting with one another, working with or alongside others, there will be times when conflicts arise, egos are bruised, and damage is done to one another or to the relationship. Key to moving through these difficult moments is your willingness and ability to apologize and to forgive—two sides of the same key. That is, apology and forgiveness are often—but not always—inseparable. A sincere apology makes the ability to forgive much easier. There has been an acknowledgment of the harm experienced. The gift of forgiveness makes the sacrifice of apology worthwhile. Because we can be forgiven, we can admit our errors and make amends.

There are times when we apologize without any expectation or hope of forgiveness. The apology itself is a cleansing experience. When we take responsibility for our actions, we can begin to forgive ourselves for our actions even if others do not or cannot. There are also times when we forgive without hearing an apology. We move through the process of forgiveness for our own benefit, not for the other person. We forgive to let go of past injuries and move on with our lives. But let's consider both sides of that key to successful conflict resolution.

Apology Offered

Often, the best thing you can do when you make a mistake is to apologize. Sometimes it's also the hardest thing you can do—to admit that you have not done the right thing. It might be an unintentional oversight, an honest miscalculation. You got busy with several office distractions and now you are embarrassed that you forgot the lunch appointment you set last week. You thought others already knew what you had been told; you didn't realize the information was confidential. You started the project without checking that others were also working on it.

Or, it might be an action you took guided by one of your lesser angels: maybe your desire to look good to your own boss or the work group, or to have more, or to grab control, or to get even. Maybe you flew off the handle at a member of the staff and recognized in hindsight that she really didn't deserve that sort of treatment. Maybe you intentionally let slip a piece of information because you thought it made you look good. Maybe you didn't include the names of others who made important contributions on the report when you submitted it to your boss. Apologies are particularly hard when you feel guilty or embarrassed or ashamed of your behavior. And yet we all find ourselves in that place at one time or another.

An apology can make the difference between moving forward and not. There are times and places when the other person cannot let go of his or her resentment or hostility until the person hears a sincere acknowledgment from you about what you did wrong and your stated intention not to repeat the behavior. That's the beginning step toward a resolution.

Acknowledgment

An acknowledgment is often the beginning of an apology. You may remember the story of Tre, the CFO, and his senior management team in Chapter 2 of this book. One of the senior managers had presented Human Resources with a long list of complaints, ending with "Either he goes or I go. And, by the way, the other SMTs feel the same way."

What followed that disclosure was a series of challenging meetings over several weeks, as the SMTs spelled out to Tre all of their frustrations, built up over the years. It was hard for Tre to listen to that, to lower his defensiveness and let go of his ego long enough to hear what they were saying. The day he walked into the meeting room and acknowledged all that they had said to him as true was a dramatic moment for everyone. In fact, you could feel the tension drain from the room. One of the team members said, "This has been life changing for everyone. We had kept our resentment from Tre for all this time, for fear of his reactions. Now that we have walked through this together, and he has acknowledged his part, we are stronger as a team than we ever were before."

Because sincere acknowledgment can be such a powerful moment, here's another example. Several years ago, I mediated a dispute in a large federal agency between a relatively high-ranking manager, Carl, and his boss, Angela. Carl had filed several complaints against the agency and was demanding $1.5 million to settle them. He talked. Angela listened. He described a series of events during his career when he felt he had been wronged. She was thoughtful and still. Then she spoke carefully, "Carl, there are things that have happened here that should not have happened." It was as close to an apology as she could get. He heard her. I watched the face of this robust and angry man soften, his eyes rimmed with tears. "Nobody in this agency has ever said that to me," he said quietly. Within minutes, the discussion shifted from "$1.5 million" to "what can we do now to fix this situation?" In this case, an outright apology could have been construed as an admission of guilt by the agency—and managers are trained to avoid any such admission for fear of legal liability. For Carl, her acknowledgment was enough—to hear that someone inside the agency could hear his story from his point of view and want to make amends.

It Takes Two to Tango

In resolving a conflict or addressing a difficult issue with an employee or a co-worker, consider the part that you played in the event. It takes two to tango. A careful reflection will almost always reveal that both sides had some role in the situation's going badly.

When he didn't get the project completed on time, maybe you didn't make the assignment or the deadline clear, or you did not prioritize the tasks that employee was juggling. When she barked a curt response to your question, maybe your own tone of voice sounded disrespectful. Did you provide enough guidance so that he felt able to perform adequately? Were you so anxious about the task or his ability that you hovered over his desk, micromanaging his every move? Are you more comfortable with the work you once did as a member of the staff than with the assignments of your new position, so that you now interfere with a subordinate's ability to complete a project? Or might you have forgotten a commitment you made in a meeting and failed to provide the information you said you would send later?

After identifying your own role in any difficulty, it's time to sit down with the person and give feedback on what he or she did wrong. If you start by acknowledging your own part with a simple apology, the conversation will take a more positive direction. A caution here: Be clear with yourself before you start the discussion. You are only owning one piece of the interaction. Avoid allowing the conversation to shift and become all about you and what you did or didn't do.

. . . .

"Sally, I want to talk to you about the Hinkelman account. Henry called me yesterday and said he was still waiting for his payment." The boss pauses to hear what Sally has to say.

"Gosh. I have been swamped with end-of-year requests. I can't do everything at once, you know."

The boss acknowledges his part, "I realize I may not have been clear with you that this was a priority. I'll accept responsibility for that." And then he goes on, "I count on you to handle all of these accounts. Customer service is vital to our success. Turnaround time for these payments is two days. What is the problem in getting that done?"

. . . .

Sometimes a manager resists apologizing, fearing to appear weak and ineffective. It seems more powerful to pretend that you are always right, that you never make errors. But that is a mistake. Rather, the ability to admit mistakes can make a manager stronger. The courage it takes to express regret is often recognized by others. An apology can create a strong bond between boss and staff. And an apology can give others permission, or even set the expectation, that they too will admit mistakes when they make them. A sincere apology takes responsibility, acknowledges the harm done, and asks for another chance to do better. Such an apology can be powerful, especially in difficult conflicts. An apology that is heartfelt and convincing can melt hardened attitudes and begin to rebuild relationships.

One of the hardest lessons for me has been to learn how to apologize, and that is true of so many of us. First, you must recognize when you have been wrong, and admit that to yourself. Then, you must walk back into the room and say it out loud to another person: "I am sorry. I was wrong. I behaved badly. I am not the person I want to be—or want to think that I am." What makes it so hard? It is the vulnerability, admitting your imperfection and putting yourself at the mercy of another person. That means you have to trust that your apology will be accepted. Or, you have to trust that you will have the strength to deal with what comes next if you don't receive forgiveness. Yes, you commit to not doing it again—to trying not to do it again—even to knowing you are imperfect—and that you may step unconsciously into that same pattern again. What you do know is that, as you learn, you step into those negative patterns less often and you catch yourself more quickly each time.

How to Apologize

Though making an apology isn't easy, breaking it down into concrete steps can make it more manageable.

1. Acknowledge what you did and what harm it caused.
2. Ask the person how you can repair the damage, or offer the other person a solution.
3. Make every effort to change the behavior that caused the harm.
4. Give the other person time to hear your apology and to process

what you have said. An apology is often an important step to forgiveness, but you cannot demand to be forgiven.

5. Be patient, hopeful, and optimistic; seek new moments to demonstrate your sincerity and commitment to restoring the relationship.

Sincerity is the key word when it comes to apologies, as these examples demonstrate:

➤ "I realize that I let you down when I didn't speak up in the meeting for the work you have been doing. You deserve a lot of credit and you have not gotten it. What can I do to make certain others appreciate your efforts?"

➤ "I should have remembered how much work you already had on your desk. I am sorry that I lost my temper over that report. I want to do a better job managing my own reactions, and I will work hard not to blast you that way again."

Consider This

☑ Consider a recent action you now regret. Using the steps outlined above, have a conversation with the person most affected by your actions.

When Is an Apology Not an Apology?

Your apology has to be sincere, or else it simply is not an apology. Here are some clues for detecting an insincere apology:

➤ The too quick, flippant "I'm sorry" doesn't carry any weight when it is said too soon, without reflection. It is likely to be heard as just a way to get out of an uncomfortable situation as quickly as possible.

➤ It's another apology from the person who apologies too frequently, for everything. This person apologizes for things he or she doesn't even control. "I'm sorry it's raining." "I'm sorry you forgot your lunch." Sometimes the person seems to be apologizing for his or her own existence. The apology is as meaningless and as empty as those who are too quick to offer one. Worse, the person makes the idea of apologizing seem weak and ineffective—giving apologies a bad name.

▶   "I am sorry you felt that way." This is not an apology. There is no acceptance of responsibility for your own actions.

▶   "I am sorry you misunderstood what I said," or "I'm sorry I didn't get that report to you on time. You didn't give me enough time to do it." These nonapologies turn the blame back onto the other person.

Forgiveness Granted

As I said earlier, the flip side of an apology is forgiveness. One naturally follows the other, as day follows night.

The Cost of Not Forgiving

Some of us carry hurts and grudges and bad feelings for a long time. Forgiveness does not come easy. In fact, sometimes holding onto those experiences becomes a mantle of pride: "Fool me once, shame on me. Fool me twice, shame on you." Often, though, that determination to carry those grudges turns us bitter and resentful. Learning to let go can release you from the past and open your heart and your mind to new opportunities.

The story is told of two Buddhist monks, Tanzan and Ekido, many years ago, who were walking together along a muddy country road. As they neared the village, they came upon a young woman stranded on one side of the road. She could not cross because the mud was so deep she feared it would ruin her silk kimono. Tanzan carefully picked her up, carried her to the other side, and the monks then continued on their way. Hours later, as night was falling, they finally arrived at their lodging. Ekido suddenly blurted out, "Why did you carry that girl across the road?!" "You know we monks are not supposed to touch women!"

Tanzan replied, "I put that girl down hours ago. Are you still carrying her?"

You may know someone like April, whom I met in my role as a mediator. Or maybe you recognize yourself in some parts of her story. Many of us hold onto grievances and wounds for so long they begin to cripple us.

> *To forgive is not just to be altruistic, it is the best form of self-interest.*
> —ARCHBISHOP DESMOND TUTU

A pril walked into the meeting carrying a manila folder bulging with paper. Three years ago her office had faced a major reorganization. Her job was eliminated; she was slotted "temporarily" into a lower grade position and had been working on a short-term assignment since then, to enable her to maintain her previous pay. Another position description was created that included some of her former responsibilities. When April competed for that job with others in the office, she was not selected. Sam was.

What was in the folder she carried? E-mails, some of them two or three years old. Performance evaluations proving her competence. She was eager to show me all the files and forms and e-mails that proved she had been wronged, deprived of the promotion *she* should have gotten. On the phone or in one-on-one conversations, she repeated her justifications. She had been victimized, denied a job that should have been hers. And she offered again and again to give me proof. She cried out in pain, "It's just not *fair!*"

She acknowledged the effort that Hank, her boss, had put into restoring her job to the higher grade, but she clung to the injury she felt, even though that decision had been made over two years ago. So, Hank complained bitterly to me about April. "No matter what I do, she's not happy. I don't even want to talk to her anymore; all she does is complain."

April spent much of her time in the office collecting data and evidence about Sam, the man who got the job she wanted. She tracked his hours at his desk, watching each of his assignments. She peppered the boss with questions (usually through e-mail): "Where was Sam yesterday afternoon?" or "I could have done that project, why didn't you give it to me?" Or, "Why did he take so long to get that done?" The more she complained, the more the boss avoided her. The more he avoided her, the more she complained.

What price did April pay for holding onto this grudge? Her anger and bitterness came with her to work every morning. She missed seeing a lot of the good and beautiful moments of life around her because her mind was consumed with how she had been wronged. When pressed, she acknowledged how she liked the field of work she was in, the luxury of avoiding the madness of metropolitan traffic, the friends that she had at work, her generous and supportive family. But, even her hours away from work could become wrapped up with the negative mood she created, the dread of going back to work after lunch or the next day, or after the weekend was over, or after vacation. She created a great deal of mental stress for herself. She alienated her boss and many of her co-workers. Others at work saw only the hostility that shrouded her face. They saw her as April, the discontented. Holding onto the resentment, she was the one who paid the price for not forgiving the boss or Sam.

. . . .

There was a cost to April's story, too, to the organization. Consider the work that didn't get done while she was busy gathering evidence about Sam. Think of the effect her attitude had on office morale. Morale drops, productivity falls, the business of the business is not getting done. And it is important to note that this victim mentality exists in all types of organizations and at all organizational levels.[1]

So, holding onto resentment over past wrongs can be pretty self-destructive. Seen from another way, there often are rewards that keep a person stuck in a negative pattern such as April's. What did April get out of holding onto this resentment? As long as she committed herself to victimhood, she did not have to take responsibility for her own happiness or her job satisfaction or her performance. As long as she could blame someone else, she let herself off the hook.

There were a few people in the office who commiserated with April, who felt sorry for her. They joined in her anger and anguish and pity. Misery loves company. They created a camp within the office of "us" against "them" and spent a lot of time and energy blaming others for any difficulties, discomforts, or challenges. As long as April could refuse to forgive her boss, she felt she could hold it over his head—somehow punish him for his mistake. What she failed to see was the terrible price that was paid for holding on to this attitude—and that *she* was the one paying the price.

> *Forgiveness means giving up all hope for a better past.*
> —LILY TOMLIN

Why Forgive?

Why should someone forgive? Forgiveness lifts the weight off; it is liberating. Letting go and moving on is in your best interest, regardless of the effect it has on anyone else in the office. Forgiveness grants you a strong sense of control and peace. There is that line from the poem "Invictus" by William Ernest Henley: "I am the captain of my fate, I am the master of my soul." You may not be able to control all of what happens to you, but you can control how you react to it. When you can forgive, you are not buffeted by the whims and actions of others around you.

Holding onto the bitterness, refusing to forgive, is a poison you take yourself, often expecting it to have some ill effect on the other person. Reliving the story over and over again is like pouring acid on your own psyche. Meanwhile, the offender is not affected at all. Even if he or she had never apologized, the gift of forgiveness is as much for one's own piece of mind as it is for the other person.

Occasionally I hear people say, "I never forgive." If we all were to live by those words, we would not be able to function in society. In reality, when we depend on other people to get anything done, we forgive all of the time. Working together, day in and day out, to meet challenging goals inevitably involves people making mistakes. A thousand times a day, we are forgiving the minor annoyances and blunders.

Wherever people need other people, and the workplace is certainly that, people make mistakes and we let them go. Someone makes a sharp remark in a meeting, you let it roll off without further discussion. At other times, there is an acknowledgment and commitment to do better the next time. Maybe an employee missed a deadline for a report. She admits the error, you forgive her, and move on. The embarrassment of forgetting a lunch date with a colleague is not the end of the friendship. Sometimes we can only shrug our shoulders and sigh.

You can't get organisms that are willing to hang in there with
each other through thick and thin and make good things happen
despite the roadblocks and the bumps along the way if
they aren't willing to tolerate each other's mistakes.
—MICHAEL MCCULLOUGH

Forgiving Yourself

Maybe the hardest person for you to forgive is yourself. The past can haunt us. Things that we did wrong years ago can still sit achingly on our hearts. The memory of those events can sometimes paralyze us in the present. Or we can acknowledge them, learn from them, forgive ourselves, and commit to doing better in the future.

When I recognize one of those parts of myself that I like the least— those habits and patterns that become traps—there is a voice in my head that is pretty harsh: "Yep, Stupid. You did it again." First, I have to tune my conscious mind to hear that voice. Then I can reframe it: "This is that part of me that drives me crazy. I'll keep working on it." This is the beginning of forgiving myself. I have found I can then more easily translate that patience and willingness to forgive to others—the clerk at the grocery store who seems painfully slow, the employee who is on the phone dealing with some personal problem. Yes, I need to talk to him about using company time to conduct personal business. At the same time, I can practice being more willing to give him an opportunity to correct his behavior: I become more willing to forgive and begin anew.

If I could ever see Cheryl again I would apologize. Some thirty-five years ago, she was a bright high school student who came in every afternoon in the work-study program to shelve books in the school library I managed. She did much more than shelve books, however. She became an indispensable right hand for so many of the tasks that were waiting to be done—that person I could turn to and simply ask, "Cheryl, can you take care of this?" Done. When school was out and the program was over, we said good-bye. She applied for a real job and listed me as a reference. She had to call me three times to remind me that the future employer was waiting for that letter of reference.

In hindsight, I have stood accused in my own mind, over and over again, of not sitting down immediately and writing that letter. Forgiving myself is consciously letting go of that guilt. Forgiving myself has also meant a personal commitment to fulfill the requests I receive now as quickly as possible. Continuing to beat myself up over it serves no one.

Consider This

- ☑ Think about your own experience as a manager. What regrets do you hold onto?
- ☑ For each regret, write down a lesson you can learn from those experiences.
- ☑ Consciously forgive yourself for your mistake, and commit instead to remembering what you learned.

How to Forgive

Sometimes the wounds are so deep that letting go and forgiving seem just too hard to do. If you recognize yourself here, if you tend to hold onto grudges and find it difficult to allow people back into your circle of trust, begin by forgiving people for some of the small stuff. As you practice those smaller moments of forgiveness, the larger ones can become more possible to consider. In those situations, think of forgiveness as a process. It is not as simple as saying, "I forgive you." It takes time, energy, and effort. Sometimes, when the pain has been particularly deep, you may need to revisit the process of forgiveness again and again. Here are some steps to follow:

1. Make a commitment to yourself to do what is necessary to feel better. Forgiveness is for you and not for anyone else. To decide to forgive is a choice for you to make.

2. Know exactly how you feel about what happened and be able to articulate what about the situation is not okay. It can help to tell a trusted person about your experience, or write down what happened.

3. Imagine as vividly as you can what the other person experienced.

4. Identify all the reasons you can think of *not* to forgive. Make a list. Write them down. Often making this list allows you to recognize how trivial some of those reasons are.

5. Think of times in your life when your wrong actions have hurt or disappointed others. None of us is perfect. None of us is without fault. It is much easier to forgive others when we remember our own weaknesses and failings. We all need to be forgiven from time to time.

6. Consider the expectations that the person didn't meet. Identify what it costs you to hold on to those expectations.

7. Accept responsibility for your own role in what happened.

8. Design and execute a ritual for completion and closure. This can be simple: throw the list you have made into a fire, or throw a pebble into the river declaring your intention for the past to be washed downstream, or bury the list in the garden, or …

9. Instead of mentally replaying your hurt, seek out new ways to get what you need. Put your energy into looking for another way to get your positive goals met.

Consider This

☑ List the people that you need to forgive.

☑ Choose one person from this list, and create a plan for how you will forgive that person.

When Forgiveness Is Not Forgiveness

When you tell people you forgive them, you are making a commitment to them to let the offense go. Holding on to the bitterness or resentment is not forgiveness. Continuing to remind the other person of his or her transgression and how magnanimous you have been to forgive is not forgiveness. Fully forgiving and rebuilding the trust between you that has been broken takes time. Not allowing that process the time that it requires, being unwilling to begin to rebuild the trust, is not forgiving. Here are some tips on how you can recognize your failure to truly forgive:

▶ You keep reminding the person of incidents in the past.

▶ You ruminate over past hurts or offenses.

▶ You use past experience as an excuse to avoid interactions irrationally.

For example, having been bitten by a stray dog, it is reasonable to be wary of strange dogs. It is not rational to be afraid of *all* dogs—those you know well or who are closely monitored by their owners. Likewise, wariness with new relationships may be wise, while being unwilling to create new relationships at all can be crippling.

Note

1. June A. Halper, "Stop the Bellyaching." *USA Today,* May 2007. http://guttmandev.com/pdf/halper_usatoday0507.pdf, viewed 11/10, 2010.

CHAPTER 10

Rethinking Anger

A nger. Some of us fear it. Some of us thrive on it. Understanding it better can help us to manage it.

Stretching across the Chesapeake Bay just east of Annapolis is the broad expanse of

> *There is no thought without feeling, no feeling without thought.*
>
> —DANIEL GOLEMAN

a bridge. If you are riding across that bridge on a clear Sunday afternoon in the spring, you can catch glimpses of a hundred sailboats. Some are headed up the bay, some down. Others are aiming for shore, on either the southern bank or the northern. All of them are using the same wind. Sailors know they need the wind to keep them moving. Too little wind and the boat sits becalmed in the water; too much wind and the boat is in danger of capsizing. But a good, steady breeze? The sailor knows how to set the sails, capture the energy, and move the boat in any direction he or she wants to go.

Think of your emotions as that same vital force. Your thoughts, your reasoning power, function as the rudder, giving direction to that emotional energy. Though you may often be unaware of your emotions, they are generating energy that affects the cognitive, thinking parts of your brain.

Here is an experiment to try with friends or family, or yourself. Ask them, "How do you feel about ... [insert your own topic or idea]?" Notice the words that each person uses to describe his or her "feelings." How often is the answer, "I think ..." or "I believe ..."? The phrase that follows "I think" or "I believe" is not a feeling—it is a thought. If the answer is, "I feel that ..." then what follows the word *that* is also a thought, not a feeling. But the answer that begins with "I feel" or "I am" and uses words like *happy* or *sad* or *scared* or *upset* is describing feelings.

Emotions—feelings—are partly mental, partly physical responses marked by pleasure, pain, attraction, or repulsion. They are not the enemy to be overcome; rather, they are an important source of information, energy, and guidance when we are aware of them. For many of us, most of the time our emotions are unconscious. Learning to be aware of our feelings, to put appropriate words to our emotions, is a skill to be learned and practiced on a daily basis. You may not know what your feelings are, yet they may be driving your thoughts and your actions without your even realizing what is happening.

It is easy to see how positive feelings move us. The sun is out this morning, the sky is blue, and a cool breeze whispers through new spring leaves. I wake up happy, excited to move into the day and find out what it might hold. The wind is in my sails, and it is a very good thing! It is sometimes harder to see how negative emotions like fear, sadness, envy, frustration, and anxiety can also give us energy to get things done. When the deadline is approaching, a little bit of fear-generated adrenaline gives us the energy to take action, to put aside the distractions and get to work. A healthy dose of fear can keep us from taking risks that are dangerous. Frustration can be an energizer, as well as an immobilizer.

In conflict, those negative emotions come to the fore. When what you want, need, and expect is getting in the way of what I want, need, and expect, emotional energy stirs inside both of us. How we manage that energy determines the direction in which the conflict will go. Often, when I am dealing with a workplace conflict, someone explains to me, "We don't have emotions here; this is the office. That stuff is for home." Or maybe, "If we could just keep the emotions out, we could resolve this and get back to work." But is this truly the case?

We must shift our thinking about emotions. They are a part of our reality at every moment, in every place, and it is dangerous to ignore that reality. Not only are emotions intimately tied to our thoughts and create the energy for our responses, but like those boats out on the bay, we *need* that energy to move us through conflict productively.

The Physiology of Emotions

Here's a disclaimer: I am not a neuroscientist. However, I do know that our knowledge about how the brain functions is expanding at a phenomenal rate. Daniel Goleman brought public attention to the world of emotional intelligence in his book of the same name.[1] In an early chapter, he begins to explain the physiology of our emotional reactions, which gave me my first introduction to many of these concepts.

Here is my brief summary of how your brain works: Just behind your forehead are the prefrontal lobes, that part of the brain we are so proud of. This is where we "think"—problem-solve, plan, build positive relationships. Surrounding the top of the brain stem are several centers that generate emotional responses. Sometimes people call this the "lizard brain." It functions powerfully and often unconsciously (see Figure 10-1).

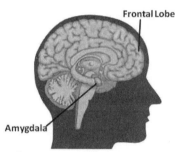

Figure 10-1. The human brain.

Back between your ears, near the top and on either side of the brainstem, there is an almond-sized area of the brain called the amygdala. This emotional response center has stored memories of our emotional life history and is primed to kick the body into action when it senses a similar moment coming around again. Small as it is, the amygdala is a powerful response center that controls our fight or flight reactions. It triggers the release of powerful drugs into our systems—adrenaline and norepinephrine. And it responds some 1,000 times faster than the frontal lobes.

One way you might understand how this happens is to remember what happens when you watch a scary movie. You sit safely in the theater, intent on the screen. Nothing much is happening at the moment. The camera slowly pans from room to room. Your palms are sweaty, your heart is pounding, you can hardly breathe. Your amygdala has triggered an alert: "Something is about to happen," and you are primed for action. You have not consciously thought (in the frontal lobes), "Oh, listen, the music is increasing in intensity, I think something is about to happen." Maybe you remember the scene in Alfred Hitchock's *Psycho*, when the woman is showering, or the ominous theme from *Jaws*. Your amygdala, without any *conscious* thought, has picked up the cues from the music and has triggered the release of adrenaline and norepinephrine, which are now coursing through your system. You are fired up, ready to go!

Most of the time, there is a healthy flow of information between these two centers—the frontal lobes and the amygdala. The frontal lobes work in synch, helping to calm the amygdala by taking appropriate action as needed. The amygdala gives the frontal lobes energy and information about what is important to us and how much it might matter. That balance is right where we want our brains to be.

Much research has been done on people whose amygdalas no longer function: they are not able to identify fear in themselves or in others. This inability can cripple a person's ability to take action when he or she needs to, to hold onto relationships that the individual cares about, and to be able to connect with other people. People need the response mechanism of the amygdala to generate energy for the cognitive areas of the brain to be able to make decisions. In other words, with no amygdala, we are those boats on the Chesapeake Bay, stranded in the middle of the water, desperately in need of a little wind.

Emotional Hijacking

Picture one of those boats on the bay when a sudden summer storm blows up. The wind takes the sails broadside, and before we know it the boat is heeling hard over, with water washing over the gunwales. The hand at the tiller struggles to maintain control of the boat. Most of us have been there emotionally at one time or another. Sparking from zero to sixty in seconds flat, suddenly we are in the middle of a heated argument, popping back hot responses. Maybe we slam the door on our way out. We no longer have access to the frontal lobes—to the thinking, reasoning part of our brains. The phrase that is often used to describe this is so accurate: emotional hijacking. The thinking part of the brain has been taken over by the emotions. Some people spend a lot of time in this zone; others rarely venture there.

Briefly, here is what happens. When the amygdala triggers an emotional response, it sends a strong dose of those chemicals through the system. The cortex (in the thinking part of the brain, the frontal lobes) gets reduced to making up justifications, or rationalizations for the emotions that have just erupted. The cortex's ability to think clearly, to create, to explore, is reduced or eliminated. When I have been emotionally hijacked, asking me to "calm down" or to think rationally is an exercise in futility—that attempt may make me even more irate. I no longer have access to the frontal lobes.

Rational thought stops. Gone is the ability to problem-solve or think creatively. Here is what I have instead:

- ➤ Flawed judgment
- ➤ Confused perceptions (seeing or hearing things inaccurately)
- ➤ Impaired ability to learn or remember
- ➤ Reduced ability to say what is true and accurate
- ➤ Deadened creativity (except for finding creative reasons to stay angry)
- ➤ Misreading of social cues (assuming that others are hostile or angry)
- ➤ Defensiveness
- ➤ Polarized thinking (people take more extreme positions than they really believe, and hold onto them tightly)
- ➤ Increased energy for blame (whatever has happened it is your fault, or somebody else's; I have no responsibility for the situation)

Before people in conflict can productively work to resolve differences, they must recover from the negative effects of emotional hijacking. If the amygdala is not retriggered, in most people these chemicals will usually dissipate in the brain in about twenty minutes. For some people, however, the effects last much longer—hours or even days.

☑ Before you read any further, think of specific examples when you or someone you know has lost their temper, either staying to fight or storming out in flight mode.

Anger as a Secondary Response

Anger is not automatic. It is a secondary response to other feelings. Think of anger as the lid on a jar. To manage anger—yours or someone else's—begin by understanding what is inside the jar, what's underneath that lid.

Confused about my own anger, dealing with my teenage children's anger, working with people who were frequently angry, I volunteered as a facilitator with my county's spouse abusers program to understand more about anger: what triggers it, and how to manage it more effectively.[2] Each week for eighteen weeks, a group, mostly men, filed into the room. Early in the program, we worked with the participants to connect their anger with their beliefs about themselves—often patterns that had been laid down early in life.

One brave man volunteered to participate in front of the class. The group leader asked him to close his eyes, clear his mind, and remember a moment when he was really upset. The man then told a story, as if it had happened yesterday, of a lamp that was broken in his home when he was a teenager. In a rage, his father blamed him for it, hit him, and sent him to his room.

Our group leader asked, "How did you feel?" He, in tears, responded, "I felt blamed for something I didn't do. I didn't do it. I wasn't even there when it happened." After identifying these feelings, the leader led him though the process of unhooking that experience from the truth about himself. That feeling of unworthiness had followed him for all those years.

My eyes as well as the students' were opened. By the end of the class they were saying, "We should have learned this in high school." So much of what they learned—what I was teaching, and what, ultimately, I learned—opened my eyes and my heart to what was happening between me and my children. This translated well to the situations I deal with in the workplaces I enter.

In Chapter 13, I tell a story from my own experience to describe a solution-seeking process. But here is the beginning of that story, as another example of understanding the feelings that undergird anger.

. . . .

In the middle of a quiet afternoon I went up to the kitchen to microwave a bag of popcorn. Eric burst into the kitchen, and he was full of eighteen-year-old energy. "Mom, get your pocket-book. We have to get to the bank before it closes, so you can co-sign a loan with me. I have found the *coolest* 1979 Camaro."

My response was, "No. I am *not* co-signing a loan for a 1979 Camaro. Forget about it."

We went from zero to sixty in two seconds flat. Suddenly we were in a heated argument, ending with something like, "You just don't love me!" When Eric was a little boy, I could sit him down on the stairs and tell him to stay there until I said he could get up. I had some control. As he grew into a teenager taller than me, I could no longer use that approach. I often felt powerless deal-ing with this new creature in my house, this proud, strong man-boy. Out of this feeling of powerlessness I frequently spun quickly to anger. The same feeling of powerlessness was sparking in him. So capable in so many ways, he felt frustrated by the lim-its that were part of his life, put on him by his mother.

. . . .

Anger starts with an <u>A</u>*tivating event*. Somebody says something or does something. Maybe it's nonverbal and barely visible—when you speak, he rolls his eyes, or maybe you make a statement and someone shrugs her shoulders. In that moment, the amygdala picks up the verbal or nonverbal cue and triggers an emotional response. Nearby, the hip-pocampus, the storage center for previous fearful situations, works close-ly with the amygdala, calming or intensifying the amygdala's responses. The amygdala translates these impulses into <u>*Beliefs*</u>: I am being attacked, or I am being accused, or I am being disrespected. When the amygdala sends those chemicals into the rest of your system, and you react—fight, flight, or freeze, depending on your own disposition, or maybe depending on your mood that day—you are experiencing the emotional _Consequence_. These are the ABCs of anger.

What are the beliefs that cause anger?

- ► I have been accused—falsely or not.
- ► I have a reason to feel frightened.
- ► I have been treated unfairly or cheated.
- ► I am not valued.
- ► I am powerless or I have no control.
- ► I have been disrespected.
- ► I am unlovable.

THE ABC'S OF ANGER

A   Activating event

B   Belief (the meaning we put on the event)

C   Consequence (emotional)

Consider This

☑ Think about the situations you identified at the beginning of this chapter. What are the beliefs that caused the anger you experienced?

☑ If the situation you identified was someone else's anger, what might have caused the person to react the way he or she did?

People Use Anger

People use anger to control, to win, to get even, to protect themselves. You probably know people who yell to get their way. Others respond by jumping into action, saying, "Just don't yell at me." And we all know someone who uses tears the same way. Those around the teary person are quick to respond, "Whatever you want, just don't cry!" How do you handle these situations?

. . . .

More than once I have been called into an office to deal with a difficult boss-staff relationship. Staff members have told me: "He's totally irrational; you just can't work with him rationally."

I respond, "Tell me what he does."

"If he doesn't get what he wants when he wants, he starts yelling. Sometimes he slams the door to his office."

"Then what happens?"

"You'd better get busy and get it done!"

What would a rational person do to accomplish his or her goals the next time something needed to get done? Probably what worked the last time! Yelling, maybe slamming the door—it doesn't seem like such irrational behavior, after all.

. . . .

The amygdala is fully formed sometime between the ages of two and five. The frontal lobes that govern rational thought and decision-making skills are not fully developed until our mid-twenties, however, so it isn't always easy going, especially when dealing with children. Remember the energy it took to control the sailboat in a heavy wind? All our lives, we practice how to respond to the amygdala's emotional energy. By the time an adult is functioning in the workplace, the patterns of response are deeply set in his or her brain. Addressing those patterns as adults requires attention and energy over a significant period of time. To begin, just consider the challenge of dealing with children's emotional responses.

. . . .

Like all small children, my two-year-old granddaughter tested her limits pretty regularly. We had such a tug of war recently. "These shorts," she demanded.

"You can't wear those shorts to bed," I started out logically, "your legs will get cold."

"I want to wear these shorts," she screamed. "*not* those pants. Not the pink ones, not the purple ones. Just these shorts." She burst into tears. I tried to hold her, tried to calm her down. She wiggled away from me and wedged herself under the bed, screaming and crying.

It was not that big a deal. She could sleep in the shorts. My "no" response was really about the power between us and who had it. It was not about the shorts. It was about who was in control. I couldn't let a two-year-old get her way by throwing a tantrum. I stood up and went into the hall. She screamed. She cried. I waited. Slowly she wound down to soft sobs. I opened the door and gently picked her up. The tears were gone. She walked to the suitcase, rifled through the shirts and pants and shorts and dresses. She picked out a pair of long, soft black pants. I helped her pull them on.

. . . .

Sometimes I watch a little boy being pushed around the grocery store by his mom, while she is struggling with his anger, feeling powerless, and he is learning that outrageous behavior works. When he yells long and loud enough, his mom will hand him a candy bar to get the screaming to stop. As I watch her relent, I groan and think, "Someday that child is going to work somewhere and become someone else's problem."

. . . .

Addicted to Anger

That child wanting the candy bar in the grocery store learns his lessons very well. He grows up and gets a job. His pattern of behavior—yelling or crying or stomping out of the room—honed over twenty years, is deeply etched into the brain's neural pathways. Changing these patterns, creating new synapses and paths in the brain, is not an easy thing to do. Whether you are the person with a negative pattern you want to change, or you are working with someone with such negative habits, know that change will be slow in coming.

For example, my granddaughter has learned to put on her own pants by now. And like the rest of us, she has developed her own pattern for getting dressed. She holds up the pants and pushes her right foot through the pant leg first. Then, the left. Some of us do it the other way around, but we all develop a pattern that is comfortable, day in and day out. After the pattern is set, we don't stop to think about it, about which leg goes in first. If we wanted to change that habit, though, first we have to be aware of it. Then, we have to consciously think each morning as we are getting dressed, "Oh, yes, I am going to switch to the other leg." We have to do that over and over and over again, until we create a new pattern, a new habit.

How much harder it is to change our anger patterns and habits! This is true particularly if they seem to be working for us a lot of the time. Particularly if we are not even aware of them.

☑   When do you experience anger in your own work life?

☑   What feelings are behind the anger that you feel?

☑   What effect does your expression of anger have on others?

☑   Are there patterns of behavior you would like to change?

☑   Think of a situation when an employee was angry. What did he or she do to express that anger?

☑   What might have been the feelings behind the anger that you witnessed?

The natural, powerful chemicals I mentioned earlier—adrenaline and norepeniphrine—*are* serious drugs. Norepinephrine is used medically as an injection to get the heart going again if it has stopped. Realizing how powerful these drugs are helps us understand that sometimes people can be addicted to their anger. For them, it may be difficult to get moving in any direction without the shot of adrenaline or norepinephrine that the amygdala produces.

There is some good news on this topic, however. Several years ago, a conference brought together Buddhist scholars with Western psychologists, neuroscientists, and philosophers.[3] The neuroscientists confirmed what Tibetan monks have experienced in practice for millennia. They reported that their research demonstrated a change in areas of the brain: through a consistent practice of meditation, an area of the frontal lobes behind the right side of your forehead enlarges. That area controls and mitigates the reactions of the amygdala. Over time, with this discipline, people are better able to manage fear, anxiety, rage, and anger. When neuroscientists reported this remarkable discovery, the Dalai Lama nodded (I paraphrase here), "Yes, of course. We have known this for thousands of years." Obviously, Tibetan monks have learned a lot about how to control their own anger. How can we manage ours?

How to Manage Your Own Anger

Any anger arousal produces physiological changes. Usually these occur before we are consciously aware of our anger. So the wise manager practices becoming aware of the changes as early as possible so he or she can understand personal emotions and begin to regulate them.

Where do you first begin to notice your responses when you are getting angry?

Head	Shoulders
Eyes	Chest
Mouth	Stomach
Jaw	Back
Neck	Hands

When you feel yourself getting angry, wherever it might start for you, here are steps you can take to manage your response.

Breathe Deeply

When you feel the first flush of anger rising, take a deep, slow breath or, better yet, take several breaths. Oxygen to the brain helps to counteract the chemical rush of adrenaline and other drugs. This practice alone can shift your response, and can give you time and space and the ability to think. A daily practice of quieting your mind through focusing on your breath, even briefly, can help you manage those moments when you begin to feel angry. The practice itself is helpful in bringing equanimity to your system generally. Then, in those moments when you do experience that rush of emotion, the daily practice helps you to remember to breathe.

> *When you notice that anger is coming up in you, you have to practice*
> *mindful breathing in order to generate the energy of mindfulness,*
> *in order to recognize your anger and embrace it tenderly,*
> *so that you can bring relief into you and not to act and to say*
> *things that can destroy, that can be destructive.*
> —THICH NHAT HANH, VIETNAMESE ZEN MASTER

Take a Break

If you need to, take a break. There are a number of ways to do this. Excuse yourself for a few minutes. Suggest coming back to the discussion tomorrow or after lunch. If you can't do that, at least inhale, count to ten, and mentally slow yourself down. Some jobs do not permit this option. If you are in one of those occupations, more practice is required to be able to respond effectively in the moment.

Take Stock of the Situation

Understand what is going on. Spend some time identifying the feelings that are behind the anger. Ask yourself, *What is going on here? Why does this bother me so much? What am I afraid of? What specifically am I feeling? What need do I have that is not being met? What principles of mine have been violated?* Try to put into words what is going on inside you: I feel hurt, or scared, or anxious . . . about. . . . Sometimes you can say it out loud, depending on who else is involved. Other times, just thinking it through or writing about it can help.

The process of putting your feelings into words moves some of the energy from the amygdala to more rational thought. Here are a few "feeling" words that may be useful:

afraid	alienated	devastated
frightened	agitated	miserable
scared	rattled	disappointed
worried	shocked	discouraged
suspicious	troubled	hopeless
panicked	uncomfortable	tense
annoyed	upset	anxious
frustrated	embarrassed	nervous
impatient	ashamed	vulnerable
disgusted	guilty	insecure
confused	exhausted	leery
lost	worn out	envious
torn	hurt	jealous

After you've identified the feeling, think about the underlying beliefs or needs that are creating those feelings.[4]

. . . .

In the meeting, each time that Rebecca spoke, Charlie rolled his eyes. The more she noticed, the angrier she got. Pausing to understand what she was feeling, she realized that she felt disrespected. As she thought about this, she reminded herself of the people in the room who did respect her, and her desire, regardless of what others were doing to maintain her own dignity and self-respect.

. . . .

How often is your anger not really about this person or this incident? Sometimes an event happening elsewhere in your life ramps up your emotions overall. Consider this scenario.

. . . .

Nichole read an e-mail directive from her boss that set her on edge. Then one of her employees walked in to ask for three hours off that afternoon. Nichole snapped at the employee. The employee was surprised and confused, not about being denied the request but by the negative energy attached to it. In hindsight, Nichole realized that she had overreacted in that moment—her reaction to that e-mail was still rumbling around in her head.

. . . .

MANAGING YOUR OWN ANGER

- ▶ Breathe.
- ▶ Take a break.
- ▶ Understand what it is about.
- ▶ Create a safe place to talk.
- ▶ Find physical outlets.
- ▶ Avoid personal attacks.
- ▶ Deal with the current issue.
- ▶ Keep talking.

Create a Safe Place

Find a neutral space to hold that difficult conversation (for more on this, see Chapter 13). Find a private spot to talk and a mutually agreeable time, when neither of you is rushed or distracted. It can help to talk through the issues with a trusted, uninvolved friend. Sometimes you will get more clarity about what is going on and how you can respond by writing your thoughts in a journal. Or you can write a letter, put it in a drawer for a few days, then reread it before deciding whether to act on it.

Find a Physical Outlet for Your Anger

Try exercise. Take a walk. Go for a run. Dance. Practice yoga. Dive into the pool and swim a few laps. Go fishing. Build a deck or drive a golf ball. Become physically involved in some form of recreation that will get your mind off the situation. *Warning: Pounding an imaginary foe does NOT reduce intense emotions.* You are simply practicing being angry.

Avoid Personal Attacks

When raising an issue, focus on the problem, not on personalities. Take the No-Name-Calling Pledge: "I will not call other people names, no matter how angry I am." Repeat the pledge as often as you need to. While you are at it, avoid the "You don't ever . . ." or "You always ..." argument, too. Name calling and personal attacks only create bigger messes that will require even more time later trying to clean up. The old saying, "Sticks and stones may break my bones, but words will never hurt me" is not true. Words count: they sting and can ring painfully in someone's ears long after physical wounds have healed.

> **NO-NAME-CALLING PLEDGE**
>
> I will not, no matter how angry I am, call other people names.

Deal with the Current Issue

Throw away the baggage. Put grudges, resentments, and old hurts away. This resolution has to start with an understanding of what you are angry about. If you are not clear in your own mind about what triggered your anger, the other stuff—the old stuff—piles on pretty quickly, before you realize what has happened.

> *Holding onto anger is like grasping a hot coal with the intent of throwing it at someone else. You are the one who gets burned.*
> —BUDDHA

Keep Talking

If you take a break, be sure to come back and address the topic after the emotions have cooled. Continue, even when the relationship is strained, to talk to the other person, to say good morning or hello, in a civil way.

How to Respond to Someone Else's Anger

Suddenly, someone is in your face, blaming you for whatever.... How do you keep your cool? Often, your first reaction is to fight back—or to leave the scene. But you can turn a potential argument into a discussion if you can hold on to your own sense of calm and stay determined not to be sucked into the other person's negative energy.

RESPONDING TO SOMEONE ELSE'S ANGER
- ► Understand your own responses.
- ► Listen.
- ► Check it out.
- ► Take a break.
- ► Create a safe place to talk.
- ► Consider the source.
- ► Set boundaries.

The boss called him into the office and closed the door. Both of them were tense; words were exchanged. As the employee left the room, he mumbled an epithet—just loud enough for the boss to hear—about the boss. Of course, the boss heard it. And the boss went off. With his fists clenched, he charged out the door after the employee. Two colleagues grabbed him and held him back. Because of the boss's behavior, it was the boss who caught flak for the incident, not the employee.

. . . .

When tempers flare, the better approach is for the boss to reprimand the employee for his actions—the language he has used as an employee. Instead, in this showdown, we can speculate that the employee walked away feeling he had won that round. What had he won? What had the boss accomplished? Remember: You can't change another person, you can only change *yourself*. By shifting how you respond to others when they are angry or upset, you can begin to shift the dynamics and patterns between you and others.

Here are some tips for handling the anger of others:

Understand Your Own Responses

Know and understand your own responses to anger, your defensiveness, your hot buttons. This is the first step in developing empathy for others. It also helps you to be aware of, and less likely to be caught by, your own triggers.

Listen

Give others the opportunity to be heard—this is a profound and powerful experience. Allow the other person to let off steam, to explain his/her perspective, to vent. This can be really hard—to listen to someone who is angry at you. But when you can do it, the results are stunning. One way to practice is to mentally remove yourself from the immediate picture. Imagine you are looking and listening through a picture window, watching a story unfold, observing a scene without judgments or opinions. The other person might be surprised that you actually want to hear what he or she has to say. You might be surprised at what the person has to tell you. Remember: What they are saying is not about you. It is about the other person—what he or she thinks, how he or she sees things. You can decide later what you might want to do about what you have heard, whether you agree with it or not.

Check It Out

"It sounds like you might be feeling frustrated, or upset, or anxious … or…? I want to know more about it." Ask it as a question, and be willing to listen to the answer. Making a flat statement such as, "So, you feel frustrated…" cuts off discussion rather than allowing it to proceed. Simply saying, "I understand" really doesn't say anything at all. On the other hand, when you can put a "feeling" word onto what you are hearing and confirm it with the speaker—"Is that it?"—the two of you can connect on a deeper level. If you are making a sincere effort to listen, the other person is likely to think, "She really is listening to me and trying to understand." Additionally, accept the person's right to be angry. Acknowledging difficult feelings does not mean that you agree with them. (There's more on this in Chapter 14.)

Take a Break

Interrupt the pattern and allow tempers to cool, without judgments or negative comments. Sometimes a short break (15 to 20 minutes) is sufficient. Other times a longer one may be needed. Perhaps you can come back after lunch, or the next day. Just be sure to come back to the topic and resolve it in a calmer moment. If someone loses his or her temper and that ends the discussion for good, then that anger has effectively controlled the outcome.

Create a Safe Place to Talk It Through

Take time to regroup, to think through your reactions and your response. Provide privacy and a neutral space within which you can work it through. Allow enough time for both sides to be heard and some resolution found. (More on this in Chapter 13.)

Consider the Source

Don't take it personally. The other person may be angry about something or someone else. There may be other issues going on with co-workers or outside of work. Keep the conversation focused on the issue at hand.

Set Boundaries

Establish ground rules or guidelines for discussion, either before a difficult conversation or along the way as needed. Propose ground rules with shared responsibility and without judgments: "I cannot hear you when you are yelling. Can we agree to use respectful language?"

When a difficult conversation comes up, when you feel your own emotions swinging into anger, or you sense that the other person might be ready to blow, remember the boats on the Chesapeake Bay. Keep a steady hand on the tiller, guide the rudder in a positive direction, and don't let a gale of anger capsize the boat.

Anger and Violence in the Workplace

News accounts of violence in the workplace amplify our fears about anger. We know that wherever people interact with one another there is the opportunity for anger to turn to violence. According to the National Institute for Occupational Safety and Health, only 7 percent of violence that occurs in the workplace is caused by disgruntled employees.[5] Still, any employee violence in the workplace is unacceptable.

What is a manager to do? Observing and reporting changes in people's behavior are the best defense against this possibility. Know the policies and procedures within your own organization for handling potentially violent employees. The better you know your employees and co-workers, the easier it is to notice the warning signs. Here is a list of behaviors that indicate larger problems of anger and violence.[6]

1. Verbal threats. The person makes direct, veiled, or conditional threats of harm.

2. Constant negativity. The person is never happy with what is going on. He or she is consistently unreasonable and overreacts to feedback or criticism. The individual blows everything out of proportion and is unable to accept criticism of job performance; rather, he or she takes comments personally and turns them into a grudge.

3. Intimidation. The person uses intimidation of others to get his or her way (can be physical or verbal intimidation)—for example,

fear tactics, threats, harassing behaviors including phone calls, stalking, and the like.

4. Paranoia. The employee thinks other employees are out to get him or her. The individual feels persecuted or the victim of injustice.

5. Not accepting responsibility. The person does not accept responsibility for own actions, makes excuses, blames others, the company, the system, for problems, errors, and disruptive behaviors.

6. Angry, argumentative, and confrontational. The person is frequently involved in confrontations and arguments with others, including supervisors, co-workers, and neighbors. He or she has low impulse control, slams doors, pounds fist, or is verbally aggressive.

7. Fascination with violence. The person applauds certain violent acts portrayed in the media, such as racial incidences, domestic violence, shooting sprees, or executions. He or she is fascinated by the killing power of weapons and their destructive effect on people, coupled with an excessive interest in guns, particularly semi-automatic or automatic weapons.

8. Vindictive. The person makes statements like, "He will get his" or "One of these days I'll have my say." The individual openly hopes for something bad to happen to the person against whom he or she has a grudge.

9. Desperation. The person expresses extreme desperation over recent family, financial, or personal problems.

10. Substance abuse. The person shows signs of alcohol and/or drug abuse.

If you are concerned about an individual's behavior, if you notice these tendencies, talk with someone in the human resources office, an Employee Assistance Program (EAP), or a mental health professional to determine what steps to take. While the occurrence of workplace violence is rare, sometimes we read about tragedies in the newspaper in which others had noticed negative behavior earlier but had failed to take any action until it was too late.

Notes

1. Daniel Goleman, *Emotional Intelligence: Why It Can Matter More Than IQ* (New York: Bantam Books, 1995).

2. Steven Stosny, *Treating Attachment Abuse: A Compassionate Approach* (New York: Springer, 1995).

3. Daniel Goleman, *Destructive Emotions: How Can We Overcome Them?* (New York: Bantam Books, 2003).

4. Marshall B. Rosenberg, *Nonviolent Communication: A Language of Life* (Encinitas, Calif.: PuddleDancer Press, 2003).

5. National Institute for Occupational Safety and Health, Centers for Disease Control and Prevention, 2006, http://www.cdc.gov/niosh/docs/2006-144/#all; accessed November 15, 2010.

6. Adapted from "The Unlucky 13: Early Warning Signs of Potential Violence at Work," National Institute for the Prevention of Workplace Violence, http://www.ncdsv.org/images/The%20Unlucky%2013_Early%20Warning%20Signs%20of%20Potential%20Violence%20a%E2%80%A6.pdf; accessed November 15, 2010.

CHAPTER 11

A Sense of Humor

D id you hear the one about the manager who walked into the bar? No, that's not really what we mean by a sense of humor as key to resolving conflicts. You really don't need to be a standup comic to manage conflict effectively at work. Rather in this chapter, I show how having a sense of humor is essential to creating a positive climate for dealing with difficult issues.

Keeping Things in Perspective

Sometimes all we can do is laugh. Or shrug our shoulders and smile. Sometimes we could jump up and down and scream, but it really wouldn't help anything. So, keeping it all in perspective by maintaining a sense of humor becomes the better choice.

> *A person without a sense of humor is like a wagon without springs. It's jolted by every pebble on the road.*
>
> —HENRY WARD BEECHER

. . . .

Everything possible had gone wrong that day. I reached into the cabinet for my morning cereal and shook the few remaining flakes into my bowl. The timer on the coffee pot took early retirement, so I had no coffee. Running a few minutes late, I slid into the driver's seat and turned onto the toll road. The day ahead made me nervous. I was working with a new client I had met only once before. I reached over to pull up the address on the navigation system. Nothing came up that matched the street I needed. I called my client to confirm with him that I was headed in the right direction. His cell phone was turned off. I have learned that when I get stressed, I forget what I know. Now that I was on my way and stressed, I could not think clearly about where the office was. I kept driving, following my nose or my instincts. At a red light, I tried calling another number, the client's office. The number written in my file was wrong. All of the technical systems I had put in place to back up my memory had fallen through. How could they all slip at once?

Stepping back from my anxiety, I was able to laugh at the ridiculous pickle I was in. In this moment I had a choice. I could launch into a grumble about "having a bad day," or I could put the situation in perspective and see some humor in it. The laughter was a great release of the tension and helped me to shift my thinking from panic to problem solving. Within minutes I had realigned my internal map, and I pulled into his parking lot with time to spare.

. . . .

Tension keeps us off balance, keyed up. We are ready to spring into action, primed for defensive mode, for attack or counterattack. Letting it go, through a sense of humor, actually brings us back into balance, increasing our flexibility and curiosity. Many studies have shown that laughter is an antidote to stress, releasing endorphins in our brains more powerful than morphine.

> *At its heart, humor is a Darwinian tool, an adaptation of attitude that helps us tame the terrors of life.*
> —GENE WEINGARTEN

Deborah, a colleague of mine, tells the story of creating a public relations campaign for her company. A rival actively worked to sabotage her efforts on every front. As Deborah sought employee input regarding a new logo, the rival issued a company-wide e-mail, eviscerating one of the proposed approaches. Not wanting to engage in a very public conflict, Deborah responded to staff and to him with a memo about the various options, written in the voice of Elvis Presley, which had people laughing out loud. Her use of humor diffused the situation. She even received a thank you from her supervisor for managing the incident well.

Angels fly because they take themselves lightly.

My grandmother used to apply the "one hundred–year rule": a hundred years from now, what the heck difference will it make? We can choose how we respond to the times when events seem to fall like dominos in the wrong direction. Keeping small things small leaves us with more energy to deal with the bigger problems that are bound to come our way.

Laughing at Your Own Mistakes

It takes a certain self-confidence and comfort with yourself to be able to laugh at your own shortcomings and stumbles. Self-effacing humor shows the ability to recognize that you are not perfect, and you are still okay. You're still a good manager. It acknowledges that you bring your skills and abilities to the job and do your best, and no one can expect any more from you—or from anyone else. It's a strategy that builds rapport with others, whether subordinates or co-workers. A manager who can be humanly imperfect is more able to allow others that same grace. This sense of humor, or positive perspective, builds a sense of hopefulness and sends ripples of stress relief across an office. A display of humor can help people like you, and when they like you, they want to work through the hard stuff together with you.

A word of caution, however: a little humor goes a long way. Laugh at yourself too much and you begin to belittle yourself—and that is counterproductive. Again, the key is balance.

Laughter Helps Us Think

Laughter brings oxygen to the brain. More oxygen to the brain helps us

> *People think of humor as being frivolous. But it's not. It's just a different kind of wisdom.*
>
> —LARRY MILLER, COMEDIAN

think more clearly, and that helps us solve problems more effectively. A sense of humor helps us to face conflicts and the people we have those conflicts with in a more positive frame of mind. That frame of mind also enables us to see more possibilities for solutions.

- -

Many times the humorous moments in the workplace are difficult to translate to paper. One of those moments occurred several years ago when I was working on an intense project with a team of five. While we were pushing against the deadline, unbeknownst to us, a repair crew came through the office to paint. This was not good timing. Couldn't they see that we had work to do? Amid the drop cloths, ladders, and paint buckets we continued our effort. The painters posted signs everywhere warning about the wet paint. During lunch, one member of the team gathered as many of those signs— PAINT DRY? NOT YET—as she could find and taped them all over a friendly co-worker's cubicle, inside and out. After lunch we had a good laugh at her handiwork. Without saying a word, she had captured our frustrations and expressed them in a funny way, releasing the tension for all of us.

- -

Humor Helps Break the Tension in Conflict

Perhaps you can remember meetings when someone broke the tension with a light remark. That burst of oxygen affects the brain immediately. Within minutes you are back on task with fresh energy to tackle "intractable" problems. Sometimes these moments happen so fast you cannot recall exactly what was said, but retracing the discussion would reveal the comic relief and its positive result.

- -

The room was hot and we were all tired. We had been arguing, and each side was holding tightly to its position. In exasperation, one woman loudly declared—again—her view. She was so worked up about the statement that she made, she banged her hand on the table and said, "The Lord can strike me down if that isn't true." Then she leaned back in her chair. She leaned a little too vigorously, and in one motion, she and the chair clattered to the floor. She came up unhurt, laughing at the absurdity of the moment. It broke the tension for all of us.

As Simple as a Smile

Something as simple as a smile can make a big difference to your sense of well-being. Smiling has been shown to reduce stress and lower blood pressure. Like laughter, it can release endorphins, changing the chemistry of your brain.

A sincere, warm smile makes you more approachable. People tend to think better of you. A smile won't make the conflict go away, but it can make the communication you need to resolve it easier to initiate and work through. A smile—an honest smile, that is—communicates, "I want to work with you, to find a way through any difficulty we might be having. I like you. I value you. I want to work this out with you."

A union local vice president related this experience: The team had engaged in a grueling negotiation with management. Finally there was a little light peeking through. Management had put forward a proposal that could unlock the stalemate. The vice president was feeling quite positive about the deal. He was startled when the chief spokesperson for the union called a break, pulled him aside, and told him, "Lighten up!" He was baffled.

"What are you talking about?"

The spokesperson then said, "From the look on your face they think you disagree with them. They are about to pull the offer off the table. You are about to kill the whole deal."

Sometimes we can become so absorbed in our own thinking that we have no idea how others may be seeing us. Employees are watching and

> *Whenever you're in conflict with someone, there is one factor*
> *that can make the difference between damaging your relationship*
> *and deepening it. That factor is attitude.*
> —WILLIAM JAMES

interpreting the boss's every move—and his facial expression. The face you wear to work does send a loud message, whether you are aware of it or not. Whenever possible, make the message a positive one.

I'm not suggesting that you should go around all the time with a phony smile plastered on your face. This is not about faking feelings. However, there is a lot to be gained by finding bright spots and focusing on them throughout your day. When you can create an atmosphere through your own attitude in which people feel more comfortable, it is easier to raise those concerns that divide us. On the other hand, when people feel like they are walking on eggshells all the time, fearful of what might break if conflicts are exposed, the problems are less likely to get addressed, and they get bigger instead.

Consider This

☑ As a start to finding those bright spots, list five things you like about your job. For some people, the list may start with "I get paid," and move to "health insurance" and "vacation days." Start wherever you are:

1. _____
2. _____
3. _____
4. _____
5. _____

To Deliver Messages More Easily

A sense of humor can help you deliver a message that will go down more easily. "I only have one nerve left, and you are standing on it" is a message that is easy to hear, respect, and respond to. A grumbled, "Can't you see I'm busy?" gets a totally different response. A manager in a large corporation I worked with was famous for his line, "Let's go get a cookie."

He explained that whenever he needed to give an employee negative feedback. On their way back from the cafeteria, he would deliver his message. Yes, they soon learned what was coming, but the cookie and conversation sweetened the moment.

Your moods and emotions have a measurable effect on the people you work with—think of it as "emotional contagion." Your *negative* mood can have a negative effect and your *positive* mood can have a positive effect on the people you work with. Several years ago, Sigal Barsade conducted studies of "emotional contagion" through a series of carefully controlled experiments with senior management teams.[1]

> *The human race has only one really effective weapon, and that is laughter.*
> *The moment it arises, all our hardnesses yield, all our irritations and*
> *resentments slip away and a sunny spirit takes their place.*
>
> —MARK TWAIN

Using a paid actor within the group, she videotaped people working together. When the actor was positive and friendly, others on the team began to experience those emotions themselves. Their positive mood then had a direct effect on the cooperativeness of the group and their constructive conflict-resolution skills. The research demonstrated that group members put in more effort and engaged in more complex reasoning and problem solving. On the other hand, the actor's negative emotions produced a negative spiral within the group. As the teams' negative moods spread, their willingness and ability to work together productively also fell.

Books have been written about the success of Southwest Airlines—and the role that expressing a sense of humor has played in that company's success. A flight with Southwest becomes memorable because of the lighthearted jokes that the flight attendants sometimes engage in during the trip. Humor is a part of the corporate culture. Even in the interview process, people may be asked to give an example of how a sense of humor has helped them. This pays off for the company in customer satisfaction. It also pays off in the workplace. Named as one of the best places to work in America, Southwest Airlines is known for its low turnover and high employee morale.

Cautions on the Use of Humor

There are good ways to use humor, and some not-so-good ways. Here are a few things to keep in mind:

► Avoid being flippant. You wouldn't try to lighten the moment when you fire an employee by saying, "So, Charlie, it looks like you'll have plenty of time for that family vacation now."

► Dirty jokes or sexist or racist "humor" have no place in the workplace. There is a lot that is funny about our humanity that is clean and respectful. Keeping the workplace safe for everyone means keeping the fun dirt-free.

► Making fun of others is not funny. Mocking people, knocking them down with "humor" to try to make yourself look smarter or better, actually makes you look worse.

► Sarcasm isn't funny. Sarcastic remarks belittle or verbally attack another person or group. Sarcasm may seem funny to the speaker, but often it is hostile and mean. Remarks like these make differences, disagreements, and conflicts harder to resolve because of the damage they do to working relationships.

Here are examples of sarcastic remarks that may have seemed funny to the sender but to the receiver they carried a destructive sting:

► He never slows down to think; it's too painful to spend time with his own thoughts.

► Anyone who told you to be yourself couldn't have given you worse advice.

► Keep talking, someday you'll say something intelligent!

► Perhaps your whole purpose in life is simply to serve as a warning to others.

► Thinking isn't your strong suit, is it?

These types of remarks, especially coming from a manager, can be particularly negative and inappropriate to employees.

Consider This

- ☑ What mind-set do you bring to work every day?
- ☑ How do the moods of others affect you?
- ☑ Are you able to laugh at your own shortcomings?
- ☑ How often do you smile at people with whom you work?
- ☑ What habit do you want to change to lighten the mood in the office?

Note

1. Sigal G. Barsade, "The Ripple Effect: Emotional Contagion and Its Influence on Group Behavior," *Administrative Science Quarterly*, 47, no. 4 (December 2002), pp. 644–675.

CHAPTER 12

Time

Time is a gift. It is your friend. In a smartphone and social networking crazed world, a world that is driven by instant messages and immediate access, this idea defies all logic. What could possibly be useful about taking time in dealing with conflict? We don't have time for that!

Patience Is a Virtue

When we talk about time in the context of a conflict, we are mostly talking about patience. Here is an example: In January, my company completed work on a project for one of our favorite clients. Back in the office, after a job well done—the client agreed on that—we submitted an invoice. Just like we always do. The phone rang in March. "So sorry, there has been a mix-up with the contracting vehicle; it's going to take us a couple more weeks to sort this out." We are now well into the middle of May—those bare branches of winter were in the full green leaf of spring—and we still had not been paid. Somewhere in the maze of cubicles in that organization, three duplicate invoices are drifting about, between desks. The frustration has built up to boiling in my office. Passersby can watch the steam com-

> *Dear Lord, give me patience. And I want it right now.*

ing out of my ears after each phone call. Losing my patience—or my temper—with them is not an option. We need their cooperation—and we want to be able to continue working with them on other projects.

> Time allows us to cool off emotionally and have a different kind of conversation.
> Time allows people to change their (our) minds.
> Time allows wounds to heal.
> Time allows an apology to sink in, and allows us to forgive.
> Time allows us to save face.
> Time allows us to check to be certain the solutions we are proposing are actually possible.

Patience may be a virtue. I've certainly been told that all my life. I wish I had it, but many times I don't. Sometimes all I can do is pretend to be patient. When my mind is spinning over a disagreement or argument, I can use a variety of patient-like strategies. A few conscious deep breaths help me get off the treadmill of thoughts. I look for distracting tasks that can get me through the moment. Maybe I can walk out to get the mail. Or check my to-do list for simple jobs that require little thought but that continue to linger, waiting to be completed. I may divert my attention by balancing the accounts or cleaning out the old folders on my computer. I might pick up the phone and connect with a friend, or find a few moments to write my thoughts in a journal.

If I can find some task that pulls my mind away from this moment, this urgency, this anxiety, I can give myself time to reconsider my initial reaction. On the other side of the simple task, my mind is clear. The moment of anxiety has faded. Not only is the stack of papers filed or the

> *When you remove time, you are subject to the lowest-quality intuitive reaction.*
> —GAVIN DE BECKER

account balanced but I can also put the disagreement into better perspective and often find a more productive way through it.

Your computer gives that familiar ping. A new e-mail is waiting for you. Interrupting your work, you open it up. Your heart races as you read. One of your employees has accused you of botching the report on a major account. How could he dare accuse you like this? *And* how could he have copied your boss on this? Every cell in your brain seems to be screaming, "Let's set the record straight right now!"

Time could be your best friend in this moment. Yes, you could type out an angry response, telling him all that he needs to know about where he really fits in the world and how right you were on this point—and maybe every other point you have made in the last six months. But you remember this: Time is my friend. You resist all of the urges to hit the send button. You save it as a draft e-mail. You wait. You reopen the message the next day and reread it—you might even ask someone you trust to read it as well. *Does my message really convey my meaning? Will the recipient understand the key points I am trying to make? Or will he only hear the venom and respond in kind, his own fingers pounding the keyboard in self-defense?*

. . . .

There is some news that's best let into your mind gradually. I have learned that, when I receive an e-mail that stirs up a hot reaction, I manage it better if I read it once, close it, move on to something else, and then come back to it a little later, to reread and consider it again. Invariably, when I slow down the process, and relax my reaction time, the news is much easier to take and my response is the better for it. What I felt in that first moment was like a huge, searing red coal that turned out to be no more than a few sparks that floated away on the updraft. Try it, try the pause that refreshes, and see if this doesn't work for you, as well.

> *Patience is the ability to idle your motor when you feel like stripping your gears.*
> —BARBARA JOHNSON

The Perry Mason Effect

How do people change their minds, especially when you believe they are wrong? That old *Perry Mason* program on television gave us the wrong idea. The show hasn't been on for years, but the lesson persists. A long time ago, my family sat each week in front of the black-and-white TV to watch the show. Life was simpler then, with only three channels and no remote, picking a program to watch was easy.

Now that I look back on it, I realize that every week of *Perry Mason* was really the same show. Each episode Raymond Burr (as defense attorney Perry Mason) spent the first forty-five minutes developing the case. Then, in the last fifteen minutes, he put a witness on the stand and badgered this person until he or she collapsed. "You're right," she would sob, "I killed them all." The next week, my family gathered eagerly in the living room again, to watch the same scenario with different actors and a different stage set. Another witness would take the stand, and again, Perry Mason would bear down on this person until he crumpled with another confession. Looking back, I realize what this routine taught us about how to change someone's mind: keep at it until the person collapses in exhaustion and agrees with you.

But our minds really don't work that way. We need time to process new information, to reflect, to decide what makes sense and to let go of old beliefs. People are much more likely to hear what you have to say and incorporate new thinking if you give them time to think it through for themselves. Talk it out, listen to what they have to say, say what needs to be said from your perspective, and take a break. Come back later to see what shifts may have taken place in their thinking. Or maybe even in your own.

Perhaps you have heard this advice, "If you want an answer right away, the answer is no. If you can give me a chance to think about it, the answer is maybe." Most of us don't think in a linear fashion. We are much more like cartoon characters (I think of Billy in the *Family Circus*, or Jeremy in *Zits*), who wander out the back door on the way to wherever and meander all through the neighborhood before getting there. Moment by moment, our brains are subject to all kinds of thoughts. Taking time to pause, to process, allows the choppy waves of thought for calm and clarity to appear.

Time Heals Wounds—Yours as Well as Theirs

Allow yourself or others time to recover from hurts or from ego injuries.

When the pain or the slight is fresh, accept that time may help to create some space for healing.

Particularly, when you offer an apology, give people time to think over what you have said and decide whether to accept it. Forgiveness doesn't come in a minute or an hour or even a day. It can help to give the other person permission upfront not to respond. "I want to tell you something. I really don't need any kind of answer from you right away. It's just something to think about."

And when someone apologizes to you, you may not feel an immediate rush of forgiveness. That's okay. Let the conversation seep in, allow yourself time to consider what has been said. You may find, reflecting on the conversation a day or so later, that you can let go of some of the pain or disruption that was created, and forgiveness begins to germinate. What had seemed so important has melted away, like the snowball you stuck in the freezer last winter to throw at Frankie at the Fourth of July picnic. Where did it go?

. . . .

Johnna and her boss Karl came into the mediation at odds. She had a list of complaints: how she had been overlooked for assignments and projects, how she was out of the loop for important communications within the office. Johnna talked. Karl listened. Then Karl spoke: "I realize now that I could have done things differently. I could have been more open and forthcoming with you. I felt like you didn't trust me, and so I couldn't bring myself to talk to you more directly. And for that, I want you to know I am sorry."

The mediator heard a sincere, genuine apology. Johnna didn't. She refused to believe it and tossed it aside, saying, "You're just trying to play me for a fool." The mediation ended without the apology's being accepted. The employee was allowed to go on administrative leave for two weeks with pay and then resign. While an agreement was reached to address the tangible concerns that were raised, the hurts between the two lived on. Afterwards, Johnna talked to the mediator: "I got what I wanted but it doesn't feel good."

The mediator asked, "Was there something that you needed

that you did not get, or was there anything offered that you did not accept?"

Johnna didn't answer. A few days later, Johnna sent the mediator an e-mail. "Now, I understand what you meant when you asked 'Was there something I was offered and did not accept?' There was, and now I have accepted it." She went on to say that she was ready to write her boss to say thank you, and that she, too, would apologize.[1]

Time to Process Feedback

When someone criticizes you or your work, take time to think about what you have heard before you respond. Criticism and complaints often sting, so our first reactions are usually defensive. We swing into retort mode: self-justifications, or shifting the blame to somebody or something else, or making a joke out of it, or making assumptions about their negative intentions. We'll do anything to keep from taking in the words and processing them, thinking about them, deciding which ones we want to keep and which we'll throw away. But this is where significant change can occur if we let it. Allow yourself time to respond.

Few of us have the grace to say "thank you" in the face of criticism, but thank you may be just what is in order. "Thank you for letting me know." "Thank you for coming to

Never be afraid to sit awhile and think.
—Lorraine Hansberry

me with this information." In other words, "Thank you for giving me the opportunity to improve." Or that noxious phrase, "Thanks for sharing." Then you back away from the conversation to consider what has been said. Is it true? How much of it is true? How much of this is about me? How much might be about the other person?

Keep in mind that your most objectionable traits are the ones about which you may be the most defensive.

Grieving Takes Time

Most of us are familiar with the five stages of grief when dealing with death and dying: denial, anger, bargaining, depression, and finally acceptance. They go something like this:

Denial: "This can't be happening." "It can't be true."

Anger: "How can this happen to me?" "It's not fair!" "Whose fault is this?"

Bargaining: "Just give me one more chance."

Depression: "I just can't go on."

Acceptance: "All right, then. It is what it is. I can handle it."

Elizabeth Kübler-Ross introduced us to these stages and refined her understanding as she worked with people through terminal illnesses. She pointed out that people don't always go through these stages in linear, one-through-five order. Some will only go through two or three. Others will loop back through some of these stages several times over many years.

We go through these stages when we face all kinds of losses, not just loss of life. You can see this in so many situations in the workplace: the promotion she didn't get, a lower evaluation than he expected, the loss of teammates during a reorganization, a difficult conflict with a peer, an uncomfortable reprimand. The ups and downs of life always bring losses, as well as gains. The grieving process is how we work through those losses.

What can we do with this information? We can allow ourselves and others time and space to grieve when bad news comes, rather than demanding a "happy face" as an immediate response. We can realize that most people will work through these stages and arrive at acceptance. For example, if someone is angry, give the person some time to live through that feeling and to cool down. It is okay to have those feelings and work through them without the anger controlling the outcome. If someone is depressed, listening to the individual may be helpful. Telling or expecting him or her to simply cheer up will not do it. To give up these feelings can also be a loss that may require letting go—and grieving.

. . . .

Ben, a man in his sixties, had filed an EEO complaint against his employer. He claimed discrimination against him due to his age, race, and religion. From the agency's point of view, he had been given every chance—he had been on three Individual

Development Plans (IDPs)—and the agency was increasingly frustrated with his job performance, or lack of it.

The agency representative came to the mediation with a new offer: The agency would give him a "clean record"—they would raise all his performance ratings from minimally successful to highly successful, remove all references to the performance plans, and give him a neutral letter of recommendation. In return, he was asked to withdraw his complaint, resign or retire, and never apply for another position with the agency. Everyone else at the meeting, including his attorney, considered this a sweet deal. To everyone's amazement, Ben said no—and not just no but "Hell, no!" He then turned and fired his attorney.

On reflection, the mediator realized what was missing. (Even mediators need a little time to think.) Ben had just returned from burying his brother, aged seventy-two. He had mentioned it ever so briefly during the discussion. Everyone present already knew about this—the mediation had been postponed so that he could attend the funeral. Ben was dealing with loss: the loss of his brother, the loss of his career, his loss of status. The mediator asked himself the question, *Why would a reasonable, rational, logical person turn down such an offer from the agency? What was it that I missed?*

In an instant, the mediator understood. What was never given time or space in this meeting was all of the losses Ben was dealing with. The agency's offer did nothing to address his multiple sense of loss. The discussion had been all about the tangibles of severance. In the mediator's words, "In the rush to settle, the emotional reality was never dealt with. I believe that had we taken time to address the loss issue we may have been closer to a real resolution."

. . . .

Time as a Face-Saving Tool

In the previous example, the two parties had dug into their positions. One was adamant in his demand. The other refused to budge. They had each held their position so loudly and for so long that neither can back down without feeling defeated. They are stuck, committed to being stuck and staying stuck.

Admitting you may be wrong, allowing another person's needs or opinions or demands any latitude of acceptability, can be really difficult. Giving in feels like losing. So, I usually call a break: "Let's come back after lunch" ... or maybe tomorrow. It still surprises me how often, when they have had the chance to withdraw, even for a short break from each other, the parties to a dispute come back to the next meeting ready to move on. Those brain chemicals I mentioned in the last chapter have had time to dissipate. One side will say, "I've thought about it, and in the interest of moving forward I'm willing to offer. . . . " The break has given them both time to reconsider. And time to find the words that allow them both to change their minds without losing face.

Time to Check It Out

Decision making in an organization takes time. The bigger the organization, the longer it can take to make decisions. Earlier in the book, I described midlevel managers as the "knees" of the organization, absorbing the pressures from staff and managing the expectations of those above. When managers are making decisions for the company or in any bureaucracy, everyone needs to allow time for the decision-making process to move up the chain, with your own boss and sometimes between your boss and her boss. The more layers that need or expect to have some authority in decision making, the more time this will take. The bigger the question, and the more complex the decision making, the longer it will take.

. . . .

Headquarters was installing new software for case tracking. Rudy's office, intimately involved in all issues regarding case tracking, was in direct line for lots of confusion and questions from other offices. While he did have a budget for training his staff and the authority to allocate it as he saw the need, these new demands were more than the training budget could accommodate. Rudy met with his boss to get the additional funding. His boss, Jessica, said, "I'll get back to you." At the same time she was also juggling multiple demands for her time from her own boss and from other departments. While Rudy waited for an answer, his employees were also impatient, waiting for some word from him.

. . . .

Employees sometimes become irritated because they cannot see the many levels of decision making that are required to get a final answer, even on what seems to be a fairly obvious need. People who don't have this understanding of the decision-making chain may think that the boss is stonewalling or being indecisive, when in fact he or she has done everything possible and is waiting for others higher up to respond. The boss's job at this point may be to manage the staff's expectations about how much time the decision may take.

The Right Time

Here's something else to think about: when is the right time to raise an issue or discuss a difficult topic? Sometimes the force is almost overwhelming. You have had a thought and you are bursting with energy to address it right now. What do you do?

Slow down and think first. Where are they? What might they be in the middle of, or on their way to? If the other person is working on a project or against a deadline, now is not the best time to talk. Maybe he hasn't had a cup of coffee yet. Maybe she's not a morning person. Or maybe she is. Or is it right before he's about to head out the door for lunch or at the end of the day? You simply won't have the attention that you want or that the topic deserves if the person involved is too preoccupied and can't take in the information and respond.

Maybe you've got an issue with an employee and you decide to raise it at the staff meeting. Putting someone on the spot in the middle of a meeting is no way to get a reasoned, reasonable discussion going. You are just about guaranteed a negative response—defensiveness, counterattack—or no response at all. Embarrassing someone in a meeting is a setup for disaster. Maybe you know what I mean because this has happened to you. No, you are likely to have a much better response if you mention it when the time is right—if it's at a time that works for others' schedules as well as your own.

This advice applies to information going in the other direction, as well. If someone storms into your office with a blast on an issue, step back a moment. Is this something that requires an immediate response? If it's a life-or-death question, the answer is yes. If it's not, in most cases you can set a time to talk that works for your schedule and for the other person's, a time that will allow each of you to think more calmly about the matter at hand. Maybe you want to sleep on that last point. (There is more on this in Chapter 13.)

Note

1. Thanks to Michael West for this story.

PART IV

Putting It All Together

If you don't know where you're going, any road will do.

—Lewis Carroll

Reaching Agreement: A Solution-Seeking Model

I n Chapter 10, I began to tell a story involving my youngest son, Eric, and his request that I co-sign a loan so he could buy "the *coolest* 1979 Camaro." When I responded with an instant "No!" we were suddenly in a heated argument ending with "You just don't love me!"

At that point, Eric knew we were stuck. So did I. With a huffy, "I'll talk to you later," he slammed the door on his way out. Shaken, I headed back down to my office, asking myself, "How did that happen?" Blindsided again. This predicament had perplexed me for years. How could this child of mine, so unspeakably dear to my heart, still catch me in these angry tangles? Shouldn't I know better?

Yet, how quickly we can get locked into a positional argument. He opened the discussion with his position, his answer to the question, "a 1979 Camaro." My instant response was my position —no. What people often do from that point is to argue over their positions, just as Eric and

I did. The longer we talk, the more we dig in, each holding on to being right. Both parties are fearful of losing something; in my case, I feared losing money and time, and Eric (I speculate here) feared losing his dream. Unfortunately, this is the point at which many people start dealing with a problem—at the end. By stating their positions, they are effectively saying "Here is the answer!"

Fortunately, our story didn't end there. Half an hour later, I was back at my desk working when my phone rang. It was Eric. He had called me from another phone line in the house.

"Mom, can we talk? Will you agree to listen to me?" By this time the adrenaline had dissipated in my own brain. "Yes. I'll try, if you'll try to listen to me." Guidelines (or ground rules) had been established—he really knew a lot about resolving conflicts—so we launched into another, very different conversation. And now we were listening, trying to understand each other and find some way forward, beyond our initial, rigid positions.

Remember, almost everyone loses his or her cool sometimes, even when the person should know better. But with a solution-seeking model, such as described next, you can still achieve a mutually satisfactory resolution.

A Four-Step Process

Figure 13-1 shows a solution-seeking model with a four-step process: prepare, discover, consider, and commit. I go through these steps in detail, and apply them to the workplace. But, first let's watch them unfold with the Camaro.

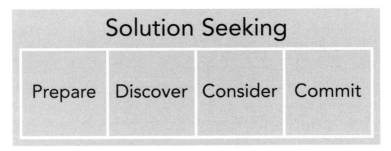

Figure 13-1. A solution-seeking model.

▶ *Prepare*: When Eric said "Will you agree to listen to me?" and I responded, "Yes, I'll try, if you'll listen to me," we established a straight-forward guideline (or ground rule) for our discussion.

▶ *Discover*: The problem, as we argued over it in the kitchen, was whether I would co-sign a loan for that 1979 Camaro. During the tele-phone call, the matter to be resolved was broadened to whether I could help Eric get a car and if so, how. In that phone call, we never used the term *interests*. But what we really had was an *interest*-based discussion, whereby each of us talked about what was important to each of us and why.

- -

Eric's independence was important to him—and the coolness factor really mattered. At the time, I was driving a ten-year-old Honda Accord, and Eric was clear. "I'm not going to get a Honda Accord, Mom." He also loved working on cars, and want-ed something he could tinker with.

For me, the matter was partly about the money. With Eric as the youngest, I already had experience co-signing loans. One thing I knew was that, whatever happened down the road, I would still be responsible for the debt. If the car bit the dust, the loan would live on. I was also concerned about safety. A parent of an eighteen-year-old has to give up a lot of the ways we can protect children when they are younger, but a car that is safe and some-what reliable does provide some added sense of safety.

- -

▶ *Consider*: As we listened to each other, we began to find ways we could reach some common ground. I, too, was interested in his inde-pendence—I didn't want to be tied to hauling him around or to juggle his schedule with mine so he could use my car. And I trusted his driving habits more than any of his friends'.

▶ *Commit*: Finally, we reached an acceptable solution: I would co-sign a loan for a limited amount, on the condition that Eric first have any car he picked out inspected by an independent mechanic (someone we would both agree on). This relieved some of my concern about the safety and reliability of the car, and some concern about the soundness of the loan. And Eric knew what he could count on from me as he looked for a car. (Eric bought a 1989 Mustang instead, after it passed the inspection, and we went to the bank. Our solution met enough of his interests and enough of mine to be acceptable to both of us.)

Why Use a Model?

Holding the solution-seeking model in your mind can help you slow down the decision-making process. When the temptation is to jump to a solution, the first rule is to *stop*. Before you jump to a discussion or rush to a conclusion, consider what you need and how you can get there most effectively.

Go slow to go fast. In this model, more time and attention is paid to the first two stages, Prepare and Discover, than to the last two stages. Most often, you will find that paying attention at the beginning has payoffs in the end stages. Not only will you reach a more sustainable solution but that solution will usually emerge more easily.

The second rule of this model is: Keep an open mind. That is, keep an open mind to what the other side may be concerned about. Keep an open mind also about what may be in your own best interest. Keep an open mind about what possible options might exist. This book provides guidance on resolving conflicts with others, focused on manager-staff disagreements. Often, building solutions by working together with employees creates more lasting and effective solutions. There are occasions, though, when the manager may have the authority to make a unilateral decision and is willing to live with the consequences of taking that approach. When you need their cooperation to implement decisions, consider using this approach.

To understand this model and be able to use it, consider each step in turn.

Prepare

As you *prepare* to take on a difficult conversation, consider how to conduct a discussion during which each person can participate effectively. Here are some questions to answer before the meeting.

PREPARE

► *What* the issue is.

► *Where* to talk.

► *When* to talk.

► *How* to make it "safe."

► *Who* needs to be included.

What Is the Issue?

Identify first the problem(s) to be solved or issue(s) that needs to be resolved. This step is key! The clearer you are about the purpose of the discussion, the better prepared everyone will be and the easier it will be to keep the conversation on track. Your notion that there is a problem, or your initial idea about what the problem is, will often be quite limited until you can hear from the others what their perspective is. That said, narrowing the focus of the discussion by providing a general common objective will allow people to be more prepared to participate.

> *If you don't know where you are going, any road will take you there.*
> —LEWIS CARROLL

An issue should be defined in neutral terms—without a built-in answer or bias toward one view or the other. The beginning of the discussion will be to define and clarify the issue. A careful dialogue here can change both the direction of the discussion and the outcome. Establish agreement on the issue to be discussed. Be clear, as well, about what the conversation is *not* about. Other issues may need attention, but not at this time. Consider, also, what is important to you regarding the relationship, as well as the issue at hand. What might be the consequences of *not* finding a mutually acceptable solution?

. . . .

When Serena sat down to complete her weekly report, she did not have the information from Jack. His report was due to her by close of business on Thursday, so that she could roll his report into hers, which was due on Friday. This was the third time in a month that Jack had not submitted his report on time. Before talking to Jack, Serena needed to be clear: Would this conversation be about what happened with this week's report, or about his pattern of late reports? Intentionally separating the two topics would enable Serena and Jack to focus their attention and appropriately address the issue at hand.

Serena sat down at her desk. Her shoulders tightened as she grabbed the phone. When Jack answered, Serena demanded that he come into her office immediately. In less than a minute, Jack was standing in front of her desk. "What do you need?"

She launched into, "It's Friday afternoon and I have to get that report out before I leave! Why didn't you get yours to me?"

Jack began to respond, "I had it on my computer and …"

Serena interrupted, "This is the third time this month you have been late. This is unacceptable. What is your problem?"

Jack became defensive. "I tried to tell you…" Before they knew it, they were in an argument about who said what to whom, and when.

. . . .

Now, consider the replay.

. . . .

Serena sat down at her desk to prepare the weekly report. When she discovered that Jack's information wasn't there, she felt the tension rising in her shoulders. In response, she paused a moment to inhale, taking a couple of conscious breaths. Somewhat calmer, she picked up the phone and asked Jack to come into her office. In less than a minute, Jack was standing in front of her desk. "What do you need?"

"Jack," she began, "I have to have the information from your report and I have not received it. I'd like to find a way to resolve this. Help me understand why the report hasn't been filed."

. . . .

She recognized that she needed a better understanding of why she had not received the report before the two of them could agree on the issue and begin to find a solution. It was possible, for instance, that there were technical problems in the e-mail system, or maybe Jack had to wait for information from someone else. Rather than make assumptions,

Serena asked for more information first. She also knew that the other question, about the pattern of late reports, must be addressed in a separate discussion.

The two had a conversation about the transfer of information through the system from his computer to hers. They then began to resolve the problem rather than make accusations or justifications, without piling on other issues.

Consider This

☑ Think of a recent disagreement with which you have been involved. State the issue that you needed to resolve. Is the language neutral, not assuming fault on one side or the other? Is an answer embedded in the question?

☑ If the answer to either question is yes, state the issue again in neutral terms that do not imply one solution.

Where Can We Talk?

To have a productive conversation, both parties have to have a safe place where they can listen, think, and respond. Standing on the shop floor, or at the copy machine, or at the counter in front of others is not the place to exchange thoughts, ideas, opinions, and concerns when the issue is significant. If you are in the middle of a meeting and harsh words are spoken, or a delicate issue is raised, wait until after the meeting to discuss it further.

Find a place that is private, where others will not be drawn in and where neither person will be embarrassed. When someone—boss, employee, customer, peer, anyone else—is embarrassed, he or she will often get defensive. A person who is defensive will spring into "fight or flight" mode. Some will escalate the exchange into an argument, some people will shut down, and some others will look for a way to get even. While many of us get defensive, others seem to enjoy the drama, performing for an audience of onlookers. Sometimes a person seizes the opportunity to create a difficult moment *because* there are other people there to watch the show. Other times, it just happens—without even realizing it, one person brings up a sensitive topic in the middle of the group and another reacts. In either case, the public space does not lend itself to a productive conversation.

Also, look for a place that is neutral and away from the distractions of e-mail and phone. Staff members may feel intimidated in the boss's office. The power that the desk conveys is real. And when one person uses a power play to impose his or her will, others are less likely to participate or to support the decision in the long run.

Sometimes a "safe place" means that you need to have a conversation, the two of you, alone. At other times, for a variety of reasons—for instance, if there is a history of emotional or even physical outbursts—there is more safety if you have another person present. That other person may be helpful by providing support to one person or another, managing the discussion so that each can hear the other, and providing expert advice or information.

Think strategically about the discussion beforehand. If another person can be helpful to the conversation, who might an acceptable person be? You will need someone you both trust, someone who will keep the conversation confidential, who will not take sides, who will keep you on an even keel and on point, and who will help you to hear each other. Sometimes this person is within the organization. This may be your own manager, or a co-worker or colleague. Sometimes the HR department may provide an acceptable alternative. Sometimes when the trust is low, the tensions and stakes are high, you may need to look outside the organization for professional help to have a safe, facilitated discussion.

When Do We Talk?

Find the right time to talk, allowing enough time to say what needs to be said, to hear what the other person has to say, to ask questions and clarify, and to reach an acceptable solution. Set up a time when both of you can give the conversation sufficient focused, dedicated attention. You need time to question assumptions and clarify intent, rather than leaping to conclusions and snapping back responses.

If someone catches you in the hall as you are headed into an important meeting, the person is likely to get a curt response. If someone comes into your office at 2 P.M., and you are working on three deadlines that are due before you leave for the day, the person is not going to get a fair hearing. If an employee is about to walk out the door for his long anticipated vacation, don't hand him his annual performance review. In short, before you can talk things through, both of you must be in a place where you can take information in and process it.

To find the right time, suggest something like, "I really want to hear what you have to say, but I simply can't right now. When is a time that works for you and for me so we can talk this over?" Acknowledging the other person's concern says a lot to that person about your interest and intention. Promising dedicated, focused time makes the other feel his or her views are respected and worthy of consideration. Note: This approach works only if *you* are reliably responsive; if each time you make this proposal to have a conversation, you return to it later. You have to keep your word.

How Can I Make it Safe?

People need clear expectations about how they will talk—and listen—to one another. We need the safety of guidelines; we need explicit expectations for behavior.

. . . .

Near my home, the county built a water park. Depending on how you look at it, it's great fun for a hot summer afternoon or a large hole in the ground filled with hazards. First, there is the water. Then, there are four slides of various heights, a couple of goofy water toys—a twenty-foot plastic snake, a bobbing donkey—two obstacle courses, various fountains, and some inner tubes and floats. Now, add hundreds of human bodies. We are talking about real danger from the other bodies and from the equipment to anyone daring to jump in. Before the county public works department trucked in bulldozers and earthmovers to begin digging this hole, they started making plans for how to keep the facility safe.

All around the grounds are signs posting the rules. Circling the edges of the pool are lifeguards wearing whistles and carrying buoys and floats. On a crowded afternoon, those whistles are blasting every minute or so. Every two hours, all the whistles blow, the splashing stops, everyone climbs out of the pool and sits on the edge for five minutes. It's in the rules. We all play by the rules because they keep us safe. That means we can keep swimming and no one drowns.

. . . .

How did they get started on that project? First, they identified what the hazards and risks were, and what made them dangerous. Then, they set up systems and plans to manage and minimize those risks, and handed out whistles. When I describe my work as a mediator, this is what I often tell people that I do: I create a safe place for a difficult conversation.

Understanding what fears and concerns the parties of a dispute may have about working with one another—that is, that their words will be twisted or used against them, that they will be insulted or threatened, that one or another will lose their temper or shut down—I help them establish a few guidelines to reduce their fears. Frequently, the tone of the discussion then shifts dramatically because they have these guidelines. They begin to trust the guidelines. By the end of the meeting, they are wondering why they needed my help at all—which I think is a really good thing.

These guidelines can be brief. If the discussion involves only two or three people, the rules need to be stated out loud and agreed to by everyone involved; then they can hold themselves and are each accountable to the others. Consider these steps for setting guidelines:

1. Identify the issues to be discussed.
2. Decide the time frame for the meeting.
3. Clarify how the discussion will be shared or not with others.
4. Clarify how decisions will be handled at the end. (Will they be written down? Will they be used as a recommendation for others to ratify?)
5. Suggest that one person speak at a time, that the emphasis be on listening.
6. State a positive intention to work together to find a solution.
7. State a positive intention to respect differing views, allowing each person to complete his or her thoughts without interruption.
8. Set an expectation that each person speak from his or her own perspective.

9. Suggest that each person trust that the other is telling the truth from his or her point of view.

Who Needs to Be Included?

Give conscious thought to *who* should be involved. This includes people who will be affected by your decisions, by your agreement or lack of agreement, and who may need to ratify decisions. There may be people you need to get additional information from—upper-level management, co-workers—or others who will implement any decisions arising from this agreement. But be careful with these conversations; you do not want to draw others into the conflict, making your case so they will take your side. That can be a sure trust wrecker.

. . . .

Suppose my boss wants to talk to me about my performance on that project. I am wondering: Who else will he talk to about this? Has he talked to anyone in HR, or to his boss? Is he going to talk to other people on the team about what he thinks I should have done?

Maybe the project, the scope of work, and the task assignment need to be addressed through a full team discussion. I want a one-on-one conversation about *my* part in it, separate from the rest of the group. Maybe the boss needs to keep HR informed. Are there others who will need to implement our decisions? This may be as simple as asking someone to reserve a room for our next meeting. Let me know that—and how that will be discussed.

. . . .

To create a safe place for a productive discussion, clarify who is involved and how they are involved, who will need to be informed, and how each of us will communicate with others outside of the discussion.

What About a Crisis?

Sometimes supervisors and managers find themselves in a crisis situation, in which they do not have the luxury of time to think through all of these aspects of planning and

Art resides in the quality of doing, process is not magic.

—CHARLES EAMES

preparation. Holding these concepts in mind, calming yourself as you enter the discussion, may be all that you can do. Even in those times, these ideas can be helpful. For instance, remembering to pull an individual off to the side for a quick conversation can help turn the exchange into a more positive one.

. . . .

R ecently I witnessed the solution-seeking model put into action at the spur of the moment. We arrived early one morning at a local hotel for a meeting. Following the signs to the meeting room, we discovered we had been assigned to a space barely larger than a closet. There would be twelve people in this room, for *three days*. Clearly, there had been a serious miscommunication between the hotel conference staff and the person on our side responsible for room arrangements.

I watched Kenneth approach the front desk, identify the person with authority (the *who* question) to make room assignments, and conduct an interest-based discussion to find a possible, though not ideal, solution. He described the matter to be resolved: adequate space for the number of people attending the meeting, not digressing into who was at fault or how the mix-up had occurred (the *what* question). The *where* and *when* questions were already answered: here and now. His own behavior and tone of voice established the model for everyone to follow, demonstrating by example the answer to the *how* question.

. . . .

Consider This

For a conflict you have recently been involved in:

- ☑ Was the discussion in a private, neutral space? If not, where could you have met instead?
- ☑ Was adequate dedicated time allotted to resolve the issue? Or was it done on the run?
- ☑ What guidelines could have helped make the discussion more productive?

Discover

People often begin a conversation about some disagreement by stating their positions—that is, they give their answers or solutions to their perceptions of the situation. For the earlier example of the missing report, that would be Serena's "Jack, bring that report to me right now." Or in the Camaro story, "Co-sign a loan for that 1979 Camaro." As a mediator, my response is "Well, that is one solution. Before we get there, let's understand the situation better."

In the Discover stage, each person is learning, gathering new information, and understanding the other's perceptions and perspectives. Now, it is time to listen, listen, listen first, and then talk, talk, talk.

DISCOVER
- ➤ Share perceptions.
- ➤ Explore the issues.
- ➤ Identify interests.
- ➤ Consider criteria.
- ➤ Avoid talking about solutions.

Share Perceptions

Begin with sharing perceptions. Explain what you have observed or experienced. Ask the other person to describe his or her own observations or experience of the situation. For example, in the scenario between Serena and Jack, the replay had Serena open the discussion with, "I have to have the information from your report and I have not received it." That was a simple description of what had happened from her point of view. Then she asked for Jack's perspective: "I'd like to listen to your perspective."

Explore the Issue

Use this time to "peel the onion," to remove each layer and consider it, to explore the complexity of the issue. In virtually every disagreement, each person involved has had some part in creating the difficulty. Listening and exploring, and explaining, enables each of you to recognize what the conflict is about and the ways in which it is important to each of you. Focus your attention first on understanding these elements. Digging deeper into this discussion allows you to define the problem more appropriately. After you both thoroughly understand the issue, only then can you begin to talk about possible solutions. If you move to suggesting solutions too quickly, you may miss important points that will inform acceptable solutions, and you may limit the possibility of solutions not yet considered.

For example, digging deeper into the problem of the late report from Jack, Serena may discover that the issue to be solved is: (1) Jack's lack of understanding of the importance of his report; or (2) a glitch in the e-mail system (I sent the report at 4:30 yesterday. I don't know why you didn't receive it); or (3) Jack has to get the numbers from Cathy, and she doesn't respond to Jack's voicemails; or (4) there was a medical emergency at home yesterday afternoon; or (5) Jack's interest in and motivation for his job is flagging; or (6) Jack was confused about the deadline; or (7) any variety of other possibilities. Each of these reasons will lead in a different direction for finding an appropriate solution.

Identify Interests

The phrase "interest-based negotiation" was made popular in Roger Fisher and Bill Ury's book *Getting to Yes.*[1] Over the years, the concept and the language have been adopted across the field of negotiation and conflict resolution. Identifying and understanding interests can open the conflict to more possibilities for resolution. The term "interests" refers to what is important to each person in the conflict—what are each person's underlying concerns, desires, and motivations that relate to the conflict and its resolution.

In a conflict, a person often has several interests in play. The more each knows about the various interests the other has, the more tools each party has to find an acceptable solution. Some of these interests may be readily apparent, while others require deeper exploration to discover. Across a dispute, two people may have mutual or complementary interests in finding a solution. Or they may discover that they have mutually exclusive or competing interests that will need to be addressed. For example, if each person wants the same week off—one to attend a family reunion, the other to take advantage of a special offer on a cruise, their interests are competing. Another way will need to be found to arrive at an acceptable solution.

There is a difference between a party's interests and its position, as shown in Table 13-1.

Table 13-1

POSITION	INTERESTS
A proposed solution to an issue, a demand	*Concerns, desires, underlying needs, or motivations*
➤ Focuses on a particular solution	➤ Focuses on problems, questions
➤ Makes a demand	➤ Articulates one of a range of needs
➤ Sets up confrontation before the problem has been clearly defined	➤ Establishes a climate and a common language for discussion so that the real issue or problem can be understood, discussed, and resolved
➤ Designed for bargaining, compromise	

. . . .

Consider a simple real estate transaction. Sammy wants to buy the house, Sara wants to sell it. One of Sammy's interests is the price—he wants to purchase the house for the lowest possible cost, keeping his mortgage payments as low as possible. One of Sara's interests is also the price—she wants to sell it for the most money she can, to maximize the investment she has made. There are other interests that can play a significant role: Sara's house has already met several of Sammy's interests: it has enough bedrooms and bathrooms and a backyard for the dog.

Digging deeper into their interests, the agent discovers more. Sammy has two children and this house is in a good school district; that is important to him. It is mid-July and he wants to complete the transaction before the next school year starts. Sara has begun a new job in another city, and is now paying two mortgages while she looks for a buyer. Carrying two mortgages has drained

Sara's finances. She has a strong interest in not picking up additional costs. Sammy is on firm financial footing and is less concerned about the upfront costs than in having a prompt settlement. Each of these interests can help shape a position for the negotiation, eventually building a solution acceptable to both: agreement on a price, closing costs, and closing date.

. . . .

Sometimes we assume to know what the other person's interests are, and we act on what we think, avoiding doing the work of actually checking it out. Even if you guessed right, the exercise of asking and listening will ensure the other person that you know and understand his or her interests.

Consider

After a thorough exploration of the issue and the interests of each person involved in the conflict, you can then begin to consider possible solutions. Sometimes, through the Discover stage, obvious solutions emerge and at this stage, then, considering the options is not necessary or can be shortened.

> **CONSIDER**
> - ► Brainstorm options.
> - ► Establish criteria.
> - ► Evaluate options.

Brainstorm the Options

An open mind is particularly useful here. Brainstorm all of the options first. My colleague, Pete Swanson, told me once that his mother had a rule: There are always at least seven options. It seems that, growing up, he was pretty stubborn—at least his mother thought so. She gave him this advice: "Any time you feel stuck, consider what the Sufis said: in any situation there are always seven ways to look at it." He presses those he is working with to generate at least seven options before they begin to evaluate them. Relax and remember that they do not all have to be good or viable options. The intention here is to open up your thinking to a wide variety of possibilities.

When only one option exists, the situation feels hopeless—it's a take-it-or-leave-it solution. When there are two options, you are likely to get caught in a dilemma, back to arguing over which one of you will win and which one will lose. Often, when people develop a list of options, they can see that the first option is not the best choice—a prime motivator in moving past the first solution someone proposes, to see what else might be just around the corner in people's thinking.

Establish the Criteria

Criteria are standards by which decisions can be made. They are used to test or judge the options that have been brainstormed. Consider the interests of everyone involved, and from those interests, as well as any external constraints, identify the key criteria for judging or testing possible options. Establishing clear criteria based on interests can provide an open route to decision making and help to ensure the sustainability of the decision.

For example, in my conversation with Eric about a car, the criteria for an acceptable solution included providing Eric with independence in picking out a car, which for him meant one that met a certain "coolness" factor, as well as one that he could work on himself; and for me, it meant choosing a car that met my concerns for safety and reliability, and was within the financial limits that I had set.

Evaluate the Options

Once you have a healthy list of options and clear criteria for guiding your selection, evaluating those choices can become a pretty straightforward assignment.

The example below, applying the solution-seeking model, is a twist on a familiar complaint. In most instances I am familiar with, both people complain of being overworked. In this situation, that wasn't the case.

. . . .

Jose was fed up. It was time to tell his boss, Sabrina, how badly things were going. Sitting in the staff meeting, he explained, "It just isn't fair. Every new project that comes along gets put on my desk. And when Howard had trouble completing that report on time, you gave it to me to do."

Howard turned to Jose: "*You* think it's not fair. What about me? I used to be responsible for a lot. Every time I turn around, I've had another duty pulled away."

In the meeting, Sabrina did nothing. After it was over, she sent two e-mails. One to Jose said, "Make a list of projects you will hand over to Howard." And one to Howard said, "Make a list of projects you will take from Jose."

She seemed confused when the two men came back into her office, still complaining. Her "decision" had not decided anything. With her proclamation, she had avoided the issue instead of finding a solution. How could she use the Solution-Seeking Model to arrive at a more satisfactory answer?

First, prepare. They agreed on a time and a place to meet, with adequate time on everyone's calendar to be able to talk through the problem, to listen, and to find solutions. Sabrina reminded Jose and Howard to bring with them their lists of the projects they were currently working on.

Second, discover. Sitting down together, the three of them discussed the problem to be solved: how to balance the workload fairly between the two employees. Then they created a joint list of the projects each was working on. They talked through additional relevant information: What were the time frames for completion of these projects? Which were ongoing? Which were one-time assignments? How were projects interrelated? How much work remained to be done on each one?

Then, the three considered the interests of everyone involved: Jose was concerned about developmental opportunities. He also had strong computer skills and enjoyed the opportunity to use them. Howard wanted to see that the work was fairly distributed, and he really appreciated direct interaction with clients. What were Sabrina's interests? Getting projects completed on time, knowing that the work would be done at a level of quality that she did not have to revisit, responding to fewer complaints from customers, and being kept informed of progress and alerted when problems arise. The group also discussed the needs of external and internal customers.

Third, consider. The three generated several options for developing a fairly balanced workload:

- ► Identify specific skills needed for each project and assigning tasks according to skill sets.
- ► Divide one project for Jose, one for Howard, one for Jose, one for Howard.
- ► Divide the projects by client—these for Howard, those for Jose.
- ► Group the projects by the amount of time each will take, and then divide the short-term and long-term projects.
- ► Allow each to choose his own projects, taking turns.
- ► Turn the list over to Sabrina for her to make assignments.
- ► Put each project title on a separate piece of paper and draw assignments randomly (remember, they were brainstorming, even bad ideas are good).

Based on their earlier conversation, they revisited the interests they identified and discussed which were key criteria for an acceptable solution. Then they evaluated the brainstormed list against their criteria.

· ·

Commit

The final step in the solution-seeking model is commitment.

COMMIT

- ► Make commitments.
- ► Implement.
- ► Evaluate.

Make Commitments

After considering alternatives and evaluating options, both parties decide what the solution will be. At this point, what everyone has is an agreement. Giving it value depends on the willingness and desire of the parties to the conflict to follow through on the solution. Often, commitments that are written down. The more specific and clear they are, the easier they are to remember—and the more likely to be kept. Writing down the agreements provides a road map; it gives everyone an opportunity to focus on the details and realities of implementation.

Implement

Before ending the discussion, look over the decisions that have been made and clearly identify the next steps. Then assign responsibility for each of those steps, with deadlines. Establish a date to evaluate the decision and implementation plan.

Evaluate

Come back together to assess the decision, and revise those elements that may not be working as well as you had hoped.

I have found that the steps in this solution-seeking model are logical and easy to follow. You might discuss them with the people you manage, making the decision-making process more transparent. This can create a common language for everyone and set a tone that makes seeking solutions part of the culture of the workplace.

Note

1. Roger Fisher, William Ury, and Bruce Patton, *Getting to Yes: Negotiating Agreement Without Giving In*, 2nd ed. (New York: Penguin Books, 1991).

CHAPTER 14

Listening Is the Place to Start

This weekend I drove to Pittsburgh for a wedding. Cruising up the Interstate, I didn't know what was ahead for me when I would reach the city. For a stranger, Pittsburgh is a challenging maze of roads that twist around ridges and hills, crossing and re-crossing its well-known three rivers. Though I had written directions and an unwavering voice in the GPS system, finding my way to the hotel, to the church, to the reception, and back to the hotel became quite an adventure. Fortunately, when I packed for the trip I remembered to include an emergency supply of calm, an order of courage, and just enough curiosity to get me through the trip.

For a few panicky moments I lost that sense of calm when I set off in the wrong direction. Before I knew it, I was across a bridge, wandering in a strange—and not too friendly looking—neighborhood. Intentionally steadying my thinking, I took a gulp of courage and moved beyond my fears, trusting that by instinct and instruments I would find my way back. Then I activated my curiosity as I scanned each intersection for clues that I could connect with the instructions from the map guidance system.

Arriving safely home, I recognized how similar this experience was to the exploration that is called *effective listening*. Effective listening is really a journey into another person's world: what someone else believes, what someone else thinks, knows, and cares about; what makes that person anxious or annoyed or eager or excited.

Listening is the single most important and powerful tool you can use to resolve a contentious issue or repair an awkward working relationship. And it is particularly difficult to do in disagreements, arguments, and conflicts, when you may not be eager to hear the person who is disagreeing with you. The boss who *listens* to employees is held in high regard.

What Keeps Us from Listening?

How many things on the following list make listening hard for you to do? Check all that apply:

- ▶ Your own thoughts—about other projects you are working on, other problems you are trying to solve, other activities you are looking forward to.

- ▶ Your reactions to what the speaker is saying—your judgments, your opinions.

- ▶ Defensiveness—wanting to be seen as being right.

- ▶ Anxiety that others might find fault with you.

- ▶ Impatience about time—how long is this going to take? How can you get to the end of this discussion as soon as possible so you can get on to the next task?

- ▶ The topic—is boring, or it's too complicated.

- ▶ Insecurity—you don't know the answer to the question being raised.

- ▶ Difficulty hearing or paying attention—because the speaker has an unusual accent, or talks too softly, or too loudly, or too quickly or slowly.

- ▶ Biases—because you have had interactions with this person before that didn't go well.

▶ You don't like the person.

▶ You don't trust the person.

▶ External distractions—other conversations, the alert beep from the computer announcing new messages, other noises in the building.

▶ Reactions to "trigger words"—words or phrases that our brains cannot or will not process, that set us off.

Many of us, at one time or another, would check every item on that list, and maybe a few that are not listed. Sometimes certain words particularly set us off. What are your trigger words—words that block your ability to hear the content of what another person is saying? For example, triggers may be "you people," "you never..." "you always..." "the girls in the office."

Add to that list of listening challenges the bad habits we have become comfortable with over the years and we've let become obstacles that keep us from listening to what another person is saying. These habits are often easier to spot in others than to recognize in ourselves. Has anyone ever done any of these to you?

▶ Helping you finish your sentence when he is certain he *knows* what it is you wanted to say.

▶ Listening just long enough to grasp a piece of context from your conversation that she can connect to something of her own experience. Suddenly the discussion has shifted from your concern to "That reminds me of the time I...."

▶ Jumping in with a solution or advice, "Why don't you just ..."

▶ Looking around the room or over your shoulder while you are talking.

These interruptions make the other person sense you are not listening. They also complicate your ability to listen to what the person is saying. Calming your own thinking sometimes requires you to catch yourself, just as you are on the edge of interrupting, and remind yourself that your first task is to listen.

Listening is not about answering. When you are really listening, you are not thinking about what you are going to say as soon as they quit talking. When you are listening, you are not carrying on a dialogue in your own head: what he ought to think about this; what she should have done; how he is wrong about this or that; how it is her fault we got in this mess to begin with, how he talks too much, and so on.

Consider This
- ☑ In the next twenty-four hours, listen to yourself. Which of these habits do you exhibit?
- ☑ How often do you interrupt another person speaking?

Listening is a skill. It is an art. It is a discipline. It requires attention and practice. And it begins with awareness. How do you listen without being caught by the judgments, opinions, desires, justifications, and stories rumbling around in your own head? Before you learn about the tools and techniques a good listener can use, let's start where good listening starts: with attitudes and intentions.

The Three C's: Calm. Courage. Curiosity.

Being a good listener begins with having the right mind-set. First, keep your mind *calm*, then have the *courage* to step into the unknown, and then be *curious* about what the other person has to say.

Calm

The first step in being able to listen to others is to calm your own mind, to hit the pause button on all of the thinking that inevitably swirls around in your head. Research tells us that the human brain runs at about 400 words a minute, and the average speaker talks about 125 words a minute. Learning this was a great relief to me. It explains what most of us naturally do—insert our own thoughts into the spaces between another's words.

In a disagreement, we are

> *I've overflowed with my own ideas, with a variety of self-motivated feelings and I see clearly how my fullness undermines my ability to be present, how it erodes the possibility of availability.*
> —SUE MONK KIDD

often quite busy thinking about justifications for how right we are, or how wrong they are, or assigning blame, finding fault, and making hasty judgments of all kinds. Turning off that thinking takes conscious effort and attention. Slow down. If you are not calm, you will not be able to hear what the other person is saying.

Here are three steps to achieving a calm mind:

1. Fix your the intention to be calm; tell (or remind) yourself that your first responsibility is to hear what the other person is saying.
2. Take a few deep, slow breaths; this can help create that calm.
3. Consciously turn away from other thoughts when they intrude.

If all of your efforts to keep your mind calm and open are not working, do not pretend. If you *can't* hear because you are distracted or upset, find another time, or place, or way to talk. You don't have to rationalize it or explain it right here and right now. As calmly and clearly as possible, excuse yourself from the conversation. "I'll get back to you soon." "I am working on a tight deadline right now. Let's set up a better time to talk." "I need to take a break." "I can't hear you right now." Acknowledge your intention to listen, "We need to talk about this. Right now doesn't work for me."

Courage

For a manager who is receiving a complaint about a behavior or action, it takes courage to listen to a message you may not want to hear, to step into the unknown. It takes courage to admit that you may not have all the information or all the answers, or that you may be wrong. It takes courage to be willing to consider changing your mind or direction. Courage is not the absence of fear but, rather, the willingness to enter into an uncomfortable situation even in the face of fear. If someone is disagreeing with you, or blaming you, you may feel anxious, nervous, or even afraid. Having courage is being able to stay with a discussion when you may hear something you do not want to hear.

. . . .

When Hal went into the boss's office to express a concern about how the new contract was being administered, he had a few ideas about ways to improve the cost tracking. Since this was the first time the office had contracted out these services, the boss was anxious about how the process might work from the start. In response to her anxiety, she stopped Hal midsentence and called the contractor to register a complaint. If she had had the courage to listen to all that Hal had to say, he would have provided the answers that she needed. In her haste to fix the problem she perceived, she did not let Hal finish his explanation and she created more confusion.

. . . .

Curiosity

In a difficult conversation, becoming curious may not be your first response. However, if you calm your own thinking, and can hold onto your courage, you can listen with curiosity: What is she saying to me? Why does he think that? What is she upset about? What did she see that I didn't see? Even silence can be golden; it can allow others to gather their thoughts. Please note: There is a clear difference between *listening* to someone and *agreeing* with the person.

> There are many benefits to this process of listening. The first is that good listeners are created as people feel listened to. Listening is a reciprocal process—we become more attentive to others if they have attended to us.
> —MARGARET J. WHEATLEY

Why bother with this curiosity thing? For one, you will probably learn a lot about what people are thinking and why. For another, they will be much more ready and able to hear you if they have had a chance to unload what is on their own minds first.

CONSIDER THAT OTHERS:

- ► Think their views are well grounded.
- ► Want to do the "right" thing.

➤ Can see things that you miss.

➤ Miss things you can see.

What Are You Listening For?

Often, what a person starts out talking about may not be what an individual really wants to express. As listener, your calm demeanor, your patience, and your willingness to hear what is said will encourage him or her to say more. Listen for the expression of needs, beliefs, and expectations—things that are often below the surface of the original statements.

What do all people need? First, we need to be heard, to be taken seriously, to be respected. We need the simple acknowledgment that, yes, who we are and what we think matters, whether we are bosses or employees, managers and supervisors or staff. As you develop your own listening skills, this is the place to start. Then you can listen further to hear and understand the needs, concerns, expectations and interests of the person you are conversing with. If you can see something from another person's point of view, it is easier to identify common goals.

HOW TO LISTEN

1. Stop talking.
2. Get rid of distractions.
3. Don't judge prematurely.
4. Listen for key ideas.
5. Ask honest questions.
6. Paraphrase to confirm that you have heard the message.
7. Suspend your own thoughts.
8. Listen empathetically. Put yourself in the other person's shoes.
9. Trust that each person is speaking the truth from his or her own perspective.

The Listener's Tools

Here is a tool kit of skills for better listening.

LISTENER'S TOOLS

▶ Nonverbal

▶ Paraphrasing

▶ Asking questions

Nonverbal Listening

When we hear the word *listening*, we usually think of those funny, fleshy listening instruments protruding from the sides of our heads. But we listen with our eyes, as well. Most of the time, we are unconscious of this nonverbal listening ability. You need to practice being consciously aware of the visual information you are receiving and of the nonverbal communications you transmit when you are listening.

Albert Mehrabian conducted a series of well-known studies on communication, through which he developed what is now referred to as the "7-38-55 Rule."[1] Though we give considerable attention to words when we focus on listening, Mehrabian demonstrated that, on topics where we have emotional energy, most of our communication comes through nonverbally and through our tone of voice. Since this book is focused on conflicts, emotions are of prime importance in this communication. In our context, his studies carry significant weight. Here is a breakdown of the 7-38-55 Rule:

▶ About 55 percent of communication is relayed nonverbally. The way that a person punches the air for emphasis, or nods his head in agreement with his own words, or lifts an eyebrow communicates to the listener what he thinks about what he is saying. The woman who stands tall sends a message that she believes in herself and what she has to say. These nonverbal signals can be so subtle that you react to them even if you don't know that you have observed them.

▶ And 38 percent of communication is carried in a person's tone of voice. That is, the quality and resonance of the voice—sharp, piercing, soft, gentle, or firm; in the volume—loud or soft or somewhere in between; and in the pacing of the words—slow, deliberate, or staccato. As you read this, think of the variety of voice tones you might use to say "thank you," and the various meanings that may attach to those differences. For example, it is possible to say "thank you" in a tone of voice that does not mean thank you at all.

► A mere 7 percent of what we communicate on matters of some emotional weight is contained in the words themselves. To clarify, if the message you are sending is the time for the next meeting, or the technical data that were in the report, these percentages do not apply. In those communications, fully 100 percent of the message may be in the words themselves. When people are discussing more difficult issues, though, the importance of nonverbal and voice tone communication dramatically increases.

Consider This
- ☑ List as many examples of nonverbal communication as you can (e.g., smiling, frowning, arms crossed, and so on).
- ☑ Which of these nonverbal communications can have more than one meaning?

Some aspects of our nonverbal communication are universal. You can read the smile on the photo of a child a half a world away and see the joy that is there. Other nonverbal communication is learned, however, or is an expression of individual personality traits. In addition, there can be several interpretations to the look on a person's face or his or her body posture. This is where the old question comes in, "What does *that* look mean?"

Most of our nonverbal listening is unconscious, automatic. When you are *not* conscious of how you perceive the moment, however, you open the way for misinterpretations. You can easily place your own assumptions on the nonverbal communication you observe. Because you are often not conscious of your interpretations, your assumptions may be wrong about what others intend. Maybe he is not making eye contact because that intensity makes it difficult for him to think—or to hear. Maybe she is laughing because she is nervous, not because she finds the situation humorous. Maybe his arms are crossed because he is chilly. Maybe the scowl on her face is a response to the bad news she got last night. Maybe she is not smiling because she did not get enough sleep.

Eye contact—when it's appropriate, when it's not; the length of time; and all sorts of other variables—is learned within our families and cultures. Though my mother has been gone for many years, I can still hear her voice saying to a much younger me, "I'm talking to you, girl, look at me." The message was clear and repeated. Other children grew up in different types of homes and heard quite different messages about eye contact—that it is disrespectful, or rude, or suggestive. In a conversation, you may assume that another individual is not listening to you because of you own cultural assumptions. Are your assumptions accurate or not—how much do you really know?

. . . .

Thirteen people sat at tables around the classroom. For the last exercise of the day, the class had a complex game designed to demonstrate cultural differences, with an extensive list of instructions. While they listened to the tape that explained the rules, I watched the group. One young woman sat back in her chair with her arms folded, her eyes at half-mast.

I thought to myself, *Okay. We only have twelve participants. She has obviously checked out.* When the instructions ended, I turned to the class to see if they understood the directions. "Could someone remind us of the rules?"

This young woman, the one I decided was "checked out," repeated the instructions almost verbatim. Her words shook me out of my automatic assumptions. She had listened and retained information by closing out the distractions of the classroom.

. . . .

Nonverbal communication can give you considerable information about the speaker. However, it is possible to misinterpret what you see. Become attentive to what you are observing and to what you infer from what you see. This is easier to practice in low-stakes settings, where you are not on the spot to listen in a tense situation. Observe the people around you in meetings. Watch people in restaurants or airports or at the mall—not listening to their conversations but just observing their body language. See how much information you can gather about their emotions and attitudes. For instance, much of the humor on TV is nonverbal. Watch for it. In a restaurant, you can see the tentative communication of a couple out on a first date. You can pick up a couple's romantic interest as they look into one another's eyes and lean into one another. You can also see the couple who has been together far too long—looking past one another, looking at their plates, avoiding eye contact.

In a group, our focus is often on the speaker. Look around the room at others while someone is speaking. Nonverbal communication reveals significant information about how the speaker's words are being received.

Awareness of nonverbal communication is not only important in observing what others are communicating but also in being attentive to what you are communicating as a listener. Observe your own nonverbal communication. Do you lean forward? Make eye contact? Sit back with your arms folded? Look at your watch or your cell phone? Do you keep one eye on the computer monitor or someone else walking down the hallway when a colleague comes into your office to talk? Ask yourself, *Am I communicating what I want to communicate to this person about my willingness to listen?*

To listen fully to another, listen nonverbally. Turn away from the computer to face the person speaking. Make eye contact—not staring the individual down, but showing calm interest in who he is and what he is saying. You can hear better if you also attend nonverbally.

· ·

Graduate school for me was two nights a week—Tuesdays and Thursdays, from 4:30 to 10:00 P.M. This made going to school possible while working a full-time job. By the time the last class on Thursday night rolled around, most of us were exhausted and listening was a daunting task. Our ability to listen was further challenged by sitting in a classroom where the world's most boring professor delivered the lecture.

One Thursday night, a friend told me before the class, "I'm just going to look like I am listening." As I sat in my usual seat in the back of the room, I observed her. She sat in the front row, opened her notebook, made eye contact, and nodded at various points.

After class she said, "You know, the darnedest thing happened—he actually had something to say!"

. . . .

Listening with your body and mind signals to the speaker that you are, in fact, listening. And it can actually help you hear what is being said.

Paraphrasing

Paraphrasing, also known as mirroring, or reflecting, is restating in your own words what you have heard the other person say. This can be a powerful tool when emotions are running high. When you are sincerely trying to hear and understand what another person is saying, paraphrasing communicates that intention.

Paraphrasing well begins with time spent listening well: listening for content, feeling, meaning, and context. It is *not* simply repeating everything that the other person has said. It is hearing what is being said, distilling it, and identifying to the best of your ability the key points of the message, and then asking as a question, "Is this what you mean?"

Paraphrasing can also be useful in turning off your own thoughts. At the beginning of this chapter, I compared how fast people think to how fast they talk. If you commit to yourself, "Before I respond, let me make sure I've understood what she is saying," it will help you to push the pause button on your own thinking. It can help slow down your judgments, rebuttals, opinions, or justifications.

. . . .

As soon as Art set his tray on the table in the cafeteria, he launched into a tidal wave of words. "I can't believe that new schedule you posted this morning. I haven't had a day off in two weeks. I have been here weekends. When I think I am going to get a day off, something comes up and I've got to come in to cover for someone else. Give me a break!"

Jan's first thought was to tell him how short staffed they were, how the home office hadn't approved hiring any new staff for the last two months, how everyone was going to have to pull their weight until they could see daylight again. Fortunately, she caught herself midstream. "Before I respond, let me slow down and just listen to what he has to say."

When it sounded like Art was done, Jan paraphrased, "Wow. It sounds like you are really exhausted. And the new schedule doesn't give you any relief. Is that it?" Art's response was not what she expected. He then told her about the trouble he was having at home. His wife was sick and his son wasn't doing well in school. He acknowledged the difficulties the team had with staffing. "Everything just seems to pile on at the same time, you know?"

Jan realized that Art was not looking for an answer, for her to fix anything. He was, in fact, just blowing off some steam. Her paraphrase told him that she was willing to listen.

• •

Paraphrasing takes thought and practice. There is no cookbook answer about how you do it. There are, however, some helpful do's and don'ts.

Some Do's of Paraphrasing

▶   Do keep your voice tentative. "So, it sounds like you are concerned about when the decision will be made?" Ask if you have understood. If you *ask* a person about your understanding of what you are hearing, she will often tell you more. If you are wrong, she can easily clarify what she has said or what you have heard. "No, I don't think I provided enough information when I submitted my application." If you have captured what she has said, she will often tell you more. "Yes, I really want that position. There is another opportunity in another department I wonder if I should apply for." Or she may simply state with relief, "Yeah. That's it."

What a relief it is to finally be understood. If there were a disagreement hanging in the air, the energy for an argument often dissolves in that moment. The genie named and seen melts back into the bottle. The wind drops out of the sails. There are lots of metaphors here for this moment of magic. Once she knows that her message has been received, her mind is clearer. She now has room to hear what you are saying.

► Do include facts *and* feelings. "It sounds like you were disappointed you didn't get that assignment. Is that it?" The fact in this case—the person didn't get the assignment; the feeling was disappointment. It may be that the person never used the word *disappointed* but as you listened and watched him talking (the nonverbal communication), that seemed to be the emotion he was feeling. When you manage to paraphrase both the facts and the feelings, the speaker hears a powerful message—that you really have heard and are trying to understand what is being expressed. Often, you have helped the speaker understand as well what they are trying to express. Here are a few other feeling words that may capture negative emotions: *frustrated, anxious, upset.*

Some Don'ts of Paraphrasing

► Don't repeat everything the other person has said. Parroting back is not paraphrasing. Rather, paraphrasing is *distilling* what you have heard into the essence of what is important.

. . . .

A student recently told me about her frustration with paraphrasing. Here is how she described the incident: She was facilitating a high-level meeting at the Department of Defense. At each statement the general said, this student said, "So what I hear you saying is…." She repeated this time and again. The general in the meeting finally exploded: "Quit repeating every [expletive] thing I say." "Where did I go wrong?" she asked. Rather than paraphrasing a few key points to clarify her understanding, she was parroting everything the general said.

. . . .

► Don't simply say "I understand." "I understand" conveys nothing. You may think you understand, but what you understand may be totally different from what the speaker intends. "Oh, yes … I understand." When someone says that to me in the middle of a disagreement, my immediate reaction is, "You have no clue what is going on with me." Sometimes I hear this remark as simply a way to dismiss the topic. If, on the other hand, the other person takes the time and thought to say, "Here is what I think you are saying ..." I hear and appreciate the effort.

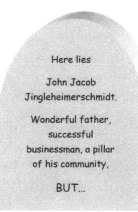

Here lies

John Jacob Jingleheimerschmidt.

Wonderful father, successful businessman, a pillar of his community,

BUT...

▶ Don't insert the word *but* at the end, as in "So, it sounds like you're disappointed that you didn't get that assignment, *but* you really don't have the skills that Joseph has." No longer are you trying to hear what the other is saying; you are now disagreeing, giving your side of the story, arguing your own point. The first task is to listen—to hear and understand what she is saying, before you respond to anything. *But* in the middle of a sentence negates everything that comes before it. *However* or *on the other hand* are just fancy ways of saying "but."

A word of caution: Using paraphrasing as a "trick" you learned in a communication class will often be heard as just that—a trick. People lose patience with someone who is toying with them, who is not sincerely trying to understand what they are saying.

Consider This

How would you paraphrase the following statements?

☑ *Situation*: The supervisor has passed on a change in work priorities from the top office.

Employee says: "This is the third time this month you have changed your priorities. I never know what you are going to want tomorrow. It's pointless to get started on this if you are just going to change it again."

☑ *An employee says to you*: "I wish I had *your* job. Every time I come to your office you are on the phone, while we have to do all the work."

☑ *Situation*: The employee is not implementing a supervisor's ideas.

Employee says: "I was on this job long before you came here. I don't need you to tell me how to do it."

Reflect on your paraphrases: Have you accurately captured the speaker's concern (content *and* feeling)? Did you include both the facts and the feelings they might be expressing? Did you avoid judgments or advice?

Asking Questions

The third skill in the tool box, Asking Questions is all about curiosity. I wonder what she is upset about? What happened? Why is he so mad? What made her smile? Why is he in such a good mood today? When we are listening with curiosity, we are listening for answers. Even if we have not verbalized a question, we are waiting to hear an answer.

Psychiatrist Bob Mauer says, "The mind can't refuse a question." What does the mind do with a statement? The mind can refuse to let a statement in, with a simple, "No, that is not the way it is." But a question causes the brain to stop and think, "How do I answer that?" When you are listening to someone and want to make a statement, pause and think, "How can I ask a question instead?" Often, asking a question may help open the dialogue. "How does that relate to our previous approach?" "Can you please help me understand?" "Would you be interested in my experience/perspective/thoughts?"

Practicing asking powerful questions enhances your ability to listen. Some questions give people an open invitation to share their thoughts; other questions are likely to put people on the defensive. "Why did you do that?" "Why did you think that was a good idea?" Questions that begin with *why* often leave people feeling that they are being grilled. You need to ask questions that encourage a person to open up, not questions that evoke an interrogation room.

Questions generally come in two categories: close-ended and open-ended. Closed-ended questions ask for a yes or no response or a specific, short answer. "What time did you get to work this morning?" is a closed-ended question, requiring a simple answer, as is "Did you call in sick?" There are times when close-ended questions give you the information that you need and may be appropriate. On the other hand, open-ended questions invite the responder to answer with a broad range of information. "What do you like about your job?" (an open-ended question) will give you more information than "Do you like your job?" (a closed-ended question).

In general, questions that begin with *what* or *how* or *why* invite more full responses. Questions are also embedded in your tone of voice. A lift on the end of the sentence can turn a statement into a question: "You thought I was disagreeing with you?" Be aware of the words you use, as well as your tone of voice when asking questions.

To open the conversation as much as possible, choose questions that are open-ended and use a nonconfrontational tone of voice. Then, to avoid the interrogation mode, ask yourself, "How would I react to the question I am about to ask?"

When you ask a question, wait for a response. Give the other person time to think, time to form an answer and to tell you. For some of us, this goes against our natural rhythms and responses. Our fear of silence is pounding in our ears. As soon as we ask the question, uncomfortable with any silence that may be hanging in the air, we rush to fill the void with our own answers, or maybe another question. The more comfortable you become with silence, the more apt you will be to practice listening and allow people to talk.

Types of Questions to Ask

- ➤ Clarifying questions: "I didn't understand what you meant by that phrase, 'loaded for bear.' Could you tell me more, please?"

- ➤ Digging deeper questions, to get more information: "What else happened that made you feel this way?"

- ➤ Questions that create doubt in the other's mind as to the viability of their positions. If we were to implement that suggestion, where would the money come from?

. . . .

Yolanda wanted to take several vacation days the following week. The company policy required that vacation days be requested at least two weeks in advance. When she asked her boss why he wouldn't bend the rules for her "just this once," he asked her a question, "How would the other staff feel if you didn't have to follow the rules and they did?"

. . . .

If you want to be a better listener, be curious. Consider: What do you know? What do you *think* you know? What do you know *really*? What do you not know? What would you like to know more about? Then think about asking questions that will help you to understand more.

Hearing a Complaint

Sometimes in a difficult conversation, the conversation comes around to the other person's views of you. She may have concerns or criticisms of actions you have taken. How do you respond? First, you listen. Consider what she is saying—give yourself time to mull it over. If you decide, after giving yourself a reasonable amount of time and energy considering her point of view, that the criticism is unwarranted, you may say so. If, on the other hand, you recognize that the criticism is fair, acknowledge it. Apologize, commit to improving, and even say "thank you" for giving you feedback that you needed.

Have the courage to hear a complaint. Begin by opening your thinking:

- ► Take a deep breath and remind yourself there may be something to learn here.
- ► Turn your back on win-lose thinking.
- ► View criticism as an opportunity for growth.
- ► Hear out the criticism without interrupting.
- ► Resist the temptation to launch a counterattack.
- ► Let the person know you understood by restating criticism in your own words. (This is *not* agreeing with the criticism but, rather, acknowledging what you heard.)
- ► Pay attention to both feelings and content.

Then, clarify what you have heard:

- ► Clarify what are facts and what may be perceptions.
- ► Clarify for yourself what harm was done and the emotional impact of your actions.
- ► Ask (with sincerity) what you could have done differently, and how it would have been better.

Most important, avoid:

- ► Shifting the blame for your actions to someone else.
- ► Justifying your actions.
- ► Making light of the situation.
- ► Attributing negative motives to the critic's actions.
- ► Distorting the complaint so you can dismiss it.

Listening takes energy, effort, and attention. There are no shortcuts. Learning to listen and to listen well takes practice over time. With patience, your skills will improve and your ability to resolve conflicts more easily will be remarkable. The rewards will be well worth the investment.

Note

1. Albert Mehrabian, *Silent Messages*, 1st ed. (Belmont, Calif.: Wadsworth, 1971).

CHAPTER 15

Saying What Needs to Be Said

S top. Right. There. Just as you are about to open your mouth. A barely audible voice—not loud enough for you to hear, but clear enough for you to feel, inside your own mind—is urging you on. You want to take action this very minute. You feel that you really *must* speak up. However, before you rush headlong into saying anything, there are some things for you to think about. If you want a productive discussion, think first about what you want to say and how you can say it.

Know Yourself First

Before you begin a conversation, give thought to your own needs and motivations, and possibly your own stumbling blocks. As a manager, everything you say carries added weight. A key to effective conflict management is analyzing your own situation and tendencies as objectively as possible. Ask yourself the hard questions and try to look at yourself from someone else's view.

Here are some questions to ask:

- What do I want or need in this situation? How does this concern fit into my short-term or long-term goals? How does it relate to the values that are most important to the organization?

- How important is this relationship to me or to the work we are doing?

- Consider the situation as it exists today. What about the situation bothers me the most? What is likely to happen if I take no action?

- What information do I need? What don't I know that I should know before I raise my concerns?

- If we fail to work this out, what are my options?

- How did I arrive at my viewpoint? What did I observe? How much of my concern is based on verifiable fact? How much is based on assumptions?

- What do I fear? What is the worst that could happen if I do nothing? What is the worst that could happen if I take action now?

- What is the effect of my behavior on others? Am I open to feedback or hearing divergent views?

- Am I overreacting? Are any of my hot buttons getting pushed?

- What is my typical approach to conflict? Is it appropriate in this situation?

. . . .

Randy knew he needed to talk to Kristin about the sarcastic remark she made in the staff meeting this morning. After all the work he had done to get that project approved, he needed every member of the team to fully support this effort. Randy knew he was taking a risk, but if this project worked out well, the rewards would be worth it for the whole team and the company.

Instead of raising his concern with Kristin at the meeting, he asked her to come by his office after lunch. He wanted a chance to settle himself and be clear about his intentions before he talked this through with her. First, he wanted to consider her remark and understand why he reacted so strongly.

For one thing, he needed to demonstrate to the team that he was in charge. A negative remark by an influential team member like Kristin could undermine his authority. He needed team members to respect and support his decision making. On the other hand, he also wanted to foster an open, collaborative workplace, so he didn't want to shut down employee comments and concerns.

What did he fear? he wondered. He feared losing face and losing control of the group or the project. He felt that he must take action to nip negative attitudes in the bud. But he also feared alienating Kristin by coming down too hard on her or embarrassing her. She was a valuable member of the team he could count on to give 110% most of the time.

Randy realized any negative comment about this pet project was a trigger for him. He had a lot invested here—in the time and energy he put into getting it off the ground. He knew it would be easy to get defensive, and he didn't want his staff to see that kind of reaction from him.

Feeling more in control of his own emotional reactions, he decided to begin the conversation with Kristin by asking her about her remark and her opinion of the project. With more information from her, he could then decide how best to respond.

Frame the Situation Accurately

How you view a conflict situation has a big impact on what you do. If you are not viewing the conflict with a mind-set that is accurate, a discussion about it can easily spiral out of control

Terry was frustrated by the crew in technical support. He'd had several run-ins with them over the last few months, and now he was certain they were out to get him. As he prepared to give a presentation to his boss and his boss's boss, he stated flatly to me, "Failure is not an option." The stakes were high and the pressure was on. Tech support would also be there to review the plan. If there was a way to make his system fail, they would do it.

Five minutes into the presentation he got into an argument with the head of tech support. Fearing another confrontation, his boss stopped the meeting at once. Terry couldn't believe that he'd been sabotaged again.

Terry had a hard time understanding the role his own mind-set had played in this disastrous meeting. Since he was convinced that he was in an "us against them" situation, he was defensive and adversarial. Certainly, there were issues to resolve with tech support, but his attitude precluded any possibility of constructive conversation.

• •

As you are entering a difficult conversation:

➤   Ask yourself how *you* can view the situation differently. For instance, had Terry considered asking tech support for their advice and opinions earlier, the tense confrontation might never have happened.

➤   View differences as a source of learning. In this example, because the security system had been breached six months before, tech support was on a strict campaign to improve security. With a different approach, Terry might have learned more about the challenges they were facing and how those challenges impacted the work they were doing together.

> *If you have learned how to disagree without being disagreeable,*
> *then you have discovered the secret of getting along—whether*
> *it be business, family relations, or life itself.*
> —BERNARD MELTZER

➤   Test your assumptions. We often make assumptions about others' motives and intentions. These suppositions can lead us to make erroneous statements that inflame the situation rather than bring clarity to the subject. When his own computer and software would not function properly, for example, Terry's immediate assumption was, "They are out to get me, as usual." Thinking through his assumptions, he might have realized that the tech support team was far too busy trying to keep their own management happy to put any energy into "How can we get Terry this time?"

Terry began his discussion with the tech support staff by making several assumptions. The conversation would have gone in a different direction if he had first asked a few questions to understand their perspective. "Can you help me understand why my system isn't working?" "Would you help me understand what your concerns are?"

> *We may convince others by our arguments, but we can only persuade them by their own.*
> —JOSEPH JOUBERT

▶ Take responsibility for dealing with the conflict—then share your concern as a problem to solve. Entering the meeting with the attitude, "We have a problem to solve. Let's see how we can work together on this," could have taken the discussion down a different track. Rather than a hostile and adversarial exchange of accusations, there might have been an opportunity to learn from each other and find some mutually acceptable solution.

A STATEMENT BASED ON ASSUMPTIONS:[1]

▶ Is made any time—before, during, or after observation.

▶ Goes beyond the observation.

▶ Is unlimited in number in any situation.

▶ Represents some degree of possibility.

▶ Is open to disagreement.

A STATEMENT BASED ON FACT:

▶ Is made after the experience.

▶ Is confined to what one observes.

▶ Is limited in number.

▶ Is as close to certainty as anyone can get.

▶ Is a way to agreement.

Consider This

- ☑ Think of a time when you felt strongly about a situation. Write down what happened.
- ☑ Read through your description of the event. Underline any word, phrase, or idea that may be an assumption or a judgment.
- ☑ Circle those that are observable facts.
- ☑ Describe the event again, using only observable facts.

Speak to Be Heard

Once you are clear about your own intentions and expectations, how do you communicate your interests and concerns effectively? How do you say what needs to be said in a way that others can hear?

Your purpose is to engage others in an exchange of ideas that is not confrontational. You want to raise issues in ways that do not make others defensive, so that you can focus on finding workable solutions.

Speak for Yourself, From Your Own Experience

Talk about what has happened and how it has affected your own work or the work of the office. For example, when Randy spoke with Kristin about her comments in the staff meeting, he said, "I want to talk with you about the comment you made in the staff meeting. I am concerned about how important the project is, and I need everyone's support going forward." Notice what he did *not* say. He didn't say, "That comment you made this morning was unacceptable," which would be a judgment, and likely to put Kristin on the defensive.

As a manager, sometimes another person will bring concerns about members of your staff to you. Proceed cautiously here. If the issue has no bearing on the productivity of the office, it is generally not your concern. Suggest that the person talk directly with the staff member.

If you determine that the complaint does have an impact on the workplace, you may need to take action yourself. Begin with direct observation of the negative behavior yourself, if at all possible. If this is not possible, gather as much information—specific and observable—as you can from reliable sources before addressing the concern. When you raise the issue with the employee, discuss the impact of the behavior on the workplace rather than discussing the concerns of the person who brought the issue to your attention.

In an earlier chapter, there was April, who was keeping close tabs on Sam's comings and goings. She was eager to report to her boss Hank any time that Sam was late or unaccounted for. Hank reminded April that Sam was his responsibility to supervise, not April's. If or when Hank decided to raise any concerns about Sam's performance to Sam, Hank assured April, he would talk with Sam, based on his own observations and concerns, not on what April had reported to him.

On the other hand, there is the situation Kelly was in. She heard complaints from several people on the team about how loudly Cherie talked on the phone. After listening herself, gathering her own information, Kelly called Cherie into her office. "I have noticed how your voice carries across the cubicles. I am concerned that your conversations may be distracting to others, keeping them from being as productive as they could be."

Be Specific

Describe the precise events that you observed and their effect on you or on the productivity of the office. Rather than saying, "You don't respond to my calls," be as specific as possible: "On Tuesday I left a message on your voice mail and did not receive a call back." What you *know* is that you called on Tuesday and left a message. What you don't know for certain is whether that message was ever received.

Demonstrate Respect for the Other Party

This is important, whatever issue you are discussing with an employee— or anyone else. Can you remember a time when someone talked down to you? Insulted you? Spoke disrespectfully to you? I have posed these questions to many groups that I have worked with. It is the only unanimous survey I have ever run. In response, everyone raises their hands. Probably everyone except the queen has been talked to in these ways at one time or another.

What do you do when someone talks this way to you? I know how I react. When someone talks disrespectfully to me, I do not hear anything else that the person is saying. I am busy inside my own head with two tasks: building a wall so you don't hit me again, and figuring out how I can regain the ground I deserve as soon as he stops talking, or sooner, if I can interrupt him. I think it is a reaction many of us have, and it contains an important truth. If you want to keep their ears open to the importance of the message you are delivering, talk to anyone/everyone respectfully.

Sometimes in a difficult discussion, I have had an (almost) overwhelming desire to let someone know exactly where he or she fit in the world. Maybe you have had this experience as well. It is easy for me to get a condescending tone in my voice, or to be disrespectful nonverbally—for instance, rolling my eyes. When I have delivered the message through my words or my attitude, "You are not as smart as you think you are," or "Let me tell you a thing or two"—and I can remember a few times when I have been pretty articulate about it, clear, direct, to the point, if I do say so myself—I have never gotten the positive response I wanted: "Thanks so much. I never realized what a jerk I am. This is really helpful information that will change my behavior from this day forward." Rather, the person has done exactly what I do in this situation: close his or her ears to any of my words. The person may see my lips continue to move, but nothing is going in. She or he is (rightly so) in defensive mode. The important points I may have wanted to make, the key concerns I have been trying to raise, are lost in the nonconversation.

So, I have to start with *respect* in order to keep the person's ears open to what I am trying to say—respect for who the person is and what he or she knows and where the person has been. I have to hold on to this thought—sometimes I have to reach pretty deep to find it. What can I respect about this person? I can respect the individual's very humanity: the courage it may have taken to show up at all, the road he or she has traveled that has been so hard, or so different from mine, or so much like mine.

This demonstration of respect comes through in my body language and in my tone of voice, sometimes even more than in the words themselves. The 7-38-55 Rule mentioned in the last chapter comes into play as you are speaking, as well as when you are listening. Disrespect can be demonstrated in that 7 percent, the words you use—name calling or labeling are obvious. Remarks that belittle others or their efforts, or statements like "you people," are also heard as disrespectful.

Disrespect can be loud in your tone of voice (38 percent), even if you are not speaking loudly. It can be easy to "take a tone" that connotes disrespect and turns off the listener to any other part of your message. Your body language when you are speaking (55 percent) can also convey a message of disrespect. A tilt of your head can be seen literally as "he talks down to me." Rolling your eyes or lifting your eyebrows can say to a person, "I don't respect you."

Much of this communication, nonverbal or in voice tone, is unconscious. To deliver a message that clearly demonstrates respect for another, begin by aligning your attitudes about the other. When you can develop this sense of respect for the humanity of others, your words, your tone of voice, and your nonverbal communication will demonstrate congruity with your intentions.

Learn Your Own Communication Style and Patterns

You may not be aware of your own communication style and its effect on others. A woman I once worked with consistently used a tone of voice that was demeaning to others. When she yelled, I cringed. Even though I knew and I reminded myself every time I spoke with her, "It's just the way she is," I continued to take her tone of voice personally. I had a very difficult time listening to her without feeling the full force of her negative attitude.

Other people have a habit of ending sentences on an up note so that each statement sounds like a question. This pattern communicates uncertainty on the part of the speaker. Listening to this voice pattern, others may easily dismiss the speaker as well as the message because of the way it is delivered.

Consider This

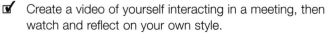 Ask someone whom you trust how effectively you communicate.

☑ Create a video of yourself interacting in a meeting, then watch and reflect on your own style.

☑ What does your tone of voice communicate?

☑ What does your nonverbal behavior communicate?

More Powerful Persuasion

When you want to persuade someone to consider your point of view, talking to them in terms that make sense to them can help them hear and understand your message. If they really understand what you are saying, they are more likely to agree. Maybe you have taken a personality inventory somewhere along the way: DiSC, Myers-Briggs, SDI, and the InQ[2] are a few of the more popular ones. From these questionnaires, it is easy to see that how people think and what they respond to varies from person to person. The more you understand these differences, the more effective you can be in your ability to persuade and convince others.

. . . .

The head of operations and the director of sales were locked in an argument. The company had budgeted money for a large piece of equipment and given decision-making responsibility to the engineer in charge of operations. The director of sales was eager to get the equipment up and running so that he could push more sales. Weeks passed. The head of operations gathered information, consulted manufacturers' representatives, and created charts of the data he collected on competing models. He wanted to consider all of the possible options before making a decision. This was a sizable investment for the company, and the equipment needed to be right for future product development. The director of sales was increasingly impatient, "Just make a decision and move on. If it's the wrong decision we can fix it later."

. . . .

What stood in the way as they attempted to communicate were the different approaches that each of them had to getting the job done. The engineer was oriented to data analysis, the head of sales had lots of energy for getting the job done as quickly as possible. By setting up a schedule for decision making and respecting the engineer's methods, the sales head would know what to expect and could support and encourage the engineer to make a decision more confidently.

In this example, the engineer was very good at focusing on the details, gathering data and considering alternatives before making a decision. To persuade someone like him, make certain that you have done your homework, that you have gathered the data and organized it accurately. Arguments over whose data is most accurate are likely to go nowhere. When you disagree you may be able to change this person's mind by considering the theory that each of you began with (in this case, the engineer's theory was that the equipment decision needed to last for ten years). Shifting that theory may provide new avenues for agreement.

Some people, like the head of sales, are focused on getting the task done. They are very good at taking action and moving on. To persuade them, take a marketing stance, that is, look for ways to sell your ideas with energy and enthusiasm. Give them the bottom line, your recommendations, or an executive summary with bullet points. And be confident about what you are saying; your confidence can be quite convincing.

Another person might be much more concerned about relationships and values. She might be the one in the office with a bowl of candy to welcome visitors, or motivational quotes affixed to the wall around her computer. In a meeting, this person is often concerned with how the decisions are being made, that everyone's voice is heard, and that the process is fair.

To persuade and convince someone like this, you might identify values that are important and talk about them. For example, I worked between two people in mediation to find common ground. One was an environmentalist who made decisions based on values and principles, the other, a developer who was much more concerned about the bottom-line viability of the project. In a private conversation, the developer talked to me about the need for more affordable housing in the county. I encouraged him to discuss these values in the mediation room, rather than the financial costs that had been his first focus. This values-based dialogue became the bridge across which the two could reach agreement.

Others enjoy the process itself and are in no hurry to make a decision, they want to look at any problem from as many directions as possible, or to play devil's advocate, before reaching a decision. To persuade people with these tendencies, give them time to look at all of the different angles and possibilities. If you appreciate the person's creative energy, he or she can bring good ideas to the solution-seeking process.

As you are working with people, listen to the language they use, the questions they raise, the information they deem important. The more you understand their approaches to processing information, the more effective you can be in translating your thoughts into terms that make sense to them. The more capable you are of doing that, the more persuasive you will be.

What to Avoid When You Are Talking

Sometimes what you don't say can be more important than what you do say. To keep their ears open to the message you really want to deliver, here are a few words to avoid.

1. *Accusations.* Making accusations is a good way to create an argument. State observable behaviors and verifiable facts. Ask for explanations. Listen for a constructive response.

2. *Generalizations.* "Everybody knows" is far too broad to be true, isn't it? "You always..." or "you never..." is likely to get an unhelpful response: "I am not always late. I came in on time a week ago Tuesday."

3. *Overkill or "proof by reiterative assertion."* Saying the same thing over and over and over again is really not as persuasive as it feels. Say what needs to be said, and confirm that the message has been received. Refrain from repeating yourself.

JUST DON'T GO THERE:

- ► you always...
- ► you never...
- ► why don't you...?
- ► you're wrong...
- ► what you need is...
- ► you're stupid...
- ► everybody knows that!...
- ► you'd better not...
- ► you ought to...
- ► why did you...?
- ► don't you know...?
- ► you should...
- ► if only you did it my way...
- ► if only you were more like me...

4. *Labels or name calling.* This is in the category of disrespect. When you use labels or call people names, they will not hear anything else that you are saying. Rather, they will jump into defensiveness or counterattack.

5. *Sarcasm.* "So, this is your idea of a great report?" "Where did you learn to type, grammar school?" It's disrespectful, and will move the listener off of the message into defensiveness.

6. *Moralizing or pontificating.* Delivering messages about the right thing to do falls into the category of disrespect. Adults in the workplace should know right from wrong. Pontificating from your soap box does not persuade or convince, it only causes people to tune you out.

7. *Assigning motives.* "I know you did this because you wanted me to look bad." Considering the action any other person takes, you are often able to imagine four or five different reasons a person might have done what they did. Stick with observable, verifiable facts. Those are the realities you can discuss rationally.

In summary, there are a few principles to hold as you engage an employee in any dialogue. Consider carefully the message you want to communicate. Speak it clearly and simply, focusing on observable behaviors and their consequences to the workplace. And demonstrate respect for the person you are talking to.

RAISING AN ISSUE

- ► Complain *only* to the person you are concerned about.
- ► Make your complaint as soon as possible.
- ► Criticize specific *behaviors* rather than inferring motives, intentions, attitudes, etc.
- ► Make only one complaint at a time.
- ► Complain only about those things the other can change.
- ► Communicate in a conversational tone.
- ► Allow the other person to respond, without becoming defensive.

AVOID

- ► Raising your voice
- ► Comparisons with other people
- ► Criticisms in front of other people
- ► Repeating points you have made
- ► Sarcasm
- ► Exaggerations, overgeneralizations
- ► Becoming defensive

MANAGE YOUR EXPECTATIONS

- ► Don't expect an immediate apology, confession, or even an acknowledgment that the message was received.
- ► You have communicated successfully if you have planted a seed of awareness in the other's mind.

Note

1. These websites have more information about a few popular personality inventories: DiSC: www.discprofile.com, Myers Briggs Type Indicator: www.myersbriggs.org, SDI or Strength Deployment Inventory: www.personalstrengths.com, InQ or Inquiry Mode Questionnaire: www.yourthinkingprofile.com (websites accessed December 1, 2010).

CHAPTER 16

The Challenge of Electronic Text Communication

L ike most of us, I begin my day checking my e-mail. What's in? What's up? Who has a question I can answer, an invitation I can't refuse, or a meeting to reschedule? There is no question about it, e-mail works. And now I can send a text message on my cell phone, making communication even quicker and easier. In the workplace, these communication tools can be great time-savers, but they require particular communication skills.

Here is a short list of things you can accomplish via electronic means:

➤ You can announce a meeting time and place so that everyone knows where to be and when.

➤ You can circulate the agenda so that everyone knows what to expect generally when they get there.

➤ You can distribute the minutes of the meeting so that everyone knows what was considered and decided.

▶ You can track the budget and increase the transparency of transactions.

▶ You can transfer data with less opportunity for human error transposing numbers or omitting lines.

▶ You can communicate with everyone on the staff, either singularly or as a group, at any time of the day or night, wherever they are, or you are, whether you are in your office or on the beach or three time zones away.

▶ When there is a policy change or a schedule change, you can communicate the same message to everyone at the same time.

The Good, the Bad, and the Ugly

Some people just love their electronic communications. They use e-mail and texting for just about everything. There are times when this works well, but there are other times when it does not

. . . .

For Steve, it was far easier to send e-mails from his office than to try to track people down at their desks. Whenever he had a new job requirement, it went directly from his keyboard into someone else's e-mail, to be added to his or her to-do list. There were a few people on the team who Steve was not all that comfortable working with. He found texting and e-mailing were especially helpful communicating with them.

There was Anita, who was always complaining at length about this project or that assignment. If he sent her an e-mail with new tasks, he didn't have to listen to Anita's complaints. And there was Ben, who never seemed to understand exactly what was expected of him. An e-mail with a clear deadline took care of that problem. What a relief to have this e-mail capability!

The longer Steve used the electronic communication, the more comfortable with it he became. Truth be told, he was much more at ease with the computer than he was with human interaction. Steve had a long list of responsibilities to juggle. He sent texts requesting status updates. If his direct reports didn't answer him quickly, that was okay. He'd just send a text to someone further down the chain of command. Sometimes, when he didn't get a response as quickly as he expected, he would send another text a few minutes later. Maybe he thought the first one didn't go through. Maybe he thought the person would understand how important the question was. After a while, maybe he really didn't think about it at all.

Staff meetings were such a bore for Steve. There was no need anymore to waste people's time in meetings. He could just tell them what they needed to know through the daily e-mail. He discovered that he didn't have to have those uncomfortable conversations face to face. Performance evaluations got a lot easier when he could e-mail them as attachments. If anyone had a problem with them, they could let him know. Preferably by e-mail.

Antoine was a bit of a pain. The two of them went round and round on a job requirement. After several e-mail exchanges, Antoine's tone got nasty. But Steve hung in there. If you keep at it, he figured, eventually employees will get the message. Then, there was that really dreadful week a couple of months ago. Facing a downturn in the business cycle, the higher-ups decided that a layoff was the only way to make the numbers look positive for the quarter. Fortunately for Steve, he had his trusty e-mail system. After he got the list and confirmation from his boss, on Thursday afternoon he e-mailed notices to three of his employees, giving them the bad news and directing them to clean out their desks. As far as Steve was concerned, it was the easiest way to handle a dirty job. He could attach the paperwork, give them necessary instructions, and he didn't have to endure any messy, uncomfortable scenes or tearful goodbyes. He thought about it from their perspective, too. He was sure they would appreciate avoiding an awkward moment.

What Steve didn't see was the negative effect all of his e-mailing had on the staff. His relationships with them became more awkward. Without staff meetings and with limited face-to-face conversations, his staff was reluctant to take on new assignments; they did not have a clear understanding of the office's priorities. Opportunities for people to assist each other on projects dwindled. When Steve reacted by pelting them with more e-mails to demand answers, they became increasingly resistant. Morale dropped as employees felt less connected to the boss, to the mission of the office, or to each other.

. . . .

Maybe you have worked with Steve. Maybe you recognize some of your own tendencies in his story. Maybe you find some of the details hard to believe. They are not fabrications, as much as we might want them to be. Like other basic elements of life—fire, water, wind—electronic text communications can be a boon to human existence, and if they get out of control, they can become destructive.

Since these communication tools are so easy to use, abusing them is easy as well. The challenge is to use electronic communication tools wisely. On the one hand, when writing an e-mail, you are not interrupted as you are getting your thoughts together. Having time to think through your response, organize your information, and reread your message, amending and revising before sending it, can help you deliver the message more accurately. This can give you added confidence, help you manage your emotions, and overcome a strong desire to avoid the situation altogether.

On the other hand, when people do not trust one another, there is too much room for interpretation—or misinterpretation—of the text. As discussed in an earlier chapter, the words themselves account for a mere 7 percent of the communication. Through e-mail and texting, people lose about 93 percent of the intended communication.

Empathy is triggered by seeing a face. This works in both directions. A manager connects with a worker and a worker thinks of a manager in more human ways when they are able to see each other. So much important information can be expressed with a smile or a shrug or in eye-to-eye contact that cannot be relayed on a bare page of letters and numbers. Emoticons can only go so far in expressing your intent. There is no opportunity to observe how the recipient is reacting to your message or to demonstrate through your tone of voice that you meant your exchange as a friendly inquiry.

If you send an e-mail and others don't trust you, immediately their negative filters shade the computer screen. In other words, they often will automatically and unconsciously read your words with a negative tone of voice. Their thought process is quite likely to be, "Who is she to be asking me *this*?" or "Where does he get off telling me *that*?"

Recently a colleague approached me as we were heading into a meeting. Waving a paper in the air, her face flaming red, she demanded, "Can you *believe* he wrote this to me?" I held the sheet steady and read the message. I shrugged. Having no history with the sender, it sounded pretty straightforward to me. She, on the other hand, had had several disagreements with him and distrusted any of his actions. She automatically read his words through her own filter of distrust.

With e-mail, you can quickly dispatch a response and have one less item waiting for action on your to-do list. On many a morning, I begin my workday by sending several e-mails. There is a sense of satisfaction that the task is done, at least until I get responses from them. However, one of the challenges of the computer system is that the send button is located so conveniently on the screen. It is easy to read a message, react to it, and immediately write a sharp reply. By the time you reflect on what you have said, and how the recipient might read it, the message is off your screen and onto the receiver's screen.

If you need to communicate something to someone you don't trust, electronic communication seems like the way to go: it's not necessary to interact with the person *and* you have proof that you sent the message. You can demonstrate later that, yes, you did send the message—and it is even automatically time-stamped. Often, you can also prove that the person opened the message, which is also time-stamped.

In contrast, if your intention is to reduce conflict and resolve differences, this approach may only drive people further away. When you do finally have to have that face-to-face conversation, you can come armed with reams of e-mails, a printout of all of the messages exchanged over the past fourteen months. You will have proof of the rightness of your cause: "See, right here. July 13, 11:15 A.M. I *told* you I could not extend the deadline." You will likely alienate the very person whose cooperation you need. Where the trust is low, using electronic communications to establish a paper trail often only creates more distrust.

The possibility of having a permanent record of those e-mail communications can be helpful, of course. If you need to retrace how the ideas have developed, being able to read through the record can be helpful. "Did I quote a cost for that project? Let me check back in my 'sent" folder to be sure that I gave them that number already." On the other hand, those messages, because they exist inside the system and never really go away, can be forwarded to others without your knowledge. In addition, once your views—or someone else's opinions—have been expressed in black and white, the flexibility to change your mind, or for them to change theirs, begins to disappear.

E-mail can be useful for communicating with many people at one time. That way, everyone gets the same information. Everyone knows that everyone else knows what is happening. However, that same capability can be used to include others in what would best be kept as a one-on-one conversation. Copying your own manager or others on the staff in an e-mail or text message ratchets up any disagreement to another level. And there are the hazards of "reply all." Without realizing who is copied on this e-mail, you can easily send a response to people you never intended to read what you have written. Suddenly, the conflict or disagreement takes on a life of its own, with rumors and misunderstandings buzzing through the office.

When Not to Use Electronic Communication

Here are some tips for when to avoid using electronic communication.

- ▶ Build positive relationships in person, so that when difficulties arise they will be easier to resolve.

- ▶ If there is any question about the strength of your relationship, or if trust is a concern, deal with differences and disagreements face to face. Communicate about complaints or dissatisfaction directly to the individual.

- ▶ If you can't meet face to face, pick up the phone and talk. Your voice tone will convey far more information about your intent than your words may express.

- ▶ If the subject matter is highly complex, direct communication can reduce misunderstandings.

- ► Do not use e-mail to communicate about confidential matters.
- ► If you have bad news to deliver, do not use e-mail or text messaging to deliver it. Talk with the person directly.
- ► Follow the rule of three: if you have responded three times through e-mail on the same topic, it is time to pick up the phone or visit the other person's office.
- ► Resist the temptation to fire off a response. Reread the original message to be clear that you are not misinterpreting it. Draft a reply and let it cool before sending it.
- ► No "flaming." Do not send messages that are hostile, aggressive, or insulting. Do not use profanity, all capital letters, or numerous punctuation marks at the end of a sentence.

How to Write an E-Mail

Face-to-face or phone communication can make exchanging views and resolving differences easier, but this may not always be possible, given the challenges of time and schedules in the workplace. There are ways to write e-mails that are effective and that avoid some of the pitfalls listed above.

Consider this e-mail message: "Not available next week." It is short and sweet—and open to negative interpretations if there is mistrust in the relationship. Revising it can make a difference in how the sender receives the communication: "Holly, next week is really busy for me. I know we need time to talk this through. What does your calendar look like the following week? Thanks."

What a difference a cordial response can make. Here are some other suggestions for phrasing your e-mails in a positive way.

- ► Use the subject line to indicate what the message is about.
- ► Begin with a salutation, using the person's name, saying "Hi" or "Hello."
- ► Express positive intention (e.g., "I want to be sure that I understand your concerns").

- ▶ Put your most important statements in the first paragraph. Follow up with details.

- ▶ Keep paragraphs short for easy reading.

- ▶ Make recommendations clear and easy to identify.

- ▶ Ask for a specific action. Tell the recipient what you need in order to complete the task.

- ▶ Re-read your message at least once more before you send it.

- ▶ Say "Thank you."

A Word About Social Networking (Facebook and Twitter)

These are marvelous communication tools, broadcasting messages to a wide band of readers at once. The public forum is not a healthy place to discuss or resolve conflicts, however. Far too many people are otherwise privy to what is best kept as a private conversation. The potential for trust to be broken, the opportunity to be misinterpreted by others, and the possibility of the conversation landing in the hands of the wrong people are multiplied. Don't even go there.

Electronic communication is a powerful tool to make life in the workplace more efficient. When it comes to developing and maintaining positive working relationships that are essential in resolving differences and disagreements, however, technology can sometimes be more of a hindrance than a help. Proceed with caution.

Bibliography

Barsade, Sigal G. "The Ripple Effect: Emotional Contagion and Its Influence on Group Behavior." *Administrative Science Quarterly*, 47, no. 4 (December 2002): 644–675.

Blake, Robert, and Jane Mouton. *The Managerial Grid*. Houston, Tex.: Gulf Publishing, 1964.

Burton, John. *Conflict Resolution and Prevention*. New York: St. Martin's, 1990.

Cloke, Kenneth, and Joan Goldsmith. *Resolving Conflicts at Work*, rev. ed. San Francisco: Jossey-Bass, 2005.

Colosi, Thomas R. *On and Off the Record: Colosi on Negotiation*. Dubuque, Ia.: Kendall/Hunt, 1993.

Dana, Daniel. *Managing Differences: How to Build Better Relationships at Work and at Home*, 3rd. ed. Prairie Village, Kan.: MTI Publications, 2003.

Dynamic Administration: The Collected Papers of Mary Parker Follett. Reprint. London: Pitman, 1973, pp. 1–20.

Feltman, Charles. *The Thin Book of Trust: An Essential Primer for Building Trust at Work*. Bend, Oreg.: Thin Book Publishing, 2009.

Fisher, Roger, and Daniel Shapiro. *Beyond Reason: Using Emotions as You Negotiate*. New York: Viking, 2005.

Fisher, Roger, and William Ury. *Getting to Yes: Negotiating Agreement Without Giving In*, 2nd ed. New York: Houghton Mifflin, 1991.

Gerzon, Mark. *Leading Through Conflict: How Successful Leaders Transform Differences into Opportunities*. Boston: Harvard Business School Press, 2006.

Gladwell, Malcolm. *Outliers: The Story of Success*. Boston: Little, Brown, 2008.

Goleman, Daniel. *Emotional Intelligence*. New York: Bantam Books, 1995.

—. *Working with Emotional Intelligence*. New York: Bantam Books, 1998.

Gopin, Marc. *Healing the Heart of Conflict: Eight Crucial Steps to Making Peace with Yourself and Others*. Emmaus, Penn.: Rodale, 2004.

Hall, Edward T. *Beyond Culture*. New York: Anchor Books, 1976.

Halper, June A. "Stop the Bellyaching." *USA Today*, May 2007.

Harrison, Allen, and Robert Bramson. *Styles of Thinking: Strategies for Asking Questions, Making Decisions, and Solving Problems*. New York: Anchor Books, 1982.

Hofstede, Geert. *Culture's Consequences: Comparing Values, Behaviors, Institutions and Organizations Across Nations*. Thousand Oaks, Calif.: Sage Publishing, 2001.

Kabat-Zinn, John. *Wherever You Go, There You Are: Mindfulness Meditations in Everyday Life*. New York: Hyperion, 1995.

Kim, W. Chan, and Renee Mauborgne. "Fair Process: Managing in the Knowledge Economy." In *HBR on Point*. Boston: Harvard Business School Press, 2003.

Kochman, Thomas, and Jean Mavrelis. *Corporate Tribalism: White Men/White Women and Cultural Diversity at Work*. Chicago: University of Chicago Press, 2009.

Kottler, Jeffrey A. *Beyond Blame: A New Way of Resolving Conflicts in Relationships*. San Francisco: Jossey-Bass, 1994.

Kraybill, Ron. *Style Matters: The Kraybill Conflict Style Inventory*. Harrisonburg, Va.: Riverhouse, 2005.

Leas, Speed. "Moving Your Church through Conflict." Alban Institute, 2002.

LeBaron, Michelle. *Bridging Cultural Conflicts: A New Approach for a Changing World*. San Francisco: Jossey-Bass, 2003.

Lerner, Harriet Goldhor. *The Dance of Anger*. New York: Harper and Row, 1985.

Mauer, Robert. *One Small Step Can Change Your Life: The Kaizen Way*. New York: Workman, 2004.

Mehrabian, Albert. *Silent Messages*. Belmont, Calif.: Wadsworth, 1971.

Mnookin, Robert H., Scott R. Peppet, and Andrew S. Tulumello. *Beyond Winning: Negotiation to Create Value in Deals and Disputes*. Boston: Harvard University Press, 2000.

Moore, Christopher. *The Mediation Process*, 3rd ed. San Francisco: Jossey-Bass, 2003.

National Institute for Occupational Safety and Health, Centers for Disease Control and Prevention, http://www.cdc.gov/niosh/docs /2006-144/#a11, accessed 2006.

National Institute for the Prevention of Workplace Violence. "The Unlucky 13: Early Warning Signs of Potential Violence at Work," http://www.ncdsv.org/images/The%20Unlucky%2013_Early %20Warning%20Signs%20of%20Potential%20Violence%20a%E2%80%A 6.pdf.

Nichols, Michael P. *The Lost Art of Listening*.New York: Guilford Press, 1995.

Patterson, Kerry, Joseph Grenny, Ron McMillan, and Al Switzler. *Crucial Confrontations: Tools for Resolving Broken Promises, Violated Expectations and Bad Behavior*. New York: McGraw-Hill, 2005.

—. *Crucial Conversations: Tools for Talking When Stakes are High*. New York: McGraw-Hill, 2002.

Redefining Employee Satisfaction: Business Performance, Employee Fulfillment, and Leadership Practices. Edina, Minn.: Wilson Learning Worldwide, 2006.

Reina, Dennis S., and Michelle L. Reina. *Trust and Betrayal in the Workplace: Building Effective Relationships in Your Organization*. San Francisco: Berrett-Koehler, 1999.

Rothman, Jay. *Resolving Identity-Based Conflict in Nations, Organizations and Communities*. San Francisco: Jossey-Bass, 1997.

Rosenberg, Marshall B. *Nonviolent Communication: A Language of Compassion*. Del Mar, Calif.: PuddleDancer, 1999.

Runde, Craig E., and Tim A. Flanagan. *Becoming a Conflict Competent Leader: How You and Your Organization Can Manage Conflict Effectively*. San Francisco: Jossey-Bass and Center for Creative Leadership, 2007.

—. *Building Conflict Competent Teams*. San Francisco: Jossey-Bass and Center for Creative Leadership, 2008.

—. *Developing Your Conflict Competence: A Hands-on Guide for Leaders, Managers, Facilitators and Teams*. San Francisco: Jossey-Bass and Center for Creative Leadership, 2010.

Scott, Susan. *Fierce Conversations: Achieving Success at Work and in Life, One Conversation at a Time.* New York: Berkley, 2004.

Stone, Douglas, Bruce Patton, and Sheila Heen. *Difficult Conversations: How to Discuss What Matters Most.* New York: Viking, 1999.

Storti, Craig. *Figuring Foreigners Out.* Yarmouth, ME: Intercultural Press, 1998.

Stosny, Steven. *Treating Attachment Abuse: A Compassionate Approach.* New York: Springer, 1995.

Tannen, Deborah. *Talking from 9 to 5: How Women's and Men's Conversational Styles Affect Who Gets Heard, Who Gets Credit and What Gets Done at Work.* New York: William Morrow, 1994.

Thomas, Kenneth W., and Ralph H. Kilmann. *The Thomas Kilmann Conflict Mode Instrument.* Tuxedo, N.Y.: Xicom, 1974.

Ting-Toomey, Stella. "Cross-Cultural Face-Negotiation: An Analytical Overview." Talk presented at Simon Fraser University, Harbour Centre, Vancouver, B.C., Canada, 1992.

Ury, William. *Getting Past No: Negotiating Your Way from Confrontation to Cooperation.* New York: Bantam Books, 1991.

Watson, C., and R. Hoffman. "Managers as Negotiators." *Leadership Quarterly,* 7, no. 1 (1996); http://www.conflictatwork.com/conflict/cost_e.cfm, accessed August 25, 2010.

Useful Websites

www.acrnet.org
www.crinfo.org
www.mediate.com

Index